Californio Portraits

BEFORE GOLD
California under Spain and Mexico
VOLUME 4

ROSE MARIE BEEBE & ROBERT M. SENKEWICZ
Series Editors

Californio Portraits
Baja California's Vanishing Culture

Harry W. Crosby

University of Oklahoma Press
Norman, Oklahoma
2015

Publication of this book is made possible through the generosity of Edith Kinney Gaylord.

LIBRARY OF CONGRESS CATALOGING-IN-PUBLICATION DATA
Crosby, Harry W., 1926–
Californio portraits : Baja California's vanishing culture / Harry W. Crosby.

  pages cm. — (Before gold: California under Spain and Mexico ; v. 4)
  Includes bibliographical references and index.
  isbn 978-0-8061-4869-4 (hardcover) ISBN 978-0-8061-9214-7 (paper)

1. Baja California (Mexico : Peninsula)—Social life and customs—Pictorial works.
2. Baja California (Mexico : Peninsula)—Civilization.
3. Baja California (Mexico : Peninsula)—History.
I. Title.
  F1246.C729 2015
  972'.2—dc23
                2015002749

Californio Portraits: Baja California's Vanishing Culture is Volume 4 in the series Before Gold: California under Spain and Mexico.

The paper in this book meets the guidelines for permanence and durability of the Committee on Production Guidelines for Book Longevity of the Council on Library Resources, Inc. ∞

Copyright © 2015 by the University of Oklahoma Press, Norman, Publishing Division of the University. Paperback published 2023. Manufactured in the U.S.A.

All rights reserved. No part of this publication may be reproduced, stored in a retrieval system, or transmitted, in any form or by any means, electronic, mechanical, photocopying, recording, or otherwise—except as permitted under Section 107 or 108 of the United States Copyright Act—without the prior written permission of the University of Oklahoma Press. To request permission to reproduce selections from this book, write to Permissions, University of Oklahoma Press, 2800 Venture Drive, Norman, OK 73069, or email rights.oupress@ou.edu.

Contents

List of Illustrations	vii
Preface	xi
Acknowledgments	xvii
Series Editors' Introduction	xix
Introduction	3
1. A Day at a Sierra Ranch	13
2. Gente de Razón	41
3. The Contest for Land	69
4. Picturing the Californios	95
5. The Sierra de Guadalupe	125
6. New Lamps for Old	153
7. A Man of the Mountains	181
Epilogue	231
Glossary	237
Bibliography	245
Index	269

Illustrations

Figures

Intro.1. Rancho Las Jícamas in the Sierra de Guadalupe	2
Intro.2. Kodalith of Californios	10–11
1.1. Uplands of the Sierra de San Francisco	12
1.2. Loreto Arce and Tacho Arce	15
1.3. Rock paintings	16
1.4. Flume of palm logs	19
1.5. Irrigation system	20
1.6. Tacho Arce gets a haircut	23
1.7. Mealtime	24
1.8. Cooking on adobe stoves	27
1.9. Tanning leather	28
1.10. Curing hides	28
1.11. Using turtle oil on hides	30
1.12. Francisco Arce does leatherwork	30
1.13. Ranch-made packsaddles filled with straw	33
1.14. Beehive	36
1.15. Kodalith of a mule	37
1.16. Bedroom shrine	38

2.1. Villa de Sinaloa	51
2.2. Ruins of Santa Ana	62
2.3. José de Gálvez	64
2.4. Cows at Santa Ana	67
3.1. Elderly vaquero	71
3.2. Riding and pack animals	72
3.3. A California mayordomo as depicted by Fr. Ignacio Tirsch, SJ	76
3.4. Opening a cattle gate	79
3.5. Date palms	80
3.6. Antonio Ríos	82
4.1. *Trajes mexicanos—un fandango* (1851) by Casimiro Castro	101
4.2. Drawings by a Japanese artist of Baja California buildings and clothing	110
4.3. Mule or burro-powered sugarcane press	116
4.4. Brass cauldron	116
4.5. William Ryan's 1847 sketch of a California homestead	118
4.6. Rancho Pie de la Cuesta	119
4.7. Arroyo Comondú	123
5.1. Guadalupe uplands	126
5.2. Rancho Vivelejos	132
5.3. Casimiro Aguilar	133
5.4. Cattle brands	135
5.5. Amador brothers	138
5.6. Arroyo de Rosarito	141
5.7. A tinaja or natural water catchment	142
5.8. Branches to feed mules	146
5.9. Kodalith of an agave	147
5.10. Switchback trails	148
5.11. Difficult trails	148
5.12. A represa or artificial water catchment	150

5.13. A seasonal or cambiadero goat ranch   151
5.14. Rancho El Zorrillo   151

6.1. Portrait of a Californio couple by an itinerant artist   154
6.2. A young sierra man prepares for a long ride   157
6.3. Young girl learning how to sew   158
6.4. Rounding up goats   160
6.5. A woman milking a goat   161
6.6. Hanging goat meat to dry   163
6.7. Domestic chores   163
6.8. Girl grinding salt   164
6.9. Mixing pulverized rock salt into cheese curd   167
6.10. Slaughtering a goat   168
6.11. Family group   169
6.12. Portrait of a mountain ranch family   170
6.13. Grandmother and child   171
6.14. Washing clothes by hand   172
6.15. Sharpening a tool   172
6.16. A traditional bed of güéribo wood   175
6.17. Chairs of güéribo wood   175
6.18. Elías Villavicencio and Juana Aguilar   176
6.19. Breaking mules   177
6.20. Three men conversing   178
6.21. A young woman and a potential suitor   178

7.1. Eustacio (Tacho) Arce   180
7.2. Tacho Arce and his maternal aunt   184
7.3. Bringing news to friends at Rancho San Nicolás   185
7.4. Filling a canteen at a pool in an arroyo   187
7.5. Mission San Ignacio   188
7.6. Santa Rosalía   195
7.7. Domitila Villavicencio   198
7.8. Tacho Arce at his grandparents' tombs   199
7.9. Tacho Arce at the ruins of Rancho San Antonio   201
7.10. Falluqueros   202

7.11. Loading and unloading pack mules	203
7.12. Loreto and Josefa Arce	207
7.13. Narciso Villavicencio	209
7.14. Tacho Arce and Tránsito Quintero	211
7.15. Condenser jacket for still	212
7.16. Germán Arce making shoes	213
7.17. A corredor or shady, open-sided sitting room	214
7.18. Hunting	219
7.19. Tacho Arce visiting a hillside ranch	220
7.20. Tacho Arce leads the cavalcade	223
7.21. Steep hillside trail	225
7.22. A sierra kitchen	226
7.23. Kodalith of a spur	228
7.24. Kodalith of a boy and a mule drawing water from a well	229
Epi.1. Rancho La Soledad	233
Epi.2. Kodalith of a horse	234

Maps

Map 1. Topography of Baja California showing the principal mountain ranges	8
Map 2. Early California settlements	55
Map 3. Missions, mission ranches and chapels, post-mission villages and ranches	56
Map 4. Missions, mission ranches and chapels, post-mission ranches	129

Preface

In 1963, after twelve years as a high school chemistry teacher, I decided to try making a living in a different fashion. I had taken up photography in order to capture moments in the childhoods of our three children. Then, as I recorded family trips and the excursions I had organized for my students to out-of-the-way places in Mexico, I became fascinated with photography's creative potential.

The following year, *California Review*, a magazine of the times, hired me to illustrate virtually an entire issue, some sixty-eight pages, each with photographs. Then a large stock photo company accepted a number of the photographs I had taken in the interior of Mexico. The following year I provided most of the illustrations for a brochure designed to attract students to the then quite new University of California, San Diego.

In October 1966 I attended a football game at San Diego Stadium. As I went downstairs to be seated, I ran into Robert H. ("Bob") Finch, an old friend from my days at Occidental College in Los Angeles who had just been elected lieutenant governor of California. He asked me what I was up to. I told him of my excursion into photography and mentioned the magazine I had illustrated, as well as my interests and activities in Mexico.

Bob Finch's reaction was immediate and surprising. He explained that as lieutenant governor he was slated to become the chairman of the recently formed Commission of the Californias, a body made up of appointees from American California and Baja California. He told me that the commission had voted to sponsor a book describing the Portolá Expedition—the undertaking that opened and led to the settlement of what would later become American California. He said the production of the book had been assigned to Copley Books, a small subdivision of the Copley Press, which also produced the *San Diego Union-Tribune* newspaper. The Copley Press was owned by James Copley, who had been appointed a founding member of the Commission of the Californias. Finch informed me that Copley Books was accepting applications from photographers who wished to illustrate the planned book, and he urged me to apply. I did so on the following Monday. My portfolio included a broad range of my Mexican photos.

Three days later I received a telephone call from the secretary of Richard Pourade, editor of Copley Books. She told me that Mr. Pourade wanted to see me, and we made an appointment for the following day. I then presented myself, expecting to answer questions and learn more about the enterprise. Instead, and much to my surprise, Mr. Pourade told me that I had been chosen for the job! My assignment was to follow the entire trail of the 1769 expedition to obtain photos at frequent intervals. Many of the photos would be used in the proposed book. I was to have the photos ready by June 1967. I assured him that I was up to the task. As I went home, I was already formulating many plans in my head.

Earlier that year I had bought a used dune buggy to which I added a roof rack and other storage facilities. I decided to use that vehicle to take me near the historic trail. I asked my former student Paul Ganster, a frequent partner on my trips to Mexico, if he would like to join me. His response was immediate and positive. We planned to set out in February 1967. I then began learning what I could about the trail followed by the Portolá Expedition. I read accounts by others relating to the trail, obtained maps, gathered supplies, and so forth.

We drove south on time and without incident. We stopped wherever we saw people and asked them how we could drive closer to the historic trail. I would always point to a tentative line I had drawn on the best map then available, a Mexican government publication on the not-very-large scale of 1:500,000. As we traveled, we inquired regularly and discovered that no one we met knew of any roads that followed that trail. We actually learned there were only a few that crossed the trail between Loreto and the U.S. border. By the time we reached Loreto, we had decided that our only recourse would be to rent riding animals and hire guides. That way we could follow the trail continuously and obtain the contracted photographs.

Unfortunately, a difficulty arose immediately: no guides or mounts could be found near Loreto. We were directed to the village of San Javier, some twenty-five miles to the southwest. There we would find a certain man who had acted as a guide for visitors in that area. We did find him but wasted two days before learning that the man had lost the trust of the local owners of riding animals. An apparently knowledgeable resident of San Javier then told us of a well-respected man who could help us. He could be found at Comondú, thirty miles to the north. We then set out, happy to have the dune buggy to cope with a rugged mountain road.

When we arrived in Comondú, we found our man, Heriberto Pérpuli. He was a local middleman who bought all sorts of local produce, such as dates grown by his neighbors, goat cheese from nearby sierra ranches, and locally raised cattle, goats, and mules. He then trucked these items to the more populated places to the south, such as Villa Constitución or even La Paz. Pérpuli's paternal grandfather was an Italian who had deserted his job aboard a ship. He found a place to work in Loreto, got married there, and stayed for the rest of his life.

Heriberto agreed to find someone to help us. We needed a place to stay that night and he found us a bedroom. He then set out to locate the guide and animals we would need, which proved to be a simple task. Señor Pérpuli called to his next-door neighbor, who came over and confirmed that in two days he would be going to La

Purísima, a mission town on the trail we must follow. He would not be going any farther but assured us that he knew local people there who could help us find our next guide. He also agreed to rent me the necessary animals until we could find and purchase our own.

When it was time to depart, we mounted our animals and headed out with our gear loaded into our saddlebags or into packsaddles on a pair of small mules. One mule was sturdy, but the other seemed old and tired. The ensuing ride was exhilarating! After a single, rather gentle upgrade we were largely on rather level land all the time, with beautiful vistas and lovely skies. We ate fruit and other cold food we had packed on the mules. We did not cook until we stopped for the night. We had traveled some fifteen miles. By then we were feeling tired and somewhat sore in areas that had been in contact with our saddles! After a good night's sleep we ate a simple breakfast prepared by our guide-host and then we were off. We reached La Purísima around noon.

When our guide explained what we needed, our story rapidly circulated. We soon hired a man who would lead us to Paso Hondo, a village some fifteen miles north on the route that matched my mapping. He promised that we would find guides and animals there. After a day's ride we arrived and began to tell people about our plans. Fernando Aguilar, the local *subdelegado* or government representative, introduced himself. He immediately began to assist us by spreading the word that we needed animals. Soon three local ranchers who happened to be in town started to inspect our animals, all the time shaking their heads. None of them could imagine how any of those animals would be able to travel such a great distance. Señor Aguilar concurred, so Paul and I worked out a plan. He would stay in Paso Hondo and guard our paraphernalia, and I would hire a truck driver to take me and our rented animals back to Comondú. I would then take a bus to La Paz, where I would arrange to have funds sent so I could buy four mules.

The return to Comondú was soon arranged, and I headed out the following morning, starting a blessedly smooth process of returning our rented animals and acquiring the funds to buy our own. When I was back in Paso Hondo, I learned that Paul had been asking around about available mules. He had found two for me to consider. I spoke with Fernando Aguilar and he agreed that those mules would be capable of completing our planned tour. But I still needed two more mules. He recommended that I speak with a man at Rancho San Martín, some thirty-five miles to the north and along our proposed trail. Don Fernando Aguilar offered to rent us two of his animals so we could continue on to Rancho San Martín, and he also arranged for a competent young local man to guide us to that destination.

We left rather late the next day. We headed north along a well-used trail and took photos whenever a compelling scene presented itself. On the third day we arrived at Rancho San Martín, where we were treated royally. I was amazed. In the span of two days we acquired the animals we needed. These two mules, along with our others, would see us to the planned end of our five hundred remaining miles of trail in Baja California.

We set out from San Martín finally launched on our quest, riding our own animals, and led by a guide familiar with our needs. Feeling ever more confident, we rode off to start examining the settings along the long trail ahead. We would stop at many places to take photos. We met a succession of capable and more than capable guides. Only one guide fell below that level and took us in the wrong direction, but it was for a relatively short stretch of our long journey. We made significant visits to more than a dozen mountain ranches and gained a great deal of information about the mountains and their trails. What was most visually fascinating was the prehistoric rock art, which is now considered by many to be the finest in the Americas.

When the adventure of traveling and photographing the Portolá Trail in Baja California was over, I left determined to pursue pressing questions that had been developing in my mind based on our fascinating encounters with the people of Baja California. What were the historical origins of the mountain people we had visited? When had they come to the peninsula? Who were their ancestors? What were their origins? As I attempted to answer these questions, I found myself inspired to write this book, *Californio Portraits: Baja California's Vanishing Culture*. I dedicate this book to them.

Acknowledgments

Back in 1980, when the original version of this work, *Last of the Californios*, was taking form, I assembled my archival research and combined that with my writings, recordings, and photographic images of my experiences among the people of the sierras involved. I had important help from Enrique Hambleton, a Mexican companion who had accompanied me on several of my peninsular mountain muleback tours. Enrique translated and explained to me the finer points of my many recorded interviews with sierra ranch people. A decade later, Hambleton convinced significant figures in the government of Baja California Sur to publish my work in Spanish, and he then provided the translation.

When my initial draft was written, I sought advice from appropriate scholars, all friends and students of related history: Dr. Iris Engstrand, Mrs. Rudecinda Lo Buglio, Dr. W. Michael Mathes, and Mr. William M. Mason. Each read my original text, contributed ideas, raised questions, and offered constructive criticism.

Thirty-three years after the publication described above, I express my thanks and profound gratitude to Drs. Rose Marie Beebe and Robert M. Senkewicz, a couple who have been my friends for decades and who created the opportunity that led to this improved and expanded version of my 1981 work. Robert and Rose Marie are insiders in my field. They have coauthored books on California history during the periods covered in my publications. They have translated and edited important earlier California works that recorded significant elements in the societies of their times. Now they are coeditors of the present work, and without doubt they are responsible for providing the impetus for its republication. Without them, *Californio Portraits: Baja California's Vanishing Culture* would never have been imagined, much less brought to life. ¡*Mil gracias, mis colegas!*

Series Editors' Introduction

We first met Harry Crosby in the early 1990s when we were in the process of translating and editing a then-unpublished manuscript on the early history of Alta California. The author, Antonio María Osio, had been born in Baja California. W. Michael Mathes of the University of San Francisco told us that Harry was working on the history of Baja California during the Jesuit era (1697–1767). He informed us that Harry could probably supply us with a great deal of information about Osio's family.

We contacted Harry and, with typical generosity, he shared with us much information he had gathered about Osio's grandfather Manuel, an important figure in eighteenth-century Baja California. That encounter developed into a friendship, and we gradually became aware of how Harry had become so interested in the land and people of what the Spanish called Antigua California.

As Harry relates in the preface to this volume, his assignment to illustrate *The Call to California* resulted in his first sustained contact with the people of the central Baja California mountains. *The Call to California* was published in 1968, but Harry continued his research on Baja California. He spent more time there, took additional photos, and visited archives in Mexico and the United

States. He published two books on Baja California in the mid-1970s: *The King's Highway in Baja California: An Adventure into the History and Lore of a Forgotten Region* (1974) and *The Cave Paintings of Baja California: Discovering the Great Murals of an Unknown People* (1975). The culmination of this phase of his work was the 1981 publication of *Last of the Californios*, a deeply personal account of the people he had come to know on his sojourns into the Baja California mountain regions. His magnum opus, *Antigua California: Mission and Colony on the Peninsular Frontier, 1697–1768*, appeared in 1994, and this was followed by *Gateway to Alta California: The Expedition to San Diego, 1769* (2003).

Harry has always had a soft spot in his heart for the mountain people whose lives touched him and made a profound impression on him. That is one of the main reasons he wrote *Last of the Californios*. The book also has resonated with readers in Baja California. It was translated into Spanish by Harry's good friend Enrique Hambleton and was published in La Paz, the capital of Baja California Sur, with an introduction by Eligio Moisés Coronado, one of the region's most significant historians.

For a number of years Harry has wanted to present the experiences of these Baja California pioneers to a new generation of readers. *Californio Portraits: Baja California's Vanishing Culture* is the fruit of that desire. Harry has composed a new foreword and substantially updated the historical sections of the work. He also has selected additional photographs that he took in Baja California, and they are included in this new edition, along with additional graphics and maps. We have updated the bibliography. We hope this volume introduces American readers to the still-too-unknown history of Baja California and to the extraordinary men and women who have inhabited the remote mountainous regions of that peninsula.

Californio PORTRAITS

Intro.1. Pioneers seeking uncontested land settled in central Baja California's mountains nearly two centuries ago. Typically, their descendants live in remote places such as Rancho Las Jícamas in the Sierra de Guadalupe. *Courtesy Harry Crosby Collection, Mandeville Special Collections, University of California, San Diego. All photographs are from the Harry Crosby Collection unless otherwise noted.*

Introduction

On September 13, 1791, only twenty-two years after the founding of the first Spanish settlement in Alta California, a Bostonian named John Green made the first recorded American contact with California soil, but the event was scarcely prophetic. Green, a gunner on one of Alejandro Malaspina's Spanish exploration ships, died the day Malaspina's expedition dropped anchor at Monterey. His entry in California's burial records assured his tiny niche in American history. Thomas Doak, also a native of Boston, has generally been regarded as the first American inhabitant of California. Doak left the *Lydia*, an American trading ship, at Monterey in March 1816 when the Spanish mission period was just at its height. He was baptized as a Catholic and lived some thirty years in the area.[1]

But there was another California—Baja California, the peninsula to the south. In the early nineteenth century, it too was visited by a few ships of the growing American fleet of fur traders, whalers, and general merchantmen then spreading over the globe. One of the earliest to drop anchor in a Baja California port was the *Maryland*, which left New York in late 1805 loaded with goods for

---

1. John Green's death is recorded in Mission San Carlos burial record #822, September 13, 1791. On Doak, see Bancroft, *The History of California*, 2:248, 275–77, 781.

sale or trade along the Pacific shores of both Americas. Although technically a smuggler, the Yankee trader was successful in eluding or bribing customs officials and doing business along the way. In January 1807, the *Maryland* put in at San José del Cabo, near the tip of the Baja California peninsula.

At that port, the visitors met and interacted with *Californios*, as the inhabitants of all California had been called since 1768 to distinguish them from mainland Mexicans. After the isolation and privations of their long sea voyage, the officers and men wrote with gratitude about how they were welcomed and how the mild weather appealed to them. Ahead of them lay the width of the Pacific, China, and then two more oceans, making at least another year of cruising before New York might be seen again. When the *Maryland* weighed anchor and sailed away from San José del Cabo on April 4, 1807, at least two of her crew had defected: the ship's carpenter, Louis le Roy, a Frenchman, and Thomas Smith, his twenty-three-year-old assistant from New York City. The pair had had enough of open seas and close confinement. The Frenchman soon found a ship bound for the mainland, but Thomas Smith cast his lot with the kindly strangers in that far corner of the world.

Smith's decision made him the first United States citizen to settle permanently in greater California. The sergeant in charge of local Spanish troops reported to the governor that on August 20, 1809, at the mining center of San Antonio south of La Paz, "the American, Thomas, was baptized, having shown a great desire to enter our company and submit to our laws." His godfather, a local hero, Alférez Xavier Aguilar, was a sixty-six-year-old retired soldier and native of Baja California. Smith took the baptismal name Javier Aguilar and used it for at least the next dozen years. The newly named expatriate American then married María Meza, a young widow from Comondú, and volunteered to serve. He first worked at the Presidio of Loreto as a ship's carpenter, then was promoted to the higher post of supervisor of all boat repairs at the Presidio of Pitic, located at Guaymas, across the gulf. Subsequent documents show that Smith-Aguilar finally settled down to raise a large family in the peninsular hamlet of Comondú, where he and his children eventually reassumed the Smith name.[2]

This previously unpublished American adventure introduces what would become a long but intermittent romance between Americans and Baja California. As citizens of the United States gradually infiltrated Alta California, they met, dealt with, and not infrequently married into families that had migrated from the original California to the south and still had relatives residing in its old mission villages. Americans occupied both La Paz and San José del Cabo during the Mexican War of 1846–48, which resulted in greater California being partitioned, the United States annexing Alta California, and Mexico retaining Baja California.

During that conflict hundreds of residents of the cape region had accepted the Americans' assurance that their land would become part of the United States. They had supplied the invaders with food and shelter and, doubtless, intelligence and directions. When the treaty that ended the war was published, these people were shocked to find that their lands would remain part of Mexico. They feared that they would face deadly reprisals from their patriot neighbors. Fortunately, the American army and navy commanders involved in that occupation appreciated the dilemma they had created with their earlier promises of safety. They arranged the only solution available to them: they obtained ships to transfer those who had aided the American cause to Monterey in Alta California, a total of over two hundred men, women, and children.

Not surprisingly, Thomas Smith's family, by then three generations, were among those who had to be transferred to Monterey to start new lives. As it happened, in less than five years it was evident that these people could return without fear to the peninsula and their former lives. Some preferred to remain in Alta California, but many, including at least two sons of Thomas Smith, returned with their families to the lower peninsula and became prominent members of the local population.

---

2. Information on Smith may be found in the Archivo General de la Nación, Mexico City, Provincias Internas 18, f. 264–95. See also Iselin, *Journal of a Trading Voyage around the World, 1805–1808*. Iselin was a crew member of the *Maryland*.

North American settlers and the great backwash of the gold rush of 1849 soon changed the face of power, once wholly Hispanic, in Alta California. This region experienced protracted economic development. But the California to the south had a very different fate. Isolated geographically and with only a small population and few obvious natural assets, Baja California was largely neglected by its own Mexican motherland and by foreign interests as well. Therefore its people, the forebears and then peers of Alta Californians, had little sense of the growing industrialization of Europe and the United States and little opportunity to change their ways accordingly. These *peninsulares* continued to live as eighteenth-century frontiersmen. What change there was occurred so gradually that visitors during the next 150 years would report on the slow tempo of life in Baja California and on its archaic ways.

As the decade of the 1970s opened, much of Baja California still had the air of a raw frontier, and casual visitors sensed little of its past. In the north, pressed against the international border, the cities of Mexicali and Tijuana had populations close to a half million each, unplanned growths that placed a heavy burden on an area with limited water, arable land, or other natural resources. Sixty miles below the border on the Pacific shore, Ensenada grew at a more modest rate and with a firmer economy based on agriculture, fishing, tourism, and port facilities. Farther south along the same coastal strip, new agricultural communities were growing rapidly, taking advantage of good land and at least a temporarily adequate supply of subterranean water.

The Vizcaíno Plain, at midpeninsula, bore many marks of recent activities. Seen from the air, this vast, once-trackless expanse of flat ground and bizarre vegetation was crisscrossed with newly scraped roads and other earthworks—scars resulting from oil exploration, agricultural developments, and the growth of fishing villages. Around Guerrero Negro Lagoon, square miles of grading marked the growth and operation of what was then the world's largest salt-harvesting complex.

Different kinds of development dotted the gulf side of the peninsula. At Bahía de Los Angeles new tourist accommodations were under construction and facilities for sport fishing were expanding. Bahía de la Concepción was already lined with camping places, trailer parks, and rental units. Older centers at Mulegé, Loreto, and La Paz all had grown rapidly, attracting and providing for tourism. The greatest display of luxury hotels and associated attractions could be found on beaches and bluffs between La Paz and Cabo San Lucas, where more than a dozen modern hotels catered to an international clientele.

Around Ciudad Constitución, a hundred miles northwest of La Paz, the Magdalena Plain was being developed for intensive agriculture, principally in cotton. Tens of thousands of acres were irrigated by pumping fossil water from sediments below. Nearby, in the southernmost foothills of the Sierra de la Giganta, large phosphate deposits were being strip-mined. Grading and trucking activities burgeoned in what shortly before had been a deserted badlands.

One development in Baja California facilitated all others, tied them together, and became the most conspicuous symbol of progress—the paved Transpeninsular Highway. Completed in 1973, it zigzagged from Tijuana to Cabo San Lucas. Side roads were rapidly being pushed out to small population centers and to areas eyed for development. Once the Transpeninsular Highway finally opened up Baja California, not even its most remote part was more than sixty airline miles from a paved road.

The newness of nearly every human endeavor visible in Baja California was matched by people who created, ran, and maintained them. When that outburst of economic growth began not many local people had funds, the needed skills, or the interest to acquire them. The rapid opening of Baja California required construction workers, vehicle operators, farmers, hotel personnel, and many other sorts of laborers and managers. Most of these were brought or attracted from the interior of the Mexican Republic. Lands were

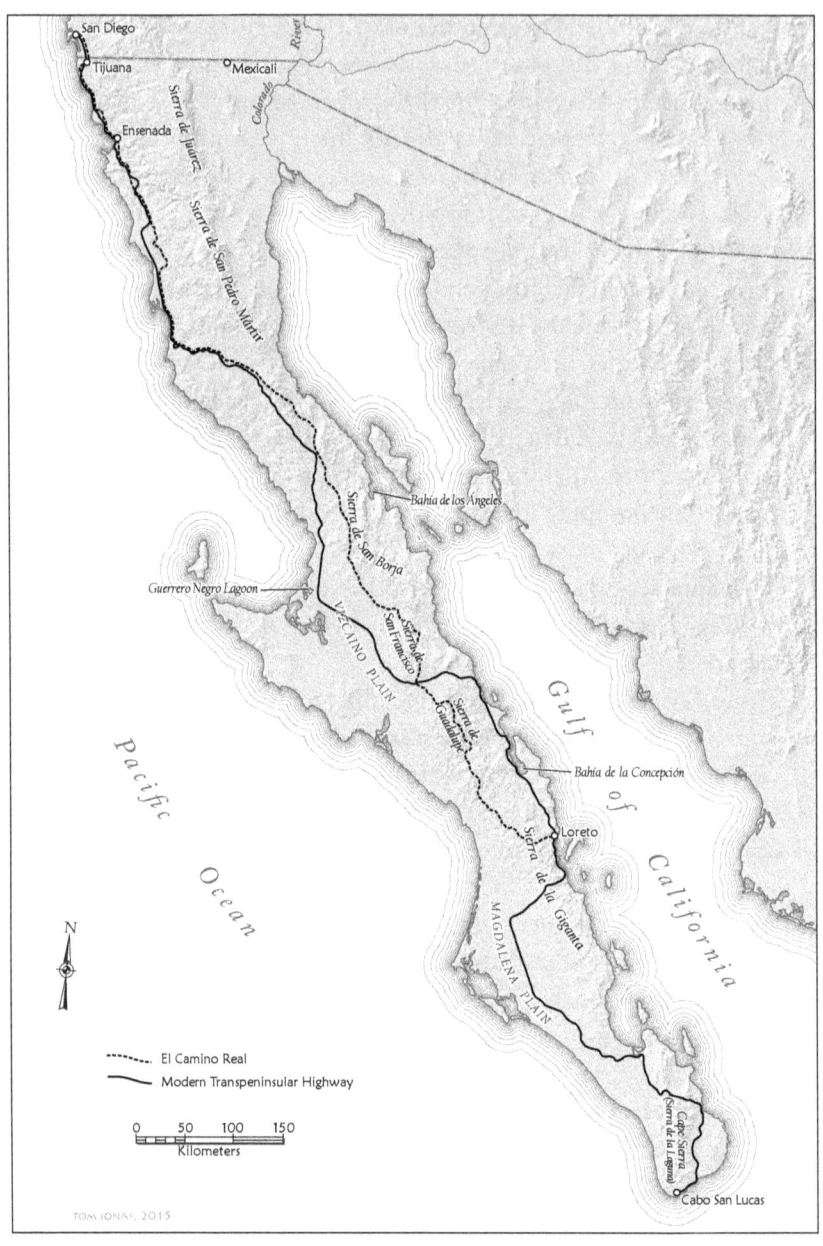

Map 1. Topography of Baja California showing the principal mountain ranges. Map by Tom Jonas. Copyright © 2015 by the University of Oklahoma Press.

made available to farm collectives—communal groups made up of unemployed men with their families enlisted from the poorest parts of mainland Mexico. The masses forming the large cities of the north likewise did not spring from native California roots but swelled with those who migrated from the interior of the republic. A measure of the newness of greater Baja California's population is a conservative estimate that soon after the Transpeninsular Highway opened, three-quarters of its inhabitants were either immigrants or children of immigrants.

The apparent Baja California of the time was a meeting place of desert and sea, rapidly becoming dotted with economic projects. The natural attractions found along gulf shores and at the cape were being exploited in a familiar pattern. The world was catching up with this oldest part of California, and it was being processed for modern needs.

Nevertheless, this description of Baja California at that time is incomplete, for significant pieces of geography and significant groups of people remained much as they had been for close to two centuries. Successive ranges of mountains form the backbone of the peninsula, and their steep broken terrain had as yet been little touched by the highway or commercial development. In these sierras, hundreds of families still lived more like their colonizing ancestors than like peoples in any other part of the changed lands or those living in their neighboring lowlands. Those mountaineers were descendants of soldiers, sailors, and other servants brought to assist in long ago missionary and military endeavors. Their ancestors provided pioneers in the original Hispanic settlement of Alta California and thus became forefathers of thousands of present-day United States citizens. However, prior to the mid-1970s and the completion of the Transpeninsular Highway, the contrasts between the lives of these distant cousins were so extreme that it was difficult to believe they were contemporaries. American California had become one of the world's most developed areas and, at the same time, one beset with all the problems associated with crowded quarters and high technology. At that time in

the peninsular mountains, the present much resembled the past. Accessible only by foot or by mule, these small but rugged sierras discouraged all but their own children from settling or even visiting their deep valleys and high places. There, ranch life was extraordinary for its self-sufficiency and its casual use of archaic practices.

Before 1980, an American visiting one of these homesteads could imagine that he had stumbled into an outdoor museum, a place designed to make him feel like an 1830s Yankee trapper emerging from the wilderness to find a Californio ranch. But it was far more than a museum display. Inanimate objects, however convincing, could not impart the disorientation, the sense of encountering a lost world that occurred when one met those ranchers and shared a few days of their lives. Then it really sank in. Those surrounding mountains were no diorama. Those buildings and implements were not historical reconstructions. Those people were not costumed actors or tour guides. Their archaic ways had the freshness of daily life and was, moreover, the only life they had ever known. And they

Intro.2. Kodalith of Californios.
Courtesy Harry Crosby.

were but vaguely aware of the incongruity of that life with the late twentieth century.

How did this all come about? How was this frontier culture planted in Baja California, and why did it persist for so long? Why did as many as two thousand people live in the same fashion in the oases of several sierras?

In words and pictures, this book endeavors to take the reader back into those mountains to visit those ranches before they were profoundly changed or abandoned. It attempts to capture glimpses of an old culture and answer questions about its origins. It is an expression of the author's profound gratitude for the opportunity to have experienced several years of extended contacts with the last of the Californios before their inevitable transformation by the bustling world below.

1.1. Pack trip crossing the uplands of the Sierra de San Francisco.

CHAPTER I

A Day at a Sierra Ranch

As viewed from the Transpeninsular Highway, the western sides of the sierras in central Baja California rise in irregular mounds, each made up of a progression of slopes topped by mesas that lead back to one or more peaks. In each case, the unseen eastern sides consist of taller, steeper rises and fewer mesas before ending in their peaks. From north to south these are the sierras of San Borja, San Juan, San Francisco, and Guadalupe. They are not tall in comparison to the world's other mountains: their elevations range from under five thousand to less than seven thousand feet. But they rise sharply and dominate views of the narrow peninsula to an exaggerated degree. Flying over gives a splendid sense of the sierras' origins. The most northerly three are irregularly rounded in outline; their dark volcanic masses still seem to pour out onto the lighter deserts. Fan-shaped mesas, especially, retain the appearance of great flows of lava frozen on their way down from the heights. Passing over the Sierra de San Francisco at a low elevation reveals that peaks are separated and mesas cut by deep ravines darkened by shadows and choked with palms.

Late in the day, the western side of San Francisco's dark lavas and tuffs commences to glow, and at sunset, when the desert floor is in shade, the sierra burns, a fiery red pile rising out of the gloom. At dusk, the mountains recede until they become no more than an inky silhouette against a dark, starry sky.

Moonrise converts the gulf to the east into a shimmering mirror, brilliant in contrast to the dark shore. Small clusters and moving dots of light show the human presence. A gaily illuminated ferry leaves its slip and glides away from the lighted town of Santa Rosalía, bound for Guaymas. Fifty miles west, an electric glow floods the plaza of the hamlet of San Ignacio, plays on the front of its old mission church, and winks skyward. Between the towns and beyond, car and truck headlamps throw long rays on the highway and shine on the margin of the desert that was brushed aside to let them pass.

Just north of these sights stands the rising mass of the San Francisco range. Even during the decade after the north–south highway was paved, few would have guessed that it contained significant human activity. But in fact, there were dozens of tiny ranches, a few larger ones, and two hundred or more people with a unique sierra way of life. Let us visit one family at one ranch, picturing all as it was in March 1973.

Rancho San Gregorio

The first sign of light in the eastern sky finds Loreto Arce on his open-air porch and wakes him as it has each morning of his life. Don Loreto throws blankets aside and sits up on his bed of rawhide thongs stretched on a hardwood frame. He puts his feet to the floor and shuffles them to find homemade shoes, which he puts on without socks. Rising, he finds a shirt hung carefully over the back of a chair and then, under it, a light jacket. Loreto tousles his wiry shock of curly dark hair and rubs the sleep from his eyes. He walks out into his garden and, quite oblivious of the canopy of fast-fading stars over his head, takes a dipper of springwater from a barrel and drinks. Then he rinses his face.

A medium-sized black and white dog has come out of the shadows and joined its master. It waits expectantly as the man makes

A Day at a Sierra Ranch

1.2. Loreto Arce talks to Tacho Arce at Rancho San Gregorio.

his way back onto the porch and feels around over a rafter for his pocket knife, a pair of pruning shears, and perhaps a ball of twine carefully set aside as he cleared his pockets after the previous day's work. Now ready to start his chores, Loreto Arce steps back into the garden and, with his dog, starts to climb cautiously down steep stairs carved into the stone cliff, which supports his ranch houses thirty feet above the bed of a water-worn *cañada*. Once on level ground, the rancher quickly finds his path among rounded boulders and cobbles in the watercourse. Man and dog head down the dry gulch between high rock walls. It is a journey that Loreto has made almost daily for forty-eight of his eighty years.

A series of small duties require the old man's attention. He tests a prop supporting a split palm-trunk flume carrying water to his lower orchard; he checks the rate of leakage at a union of two sections of this open "pipe." They are rotting, and he knows that soon he or his sons will need to make a bypass and effect repairs.

1.3. Rock paintings a few hundred yards upstream from Rancho San Gregorio.

As he emerges from the two hundred yards of shut-in canyon, the proprietor of Rancho San Gregorio catches sight of a work that has consumed most of his life.

In a wide spot of the capriciously water-carved cañada, a level area some two hundred feet wide and eight hundred or a thousand feet long, Loreto Arce, his wife, his children, and employees, when he could afford them, have laboriously created about two or three acres of productive land. All of it was once a rock-studded wash littered with uprooted *palo blanco* trees (*Lysiloma candidum*) and other more minor flotsam, its condition reflecting the typical aftermath of the most recent in an intermittent series of *chubascos*, the cyclonic summer storms that periodically lash the region.

Before 1928, this place showed only slight evidence of human activity. A series of shallow depressions in the walls of the narrow part of the cañada displayed remains of giant rock paintings, works thousands of years old by prehistoric people who made the sierra part of their annual rounds of hunting and gathering. They returned for such long periods that their stone artifacts litter every level. Their impressive ceremonial art—paintings on rock walls, usually under overhangs or in open caves—has been found at hundreds of sites. Their paintings are related to those found in the sierras adjacent to the north: San Francisco, San Juan, and San Borja. The huge and impressive murals found in these three ranges have received worldwide recognition for their unique artistry and great age, at least five to seven thousand years. They have been named "The Great Murals" by the Mexican government's National Institute of Archaeology and History.

During the late 1920s, Loreto worked as a goatherd, sharing a ranch with his father, Patricio Arce, at San Gregorito, a few miles away. Young Loreto ranged over the entire area, either rounding up goats or hunting deer and mountain sheep. At a place they knew as San Gregorio, he became familiar with a good little running spring that issued from a split in the volcanic rock and soon disappeared into the porous cañada floor. Loreto was by no means the discoverer of the spring. Indians found it in ancient times, hence the area's prolific display of art. The water was known and used occasionally all through the region's mission period, from about 1748 to 1810, and during subsequent years when the greater area was nearly depopulated. But Loreto Arce was the first man who decided to use the spring and pipe it half a mile to the nearest level terrain. He felled palms, split them in two, and hollowed the halves for his flumes. He built trestles to support them and hold them up on the sides of the waterway, out of reach of seasonal flooding. The whole system mirrors agricultural practices that the first missionaries brought to California before 1700. In those times, surface water always was conducted from its source to the site of its use rather than subterranean water being lifted up or pumped up out of wells.

When Loreto had arranged a supply of water at his level area, he still lacked any semblance of cultivable earth. To supply this, he brought in mules and burros and equipped them with *alforjas*, open rawhide pack-boxes. He and his relatives scoured the slopes and washes to find every small deposit of soil or even sand that could be scooped out and put into the alforjas. At the same time, Loreto Arce undertook a major civil engineering chore, nothing less than forcing the occasional runoff water flows in the cañada to follow a certain path and thereby spare the remainder of the level area from flash-flood devastation.

The last such deluge, before Loreto began his work, had left the open area not quite level; a discernible waterway had formed in a serpentine pattern as the flood caromed off one high sidewall and sped toward the other. This seasonal riverbed was a few feet lower than the rocky terraces on either side, and Loreto planned to use this to his advantage. About 1930, he began the monumental task of raising two-hundred- to four-hundred-pound boulders from the deeper parts of the waterway and lining them up as a levee to protect the higher levels during future floods. Gradually his three or so acres were cleared of their larger stones and surrounded with rock bulwarks five feet high and three to four feet wide. Then he brought his hard-won soil by burro-back in the leather hampers and created shallow but usable planting areas within his walls. Out of an intensely dry, barren-appearing wilderness, Loreto created one of the elaborate *huertas*, or orchard gardens, that may be found scattered through the midpeninsular sierras.

All of these labors were part of a local tradition reaching back to the early eighteenth century. At Comondú, about the year 1714, pioneer missionary Juan de Ugarte employed the same methods. He used pack animals to collect earth, and men with wooden and steel levers to roll great rocks into protective walls. Such dikes and backfills became standard installations at missions and mission ranches. Their remains are still visible at more than a dozen places. Post-mission copies are found at nearly every ranch where a huerta has been attempted, and in some ways the ranchers' efforts are more remarkable than those of the missionaries were. In mission times, dozens or even hundreds of Indians could be pressed into service, but during the nineteenth and early twentieth centuries, private citizens of these sparsely populated sierras could muster

1.4. A flume of split and hollowed palm logs crosses the seasonal streambed at Rancho San Gregorio in the isolated northeast corner of the Sierra de San Francisco.

1.5. Loreto Arce cleans dirt and leaves from his open irrigation system, here elevated atop a rock wall to maintain its gradual fall from a distant spring.

no such forces. It took tenacious men like Loreto, and they would dedicate years to achieve this goal. As a reward, each of the persistent ones became master of a livelihood: a huerta full of oranges, limes, grapefruit, pomegranates, figs, and grapes. These and many vegetable crops grew steadily here with liberal irrigation.

Just such an oasis spread before the old man's eyes as he walked carefully down the cañada. His flume, now ten feet in the air, crossed from one bank to the other over his head, and under it he could see the almost white rock wall that surrounded the nearest of his garden plots. Dark green columnar forms of eighteen-foot orange trees speckled with fruit rose from behind it. Above and beyond could be seen groups of the lovely white-barked and slender-trunked palo blanco trees native to the region. Even though their wood is useful for construction and their bark is indispensable in tanning leather, the Arce family has spared a number of nearby specimens, retaining them as grace notes to the canyon's charm.

Loreto spends no time savoring or even taking note of the scene. He has to cross the flood channel, and the path is rough. At his age, he prudently avoids a mishap by picking his way slowly among the uneven cobbles. Once across, he climbs a crude stile that puts him inside the huerta's great retaining wall. There, at the very top of his handmade orchard, is a critically important element in his irrigation system, a *pila* or reservoir made of stone and lined with concrete plaster. This open tank, some eight feet wide, twelve feet long, and three feet deep, holds over two thousand gallons of water that have accumulated since he irrigated the night before. His first act is to pull on a cord attached to a plug in the floor of the lower end of the pila. This releases the water, but the three-inch outlet pipe prevents too great a rush. The water enters the ditches of a distribution system and heads out into the grove and garden patches. Loreto quickly finds a hoe, which he had laid atop the wall, and in a moment he is busy changing the flow of his irrigation water by breaking down little dams and building others. Once his irrigation pattern is activated, he turns to hoeing weeds among his squash, horse beans, and onions. Another day of work is under way at Rancho San Gregorio.

San Gregorio lies in the northeastern foothills of the Sierra de San Francisco, almost exactly in the center of peninsular California. Just eight miles down the watercourse from the ranch one can see remains of the old Camino Real, the mission trail built in the mid-eighteenth century to facilitate north–south communications and the passage of supplies. Today, most of the small amount of traffic in the area is headed to or from Loreto's ranch. El Camino Real is quiet. Only an occasional rancher headed to Santa Gertrudis unwittingly duplicates the constant journeys of earlier times. The auto road nearest to San Gregorio is a rough and rocky pair of wheel tracks recently built into Rancho Santa Marta, twenty miles away. Loreto's sons dream of bringing this link to a point near San Gregorio, but the terrain is truly forbidding, and they probably will not succeed. Meanwhile, the family must sell or trade its products with other sierra folk or pack them for a long day's trip by mule or burro to Santa Marta and there negotiate for a truck ride to cover the remaining forty miles to San Ignacio. This route must be traversed whenever supplies or medical treatment are needed. No one complains. Only five years ago, the trip was all by mule and required three days.

At about eight o'clock, after a brisk two hours' work in his huerta, Loreto barks out a monosyllable to his dog and the two begin to retrace their steps to the ranch, both moving more freely over the rocks, which are now brilliantly illuminated by the morning sun. As they round the last bend of the *arroyo*, or watercourse, that had hidden the houses from their view, a serenade of ranch sounds greets them: another dog barks a welcome, a rooster crows, women talk and laugh, tortillas are slapped, and a radio emits a brisk flow of *la música norteña*, the typical musical fare heard in all rural northwest Mexico. Loreto hears all this but gives it no thought. He climbs carefully up steps in the bedrock bank and heads for the kitchen.

The cooking facility is housed deliberately in San Gregorio's least substantial structure. Three other buildings have concrete floors, plastered and painted adobe walls, doors, windows with glass, and

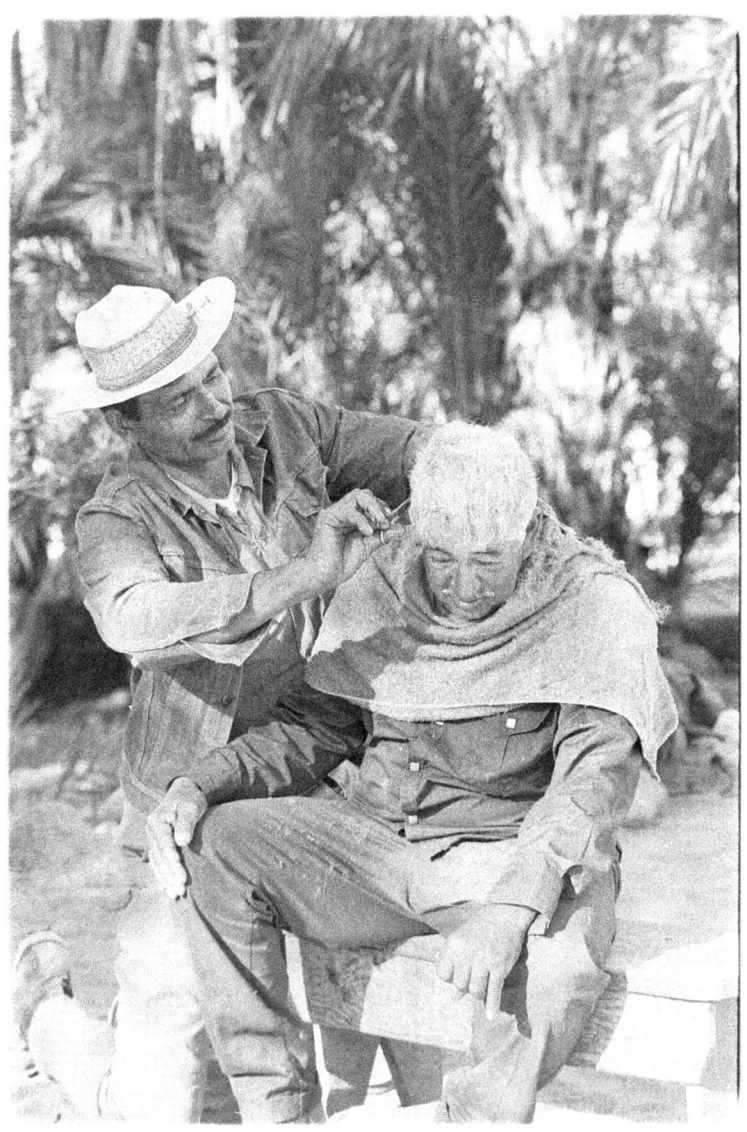

1.6. Tacho Arce gets a haircut from a friend at a ranch outside the town of Santa Gertrudis.

1.7. Following an ancient custom, meals are cooked and served by the women, who do not sit down to eat until the men have finished.

heavy thatched roofs. The kitchen, by comparison, is only a *ramada*, a framework of palo blanco trunks topped by a thin palm thatch, dirt-floored, and walled in on three sides by woven mats and laced branches. Such an open kitchen is essential: nearly every day at San Gregorio is warm, and during the long summers, they are stiflingly hot—120 degrees Fahrenheit is not unusual in July, August, or September. Even in that heat small pieces of hardwood branches must be burned to cook food in pots, to boil water, or to heat the *comal*, or griddle, on which the indispensable tortillas are cooked. Then the open-air character of the kitchen is essential to dissipate the heat. During the chill of winter mornings, women crowd around the stove to do their work. Another common practice is to take a shovel full of coals from the stove and put it in the center of the kitchen floor. Then all the ranch's people, men and women, stand around the glowing pile while they drink their first coffee of the day.

Loreto goes to the kitchen to greet his wife, Josefa; his youngest daughter; and a daughter-in-law. His hands are filled with onions and summer squash he has brought up from the huerta. He accepts a cup of coffee and sits at the dining table on the *corredor*, the shaded porch immediately outside the kitchen and sleeping rooms. Two of three sons now in residence at the ranch drift in from their occupations. Breakfast follows in a series of leisurely courses as different items are prepared and brought out to the table. Following an old custom, the men are seated and all three women remain in the kitchen, chatting as they pound, slice, grind, and cook various foodstuffs.

When the men have excused themselves and gone back to work, the women bring refilled serving dishes to the table and take their own breakfast. This custom of eating in two sittings apparently arose from a tradition of male preeminence and men's more pressing needs after a stint of heavy work. It seems to have little connection with any taboo against women sitting in men's presence, because when the women do sit to eat, a man may come and stand or sit to talk to them without in any way disturbing the seating arrangements or the progress of their meal.

A staple of Baja California sierra cooking is the *sopa*, a dish of such varied contents that its only constant ingredients seem to be warmth and wetness. Sopas may consist of watery rice containing sauteed bits of pepper, onion, and dried meat or fish, or a sopa may have a base of pasta such as elbow or shell macaroni and much the same seasonings as the rice. Still other sopas contain chunks of meat, potato, squash, or *chayote*, a squashlike member of the cucumber family.

Another dish that may be served at any meal is a gruel of pinto beans mashed somewhat to form a fairly smooth semi-liquid. And a component of all meals is a succession of freshly prepared flour tortillas cooked one after another on a hot griddle and brought to the table in threes and fours until no one present can eat more.

After breakfast, the kitchen chores are divided. One younger woman washes dishes while another sweeps the dining area and adjacent yard. Doña Josefa goes out to begin her daily garden ritual: watering her many potted plants, feeding caged birds and squirrels, cutting flowers for the table and the family shrine and, finally, hosing down the whole yard outside the kitchen and corredor. This relatively lavish use of water is a much-appreciated luxury. Only two or three other ranches in the entire Sierra de San Francisco have such an abundant supply so conveniently piped into the living area.

Loreto's youngest son, Francisco, is a handsome man in his late thirties, quick, smiling, intelligent, and immensely capable at every skill required in sierra ranching. He is a true heir to Loreto, and it is his presence more than anything else that keeps Rancho San Gregorio in such splendid condition as its creator passes eighty years of age. Francisco's decisive hand is seen everywhere: in repairs, new construction, trail building, leather curing, and all the other crafts that make the ranch work or help to pay its bills. Leather curing and leather working are the trades for which Francisco is best known in the sierra. Even in San Ignacio his handwork is admired, as was that of his father before him. Just now, he is engaged in moving a series of hides through the tanning stage, a long process that requires his attention one or more days a week.

1.8. Food is cooked on adobe stoves fueled by small pieces of dry hardwood. One or two cooks simultaneously prepare tortillas, two or three hot dishes, and coffee.

The exact procedures are fascinating because they perpetuate the practices of long ago, the eighteenth century, at least, and because they employ only materials available in the area.

San Gregorio produces few hides, even though Loreto's clan has a small herd of cows for milk. Each year a small number of bull calves are born and eventually provide hides, but the majority that Francisco cures come from ranches on the western rim of the sierra. Owners of large herds regularly send hides to San Gregorio in exchange for finished leather goods.

Top: 1.9. Leather is tanned at San Gregorio today in the same way that it was in all California two centuries ago.
Bottom: 1.10. Using homemade vats, Francisco Arce cures cow, goat, and deer hides in tanning fluid brewed from the bark of palo blanco, a common tree of midpeninsular arroyos.

When enough raw hides, usually eight or so, are on hand to make starting a batch worthwhile, they are immersed in limewater, a saturated solution of quicklime, for fifteen to twenty days. The vats used for this liming treatment are a prominent feature at any sierra ranch where leather is cured. They are usually chiseled out of soft bedrock close to a natural water catchment or a spring. They are very conspicuous because the tanner must work and agitate the hides during their two- to three-week soak, and after years of use, lime builds up all around the vats, often staining an area of two or three hundred square feet, as if all had been whitewashed many times.

The lime itself was traditionally prepared by burning limestone chipped from central Baja California's numerous local deposits. One still sees the little pile-of-rock kilns that were fired with dried local hardwoods, principally mesquite (*Prosopis palmeri*). Once fired, the dehydrated lime was reduced to a powder by grinding on a large *metate*, a stone mortar, using a heavy handstone, or *mano*. The same lime, called *cal*, was used to convert cornmeal to the *masa* from which corn tortillas were made. Nowadays, most tanners are able to get sacked lime, their trade's only concession to the twentieth century.

When liming is finished, the hides are scraped with the dull backside of a knife. The hair is removed from one side, and all the saponified fat and membrane from the other. Then they are rinsed in clear water for four or five days to remove lime and various soluble by-products of its action on rawhide.

The hides are now carried up from the area of the spring and the lime vats and are immersed in a solution of tanbark. This is a picturesque activity because the homemade tanning vats are unusual, eye-catching structures and because the tanning solution is a deep, rich, blood-red color. Each tanner makes his vats, or *tinas*, in the classic manner of the region. From palo blanco branch wood, two to three inches in diameter, he builds a square frame on legs, a sort of table without a top, four feet on each side. The legs and crosspieces are mortised together and lashed in place

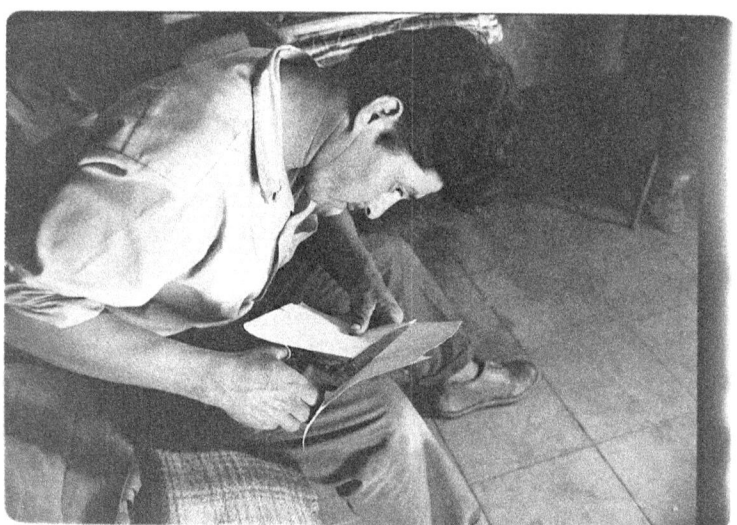

Top: 1.11. Partially tanned hides are smeared with oil prepared from turtles taken from the nearby gulf.
Bottom: 1.12. Francisco Arce, Loreto's son, does leatherwork.

with rawhide thongs. Over the frame a large cowhide (or two hides stitched and caulked together) is loosely slung so that it collapses inside the frame and forms a great open pocket. The edges of the hide, or hides, are then stitched to the frame with more thongs. When this tina is filled with water, the hide is stretched taut and bellies down nearly to the ground.

Tanning solution is made by filling the tina with fresh-hewn chips of palo blanco bark and letting them brew for days in the water. Just before the solution is used, the chips are bailed out, leaving a rich, red-brown liquor called *tinta*, or ink.

Actually, the lime-treated rawhides are started in a used or partially spent tanning solution. For the first week or two, they are manipulated frequently, perhaps every second or third day, in order to insure that the tanning ink reaches all surfaces and penetrates evenly. After two to three months, the hides are removed from the tinta and hung wet over cords strung between trees or posts. Oil from sea turtles taken in the gulf is rubbed liberally on both sides of each as soon as the liquid has dripped off. The oil-slathered hides are dried for five days and then returned to a vat filled with fresh, full-strength tinta. After a month they are pulled out for the last time and rubbed all over with turtle oil or a paste made of animal brains, or a mix of both. When thoroughly dried, the tanned hides are ready to be cut and worked.

Today Francisco has one tina to agitate. To do so he must remove the hides, then turn and re-immerse them. The contents of another tina are ready to drain and oil. These operations require two hours. He then proceeds to his own little house where he has a worktable, various shoe lasts and other wooden forms, and a variety of leather-working and cutting tools. Here he will cut hides into pieces appropriate for making saddles, belts, shoes, *polainas* (the leather leggings worn by every sierra man), and whatever other trappings are needed for ranch men or beasts. However, Francisco Arce's next chore is not to create a new object but to renovate an old one. An *aparejo*, a packsaddle for a burro, needs to be emptied of its old, matted straw stuffing and repacked with fresh, dry, resilient straw.

The aparejo has not been used for days and, in San Gregorio's ultra-low humidity, has become thoroughly dry. Francisco pries open the slits through which the stuffing was introduced and pulls it out by handfuls. In a few minutes he has cleared both sides, each a separate container. Now he takes bundles of straw, each the size of a mature celery plant, bends them in the middle and forces that middle first into the slit. This way he avoids crumpling the loose ends that would catch if they were introduced first. Once inside, the bundles are straightened out and arranged to fill the cavities efficiently. As each side of the aparejo fills, it is increasingly difficult to push in additional bundles. Francisco uses a blunt hardwood stick and a mallet, driving home the straw until the packsaddle is plump and hard. This new straw will remain resilient enough for at least a season to protect the burro from the jabs and buffets of his loads—principally *huacales* or homemade crates used to take ranch produce to market and then to bring home supplies. Francisco, satisfied at last with the condition of the aparejos, carries them down to the tackroom located near the bed of the arroyo and slings them over a rafter along with assorted saddles, saddlebags, bridles, spurs, halters, and other gear used on riding or pack animals.

Characteristic of the tradition from which they spring, all of these leather items and the craftsmanship that produces them descend little changed from the days when Francisco's forebears came to help the mission founders. Jesuit Fathers Miguel del Barco and Johann Jakob Baegert, describing their missionary experiences in Baja California before 1767, mention the preparation and tanning of leather and the specific use of the palo blanco tree to provide tanbark. When Alta California was opened, the practice of leather tanning was put to use as soon as its settlers had a supply of hides. Every mission had a kiln to burn limestone and create lime. When finely ground, this served in making mortar for construction, in treating corn to make the masa for tortillas, and in removing the fat from hides to be tanned. By 1792, two thousand hides were reported to have been cured at Mission Santa Clara. At the Presidio of Santa Bárbara, a corporal was paid 150 pesos a

A Day at a Sierra Ranch

1.13. Ranch-made packsaddles are periodically stuffed with fresh straw to ensure that they act as effective buffers between pack animals and their loads.

year to attend to the tanning. There was nothing peculiar about a corporal who was also a tanner. Nominally soldiers, the first Hispanic settlers of both Californias were actually frontiersmen with the skills to provide for many needs out of native materials.

Since breakfast Loreto has done nothing but odd jobs. His workbench in the shady corredor is piled high with objects that need attention: a little sewing here, a rivet there, a new handle to be carved for a valuable kitchen knife. Loreto has put on his glasses for this fine work. They are what most people call reading glasses, but Loreto would never use that term. Like most sierra people, he can read, but slowly and with little pleasure. Few books, magazines, or even comics are ever brought to the ranch. While the old man works, he visits intermittently with another of his sons, Agustín, who works every day in the corredor.

Agustín has been blind since childhood, apparently a victim of complications arising from measles. His contribution to the family economy is untwisting the three bundles of nylon fibers that form heavy nylon rope and then dividing the bundles into suitable smaller strands and braiding them into lead ropes for horses, mules, and burros. Agustín wears a wide leather belt while he works. He wraps the lines he will join around his body in such a way that he can lean back and allow his weight to draw the braiding very tight. He also taps it with a mallet as he goes along, thus further "setting" the fibers and making the final product extremely firm, a characteristic that is prized and creates a large demand for the blind man's work.

Agustín's life is very quiet. Because of the wildly craggy and rocky terrain around San Gregorio, he has nowhere to go for even a short stroll. He is overweight and seldom rides muleback, as no one has time to take him out for pleasure jaunts. Only once every two or three years does he join a brother to make the long ride to Santa Marta. He then goes by truck to visit San Ignacio. When he is not working, he listens to a battery radio turned up only enough for his acute hearing, or, late in the day, he may play softly on his guitar. When visitors come, Agustín listens attentively to all the gossip, the inevitable "catching up" that takes place among friends and neighbors who may go weeks or months without seeing each other. But the blind man is very shy, and his isolation gives him very little to add to conversations. Everyone greets him ceremoniously and takes pains to say goodbye, but when they shake his hard, work-worn hands, that comes as close as they know to how to establish contact, to make him feel part of the sierra community.

Just as the midday meal is being put on the table, another of Loreto's sons returns to the ranch. After waking at first light like his father, Juan Arce, called only by his nickname "Rango," was off into the cañadas above the ranch to collect wild honey. Such a chore suits Rango, who lacks his various brothers' aptitude or taste for repetitive work.

Every ranch man and boy is alert to any signs that indicate a source of wild honey. All know how to follow bees in flight, to notice the hum from their hives or the stains that run from these hives even when they are in high crevices in the bedrock canyon walls. Once found, these bees' nests, called *enjambres*, are never forgotten. If they can be reached, part of their honey is confiscated twice a year, but with enough left to sustain the hive. No effort is spared to reach as many as possible. A good enjambre yields two or three gallons of honey, and a man will build tall ladders, drive steel bars into rock crevices, swing from ropes, or climb precarious hand- and footholds to reach one. Having arrived, he starts a small fire below the hive using fuel that he takes from a sack slung over his shoulder. When the blaze is strong, he damps it with greens from the same container until smoke billows upward.

Once the bees are stupefied, the honey gatherer reaches into the hive with his hands. Or, if necessary, he uses improvised tongs and scoops out pieces of comb and honey that are then dropped into an old-fashioned, square five-gallon tin. After lowering this precious load to a safe landing, the collector retraces the steps of his usually difficult approach.

The bees are a European type gone wild. Since no mission records mention their culture, it must be assumed that they were brought into the area during the latter part of the nineteenth century. A probable source was American California, just north of the peninsula. In San Diego County, as early as the 1880s, honey was a major industry that could boast of twenty thousand hives. In the Baja California sierras today, not even the eldest can recall when the bees first came and, in their lifetimes, honey has been second only to deer flesh as the most prized harvest among all the wild food.

Rango's spirits are high. He was not hurt in his climbs, was stung only twice, got a fair cache of honey (a little over two gallons), found some lost goats, and got back in time for the midday meal. During this dinner, which is not significantly different from breakfast, he describes his adventures. Old Loreto clearly enjoys every detail. Although his honey-collecting days are over, he had first discovered that enjambre many years before, had visited it often, and still recognizes every branch and crevice of the described ascent.

1.14. A beehive waiting to have honey removed.

Since it is still winter and relatively cool, no one but the tired Rango takes a siesta. After their meal, the women begin preparing the evening's supper or doing other chores. Agustín returns to his rope making, and Loreto goes off to do the few weeding, watering, and picking chores in his small upper huerta just across the cañada from the houses. Francisco begins to collect the gear that he will need for a long ride. Early the following morning, he will leave for San Ignacio. The family needs some supplies, and he has leather goods to deliver to his customers. He feels that neither the load going to town nor the one projected to return requires that

1.15. Kodalith of a mule with packsaddles.
Courtesy Harry Crosby.

he hire a pickup truck and driver for the stretch between Santa Marta and San Ignacio. He will take his riding mule and a couple of pack burros on the hundred-mile round trip, a day and a half in each direction.

Late in the day, Francisco is off to round up his mule and the burros. Loreto starts again his long walk down the winding cañada to the great lower huerta. The other half of it must be watered, and Loreto hurries because winter shortens his workdays. When he arrives, puffing a little, he notes with satisfaction that his pila has filled properly. Apparently there is no serious leak in his flume. He opens the gate, releasing the pent-up waters, and begins the work of building and breaking down the little dams that control the flow in the tiny canals. The huerta is now in deep shadow and not even the high hill to the east reflects the sun. To the west, the great wall of the sierra blocks out any sign of a sunset.

As Loreto finishes his duties, sounds can be heard on the rocky floor of the canyon. Francisco is leading his animals and waits while Loreto plugs the pila. Together, father and son pick their way back up the dark but familiar path to the house.

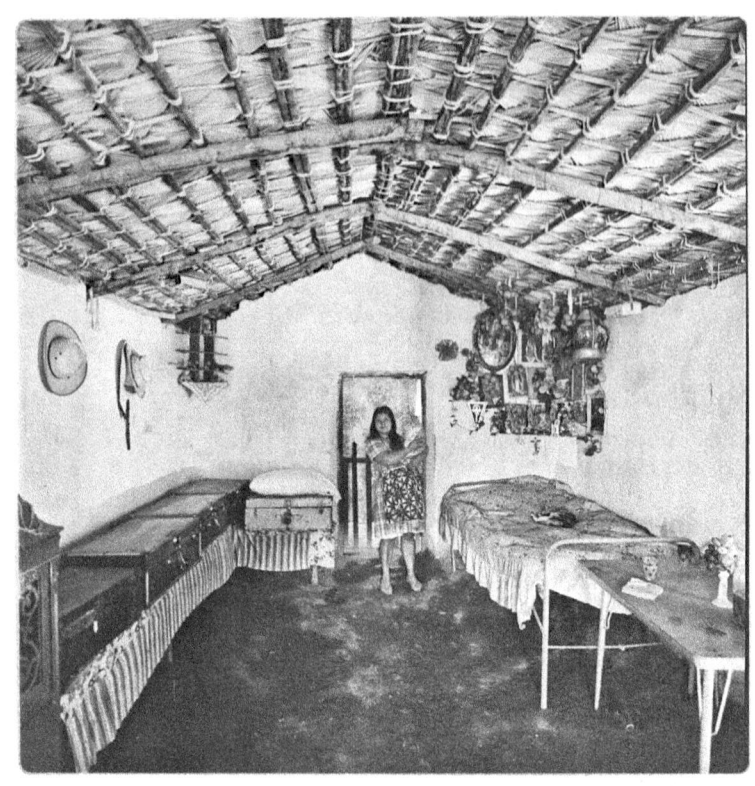

1.16. Josefa Arce's bedroom shrine is typical of an alcove or corner in each ranch that is crowded with religious objects and used for private devotions.

The radio provides a musical background at supper, which is the lightest and simplest meal of the day, consisting of a sopa, beans, and a few leftover tortillas. After they finish eating, the men move their chairs back and converse with the women, who then eat and clean up. Francisco and his wife go off to bed, Agustín strums softly on his guitar, and Rango sits by him, half singing the words suggested by the tunes. One in particular recurs in Agustín's playing, a slight, mournful melody to which Rango intones:

> The huitlacoche *sighs*
> *And sighs and cries*
> *For Catalina....*

The *huitlacoche* is a small bird with a large head, the warbler of the mountains and plains. This song was written by Germán, the eldest son of Loreto and Josefa. If the old man were listening, he could be depended on to chuckle and remind everyone that Germán's wife is named María de Jesús.

By 7:30 everyone is on his way to bed. Doña Josefa lights a candle and goes into a bedroom where a little shrine is set up. Lighting two votive candles, perhaps for children who died in infancy, she sits very quietly for a few minutes quite alone with her thoughts. Finally, she pinches out the candles and goes to her room. Loreto has rolled into his bed on the porch. The dog crawls under it and the day has ended. The only sounds are those of the mule and burros tied up below and chewing steadily on branches of fresh green mesquite that has been cut to fortify them for their journey ahead.

CHAPTER 2

Gente de Razón

The faces and ways of the mountain people of Baja California manifest a culture established in this area three centuries ago. Over those long years, their geography and the quirks of history left these frontier folk socially isolated and nearly untouched by the tumultuous epochs that utterly transformed most of North America. These are a people whose story is not easy to obtain, for the same forces that created their isolation also tended to inhibit the production and preservation of records on which local and family histories depend. Nevertheless, a thorough search of the relatively few surviving documents—church registers of baptisms, marriages, and burials, military rolls and reports, civil records of deeds to land, and a few other miscellaneous documents—yield enough facts to provide the basis for a descriptive history. Other information and color can be gleaned from the writings of occasional outsiders. A series of Spanish, English, French, American, and even Japanese visitors recorded their experiences with the California peninsula and its people during the century that began with 1769. During that period, its ports were backwaters, and its mountains were vacant spaces on maps derived almost entirely from drawings and reports made by navigators, not by explorers of the land.

We will look at those accounts, but first it is important to review briefly the events related to Baja California that took place during the 150 years before any people of European culture permanently occupied what had become a fabled land.

In 1521, Spaniard Hernán Cortés conquered the Aztec Empire, whose capital, Tenochtitlán, lay in the region that would become Mexico City. Further conquests of areas to the north, south, and west created Spanish holdings that would soon bear the name New Spain and would continue to grow for decades to come. However, within ten years, Hernán Cortés had heard reports of a landmass lying offshore from the most northwesterly Spanish holdings. In 1535, after receiving reports from men who returned from a somewhat aborted exploration, Cortés personally sailed across the intervening water and tried to plant a colony on the new discovery; the site he chose eventually became the Baja California city of La Paz. The conquistador soon returned to more pressing mainland affairs, and the colony languished for lack of every imaginable necessity. The Spanish colonists had never seen or dreamed of such an inhospitable place: hot, dry, sterile, occupied by hostile natives, and lacking in exploitable resources. Many died before the settlement was abandoned in 1536.

Shortly before the conquest of Mexico, a Spanish author named Garcí Rodríguez de Montalvo had written and had published *Las sergas de Esplandián* (*The Exploits of Esplandián*), a romantic adventure that featured a fabulous island replete with gold, pearls, and Amazons—standard ingredients in such literature during those times. This place was located "on the right hand of the Indies," an ambiguous phrase that seemed to describe the island location visited by Cortés, since people still believed that "the Indies" lay not far to the west of New Spain. Not surprisingly, this "island" was soon called California.

During 1542 and 1543, Juan Rodríguez Cabrillo sailed north from the west coast of Mexico, passing this supposed island without noting its true nature as a peninsula. He continued along the coast, perhaps as far as present-day Oregon, claiming the land for Spain as he went. Many geographic details remained vague after that voyage, but at the same time, the concept of California clearly had been extended beyond the tiny area explored by Cortés and his men.

A Religious Colony

Naming the new land was one thing, but possessing it was quite another. The Spaniards certainly had incentives to possess it: Cortés had returned with pearls, and ironically, California's gold had been foretold by the same romantic book that gave the land its name. Spanish pearlers operated profitable businesses in the lower regions of the gulf east of California, but made no attempt to occupy the land itself. Trade galleons bringing Asian goods to Mexico from Manila in the Philippine Islands, began to sight California shores almost annually after 1565 while returning from their epic round trips, Acapulco southwest to the Philippines, then north almost to Japan, then east to the shores of North America before coasting south to Acapulco. When these great cargo carriers reached the California coast, their crews were in crucial need of water and fresh food. Spain planned endlessly to create a base to relieve the distress of those vessels so vital to her trade. But money was short, men were few, the distances immense, and the winds adverse. For the century and a half following Cortés's visit, the efforts to establish a Spanish presence in California all failed, and the place remained an aloof, romantic legend.

All Spanish conquests in the New World had two elements—military and religious. Each major campaign began with Spanish armed forces attempting to establish supremacy in the area. The Spanish military was generally accompanied by priests, and the conversion of native peoples was largely entrusted to priests drawn from the most prominent Catholic missionary orders, namely Franciscan, Jesuit, and Dominican. Franciscans would establish the greater part of the mission areas in northern New Spain. However, during the 1590s, the Jesuits began to establish a series of missions on the mainland coastal plains just east of the

Gulf of California, beginning in the southern area of what today is the Mexican state of Sinaloa and working north through today's state of Sonora.

From 1683 to 1685, Jesuit missionary Eusebio Francisco Kino took part in an unsuccessful effort to colonize California. After that failure, Kino pioneered the locations for new missions in northern Sonora and what is now southern Arizona, but he never forgot California. Kino helped to inspire another Jesuit in Sonora, Juan María de Salvatierra, to launch a successful California mission campaign in 1697; its landing place was a midpeninsular base he named Loreto.

Padre Salvatierra's missionary career had begun a decade earlier in the rugged mountains of eastern Sonora. There, for almost a century, Jesuit missionaries had shared regional authority with the captains of local presidios. The missionaries were well aware that these military men protected not only their missions but also mining camps and ranches against bands of unconverted Indians. In Sonora, determined to guard and retain the lands and rights of their missions and to shield neophytes from exploitation, the Jesuits put themselves into direct conflict with the area's miners, ranchers, traders, and, at times, even military authorities. Those groups formed the coalition that dominated the area's private economic sector. That coalition constantly petitioned higher powers for access to resources controlled by the Jesuits, principally Indian labor and the best range and agricultural land.

Because previous attempts to establish a Spanish presence on the fabled island of California had been so costly to the Crown, the Jesuits proposed to undertake this occupation at their own expense. And aware of the advantages that should result from this promise, they petitioned the Spanish Crown for unusual authority. They requested and were granted control of all temporal matters, military and civilian, as well as the usual command of the spiritual crusade. These unusually broad powers led to almost half a century of California history dominated by religious activities that excluded colonization in the usual sense of the word.

The popular image of the Spanish Colonial mission frontier is peopled only by missionaries and Indians. The Jesuits themselves would have preferred such purely religious communities, but a century of missionary experience in the greater region had taught them the need for military escorts and servants skilled in essential lines of work. Experience also dictated that these should be married men accompanied by wives and families. Otherwise they could not be retained for long periods without having undesirable interactions with newly converted Indian women. Therefore, the Jesuits based their California mission system at Loreto by founding a fortress, the Presidio of Loreto, which soon had a roster of twenty-five soldiers, four or five shipwrights, a similar number of sailors, and several servants. Families of Hispanic people would become a significant and gradually increasing social element within the first decade or two of the conquest.

In those early days of the California missions the number of Indians was relatively large, and the little colony of Spanish-speaking people made up a minor population statistic. But many of the Indians did not adapt to the new ways. The newcomers introduced new diseases, and the native population declined precipitously. Meanwhile, the families of soldiers and servants flourished. Their offspring were quite incidental to the planned conquest, but from them arose a Hispanic population that ultimately would supplant the Indians and outlast the missionaries. The story of Baja California's old-fashioned sierra cultures begins with the people originally chosen solely to assist missionaries in opening a raw new land.

Frontier Culture in Northern New Spain

Frontier life was not popular in the Spanish world. By contrast with areas settled by northern Europeans, Spain's possessions produced sparse scatterings of frontier settlements. Even when inducements were offered, the government had difficulty in attracting colonists to remote areas. Hispanic people traditionally preferred an urban environment, and if they could not live in cities, they gravitated at least to towns. Isolated ranches, so common in places like Canada, the United States, or Australia, were never a prominent feature in the Hispanic scheme of things. As the frontier developed in northwestern New Spain—the name given to today's Mexico during its colonial years—most settlers lived in widely scattered villages and towns, few with populations as large as one thousand.

A surprisingly large percentage of the people willing to live on the west coast of New Spain were descendants of men who had come there as Spanish conquerors, or conquistadors, during the mid-sixteenth century. Most of them were poor men seeking fortunes and prestige with which to return to Spain, a dream realized by only a few. Most stayed on because here they had acquired land and better opportunities than they had enjoyed in their homeland.

Since these pioneers of European descent shared the frontier with mission Indians, the need arose for a name by which they could be distinguished, a name implying their European background and "old Christian" character. In the Spanish of those times, the term *gente de razón* had those connotations. It came into use all along New Spain's northern frontier and was retained by those who became entrenched in California.

The term *gente de razón* conveys complex and subtle ideas. Literally, it could be said to mean "informed people" or "people of reason," but that translation sheds little light on its historical connotation. Some reference works give its meaning simply as "white people," or apply it to natives of partly European descent along a largely Indian frontier. Neither definition adequately reflects the original usage or the realities of racial mixture on the frontiers of this new Spanish colony.

New Spain's northwestern areas were invaded not by families of Spanish colonists but by troops of Spanish soldiers. As they seized or claimed land and settled on it, two marriage patterns appeared and immediately established divergent racial and social lines. Men who were already married or had any wealth were able to bring in women of at least part Spanish descent. However, many early frontier settlers commingled with local Indian women. Children of these latter unions were called *mestizos*, and they became a growing element in the population of the rather isolated west coast of New Spain. Also, before any of these people colonized California, men of African descent came or were brought to the mainland frontier, some as slaves to work mines and some as free men seeking opportunity and relief from harsh racial oppression. In time, these blacks also commingled with Indians, adding a third genetic strain. On the mainland, people who descended from any black mixture were typically called *pardos*, "dark or dusky ones," but in California the preferred term was *de color quebrado*, "of mixed or diluted color," referring to the range of hues apparent in the skin of people with varying amounts of African, Indian, and European blood.

Despite their racial differences, all of these newcomers on the frontier scene bore a transplanted Spanish cultural stamp. Even if they or their descendants married Indian women, their children were born Christian and took on the customs, forms, and practices of the Hispanic heads of households. All were accepted as gente de razón in frontier societies. Therefore, the most informative definition of gente de razón might be "people who were born as Christians and whose lives followed a recognizably Hispanic cultural pattern."

This frontier society from which California's pioneers would largely be drawn was far from homogeneous in anything but basic culture. Social stratifications existed and were perpetuated but in a distinctly gentler fashion than in the older societies of central New Spain. This difference occurred in nearly every colonial setting in the New World, reflecting the interdependence of people taking over remote places.

In the older, longer-settled population centers, a continuum of family and social ties could be traced from the highest to the lowest status levels in the community, and the gente de razón's modest cultural and social attainments corresponded closely to status. Only people of relatively high standing corresponded with or entertained officials or other men of culture and thus learned some refinements of language and thought. Lesser gente de razón typically showed lesser degrees of sophistication.

At the top, in matters of political or economic power, were the principal landowners. A few of them were Spaniards by blood, and a larger number were of more or less white New World people somewhat loosely called *españoles*. Ranging down from them on the social ladder were mestizos with smaller landholdings, many of whom were relatives of important ranchers. And below them was a laboring class, with varying degrees of European, African, or Indian descent, which included cowboys, carpenters, masons, miners, sailors, servants, and the like. Most Indians lived in tribal or mission communities, but significant numbers became attached to the lowest level of gente de razón society, providing a pool of laborers and helpers to the humbler artisans.

In spite of these valid generalizations, this colonial society was not a sealed system in which each person was frozen into place according to his racial or cultural background. Capable, productive men at the lower end of those scales often heard the call and migrated to isolated, difficult frontiers where demand for their skills and devotion allowed them to rise socially regardless of race or caste. Some achieved relatively high status along with wealth. All in all, the population at the extremity of the road to California was typical of such frontiers found all over Spanish America. Generation after generation, these people adapted to their environment, yet they were clearly part of the greater Hispanic culture.

That said, it is important to note that a special factor helped to mold the society of those who went to assist the missionaries in California: Jesuit perceptions and needs.

Recruiting for California Service

Experienced missionaries planned and directed the physical occupation of California. These men understood that soldiers and servants must be chosen wisely because they would associate constantly with newly converted Indians. Soldiers were responsible for discipline and, for better or worse, in their daily lives they served as examples to new converts. And missionaries had another compelling and personal stake in these selections: missionaries and soldiers would be thrown together for company. At isolated missions this usually meant one priest and one soldier. Indeed, for weeks or months on end a soldier might be not only the padre's protector, but also the only person with whom he could have any real conversation.

Missionary needs dictated the hiring of men who could help missions to live off a difficult land—men who could eat its fruit, build with its materials, raise stock on its forage, and cope mentally with its isolation. A source of such people lay no farther away than the width of the Gulf of California. Sinaloa was a land not unlike California, and the communities that had grown up around its presidios were reservoirs of young men, many born into soldiers' families. These families, who were often parishioners of Jesuit priests, were better prepared for the harsh exigencies of California life. Their ambitions were less grand and more realistic than those of European fortune-seekers. Padre Jacobo Baegert spent seventeen years as a missionary in California. After he retired he wrote an account of his experiences with several useful passages devoted to gente de razón, including the following picture of the men of the Presidio of Loreto.

> Their officers are a captain, a lieutenant, a sergeant, and an ensign. Their weapons are a sword, a musket, a shield, and an armor of four layers of tanned, white deerskin, which covers the entire body like a sleeveless coat. Otherwise they wear whatever they like; they have no uniforms. They serve on horseback or on mule, and because of the rugged trails, each man is obliged to keep five mounts. The soldiers have to buy these animals as well as their weapons, clothing, ammunition, and all their food.
>
> Their duties are these: to serve the missionary as a bodyguard, to accompany him on all his travels, to keep watch during the night, to keep an eye on the Indians, and, if a crime is committed, to carry out the punishment. They take turns riding out every day to see that their horses or those of the missionary do not stray, for these animals roam freely in the field. And finally, the soldiers have to obey the missionary in everything which concerns good discipline and the affairs of the mission. Such were the wise and beneficial orders issued by the Catholic kings, Philip V and Ferdinand VI. These orders keep the soldiers from

roving through the land at will, using the Indians and their wives for pearl fishing and for other work, or abusing them in any other way.[1]

California Jesuits were particular about their employees and regularly discharged those who did not meet their standards. To maintain the numbers they needed, they were in constant communication with their mainland brethren, who not only informed promising young men of those opportunities but also sent California Jesuits their own assessments of any men who indicated a desire to apply. In addition, the young men of Sinaloa and other nearby areas of New Spain profited from accounts they received from visitors to the peninsula, usually Jesuit employees.

Therefore, young men of the coastal provinces knew that, although times were hard in New Spain and long-term employment scarce, the Jesuits were offering an inducement rare in that part of the world: fair wages paid regularly. A trend was soon established, one that would persist throughout the first two-thirds of the eighteenth century: California's recruits were enlisted primarily from old centers on relatively nearby western slopes of the mainland—Tepic, Compostela, Rosario, Culiacán, Villa de Sinaloa, and El Fuerte.

In practice the missionaries were able to exclude workers from the lowest levels of mainland society because they could use California Indians to perform humble jobs. That fact alone created a notable difference between early California society and that of Sinaloa, just across the water. And if the lowest class was absent from California's gente de razón, the highest was also represented to a very minor extent. Few who had status or wealth in more conventional Hispanic centers cared to submit to the regulations imposed by the Jesuits in California.

In fact, the missionary order, armed with its unique charter, had authority to indulge its prejudices and to change employees as often as it saw fit. When a man failed to perform satisfactorily, he was returned to the mainland. Another then took his place and was tested in turn. Some men came and gave good service but tired

---

1. Baegert, *Observations in Lower California*, 146–47.

2.1. In the seventeenth and eighteenth centuries,
Villa de Sinaloa was a fortified town on the Sinaloa River
and the greatest single contributor to California's pioneer population.

of the restrictive atmosphere. Many left California voluntarily. The absence of those who could not live up to Jesuit expectations and those who did not care to live within the Jesuit system created further differences between California's gente de razón and their more casually assembled counterparts elsewhere. These differences would become more significant as time passed. The men who survived all these selection processes were destined to do more than merely serve a stint in California. Many had come to stay, and they would found the pioneer families that gave substance to Spain's foothold. Years later, some would go north for the founding of San Diego and Monterey, helping to open and populate a new California, and would become some of its more productive citizens and progenitors.

Closed and Regimented California

California's diminutive colony of gente de razón grew slowly under the Jesuits' tight control. Their employees were severely regimented and also unusually isolated, even for people dwelling far from the centers of their civilization. The missionaries used the power of their order and the influence of their wealthy patrons to keep nearly all sailing traffic from the outside world away from their shores. They feared the influence of miners and pearl seekers, merchants and sailors. Their concern was due primarily to a genuine concern for their Indian initiates and the conviction that those converts lacked the skills to deal with outsiders interested in increasing their own wealth.

In addition, the Jesuits' paid helpers were forbidden to gather pearls or to employ Indians to do that or any other labor. Soldiers were not allowed to import commodities to sell or trade. Their employers specified the low rates they could charge for private services as shoemakers, tailors, carpenters, and the like. They were excluded from owning land or domestic animals beyond the usual backyard fowl. The argument for these restrictions was that labor, water, pasturage, and livestock were so scarce that the missions needed all that were available. In fact, private grazing could have been practiced at a distance from missions and might have added significantly to food supplies. But in this regard, as with pearling, the priests feared that it would lead to absenteeism from soldiers' normal posts and misemployment of Indians outside the missionaries' paternal control.

Under these circumstances the men who had cast their lots with the Jesuits were increasingly frustrated as their families grew. In spite of growing expenses, they had no means to augment incomes or see that their sons were gainfully employed. The mission system had not foreseen what the presence of its homegrown civilians would mean in a generation or two. As the male offspring of soldiers and servants became too numerous to simply replace their parents or to be absorbed into the strictly mission economy, they became a problem generation. Since these young people were not in the direct pay of the missionaries, they were more difficult to control. They aspired to families, lands, and possessions. However, the Jesuits who directed California affairs probably did not even want to think of these matters as their problems. The secular group had been brought to help them, not to create administrative headaches. Under the circumstances it was no wonder that friction developed, but for over three decades, one side prevailed: the priests ruled the peninsula.

The Growth of Outside Influences

The first step toward the Jesuits' gradual surrender of control over California arose from royal demands that the missionaries carry out their promises to create landing places where Manila galleons could find food, water, and shelter.

Since the late years of the sixteenth century those trading vessels were loaded with veritable treasures in Manila Bay in the Philippine Islands, headed north to enter and sail with the Japan Current, then cruised down the west coast of North America until they reached Acapulco. Among the principal reasons for the successes and failures of this precarious trade had been problems of locating fresh water and other supplies along the way. When the Jesuits received royal permission to occupy California, one of the conditions imposed was that the missionary order make it one of their goals to locate and occupy ports suitable for the assistance of Manila ships.

The first leader of the Jesuit project in California was Padre Visitador Juan María de Salvatierra, who served in that position from 1697 to 1717. However, Salvatierra's primary concerns necessarily had been the expansion of missionary influence, conversion of natives, and establishment of a progression of missions. Certainly, a principal reason for his success as a missionary had been his acumen in selecting likely locations and Indian bands as he planned new missions.

At the time Padre Visitador Salvatierra launched his campaign, the California peninsula apparently had a native population of twenty to thirty thousand. The 1683–85 expedition, which had included Padre Kino, had learned important facts about these people, and more were taken from occasional reports made during the previous century by Manila ships and privateers who had made necessary landings in California and interacted with bands of local inhabitants. Thus Salvatierra knew that the peninsular peoples were divided into three major groups, named, from north to south, Cochimí, Guaycura, and Pericú—entities totally unrelated racially, culturally, and linguistically.

During his two decades in California, Salvatierra had ordered searches for usable ports whenever he had available the manpower and supplies needed to survey the peninsula's Pacific shores. However, those opportunities had been few, and the natives encountered had been unusually contentious. Hence, during the years of his leadership, most Jesuit conversion efforts were made among the Cochimí in the north, while the southern tip of the peninsula remained little explored.

Salvatierra died in 1717 and was succeeded by his longtime follower and friend Padre Juan de Ugarte. As Ugarte's appointment was finalized, royal pressure was being increased on the California Jesuits to found the long-overdue galleon ports. Padre Ugarte was determined to comply with those demands. By early 1719 he had instructed the commander of the Presidio of Loreto, Captain Esteban Rodríguez, to organize an exploring party. Their instructions were to locate a great port site that the explorer Sebastián Vizcaíno had discovered in 1602 and named Bahía Magdalena. Their initial search was a major effort, but it failed because the

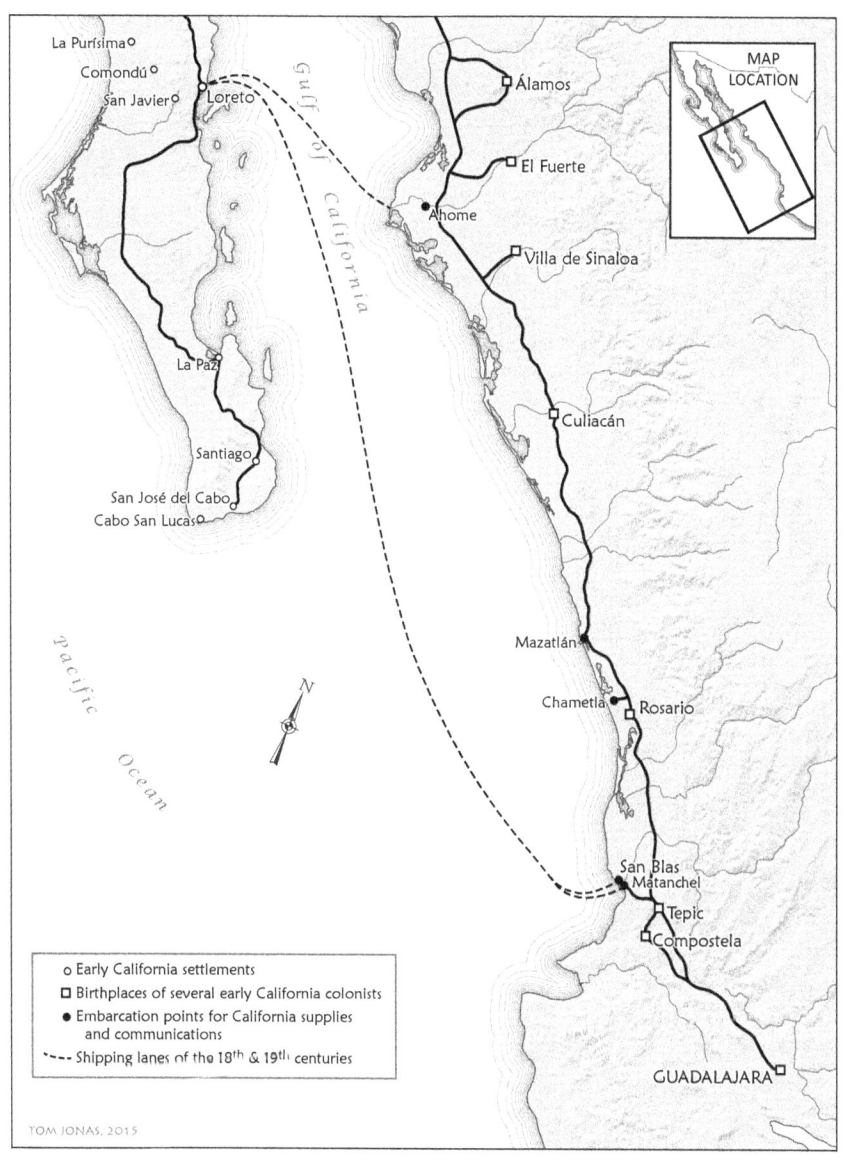

Map 2. Early California settlements.
Map by Tom Jonas.
Copyright © 2015 by the University of Oklahoma Press.

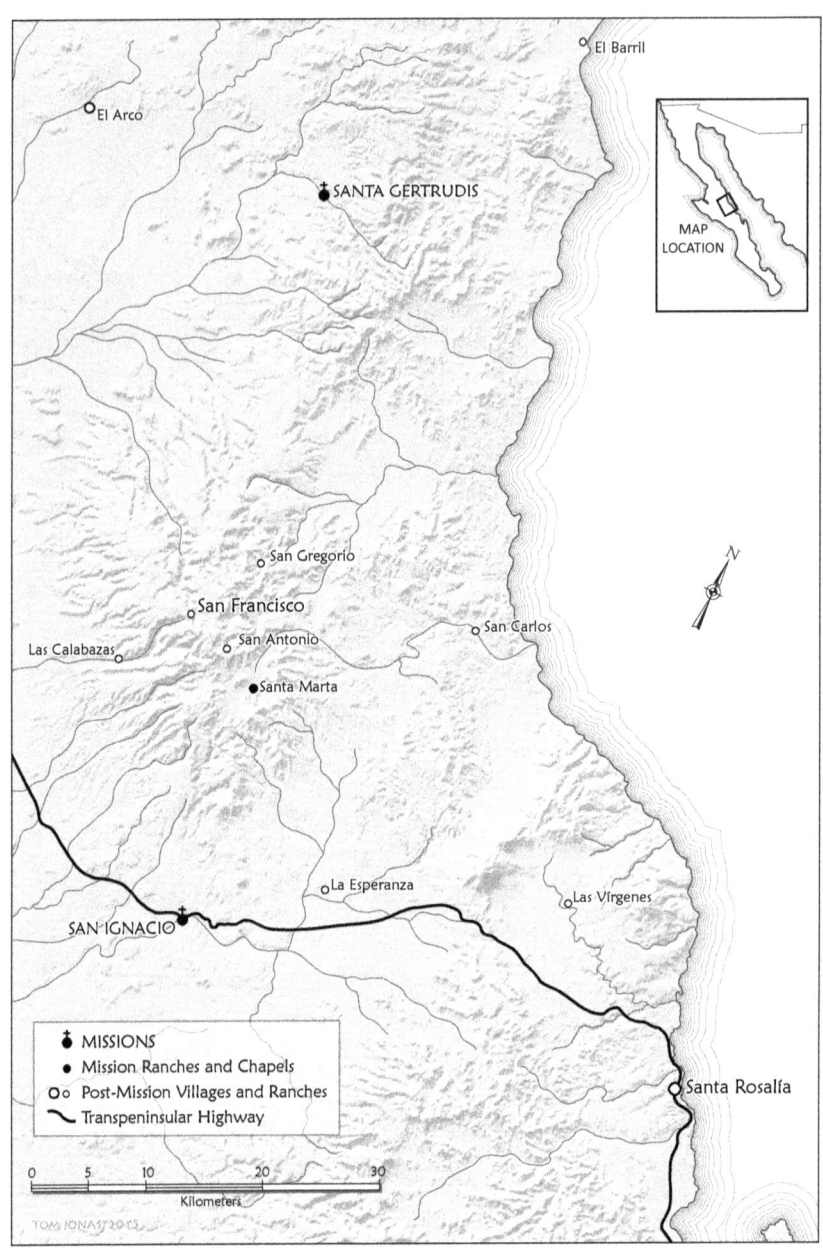

Map 3. Missions, mission ranches and chapels, post-mission villages and ranches. *Map by Tom Jonas.* Copyright © 2015 by the University of Oklahoma Press.

great bay proved to offer no sources of fresh water or wood, which were items needed by every Manila galleon.

Thus began a trying decade. Ugarte indicated the sincerity of his commitment by sending missionaries, troops, and the needed helpers to undertake the conversion of the inhabitants of El Sur, or the South, as the cape region was called. In remarkably short order, missions to convert the Guaycura were established at the Bay of La Paz in 1720, at Los Dolores in 1721, and Santiago in 1724. However, those efforts required all the available soldiers and a great deal of expense. As a result, installation of missions among the Pericú had to be delayed, and the first, Mission San José del Cabo, was not inaugurated until 1730. The second, Santa Rosa (later named Todos Santos), was opened in 1733. Only these two missions were located where they could offer assistance to Manila ships.

However, neither royal interests nor the best missionary efforts could assure that missions in El Sur would avoid a problem long foreseen and feared by California Jesuits. Their new missions, whether in the area occupied by the Guaycura or that of the Pericú, must bring together peoples of independent bands, groups that had traditionally competed with each other and had at times engaged in battle.

The Guaycura occupied most of the area between Loreto and the plains areas south of La Paz. The missionaries and soldiers exploring their area soon found that these natives were fragmented into half a dozen subdivisions, each with a distinctive dialect. Those major subgroups were, in turn, split into widely scattered and competitive *rancherías*, groups made up of extended families and usually numbering from eighty to two hundred members.

Soon thereafter, other padres and their support troops found, south of all the Guaycura, the third totally distinct cultural group in El Sur, the Pericú. These people occupied a three-thousand-square-mile area that ended at Cabo San Lucas and, in addition, included the gulf islands from Isla de San José southward.

The Guaycura proved to be particularly difficult to attract and retain by conventional missionary methods. All were nomadic, and most of the lands they occupied were among California's poorest in water and food resources. Their bands were small, highly mobile, and unusually antagonistic. The northernmost Guaycura traded raids with the Cochimí along an uneasy frontier. Those of the south regularly attacked or defended against the Pericú. And the splinter groups of the southern Guaycura not only spoke variant dialects, but also incessantly warred or skirmished with each other. The fiercest Guaycuran subgroup, the Uchití, occupied a large open area south and west of La Paz. In all, the Guaycuras may have totaled five thousand people, but no group was large enough to justify its own mission. Any mission in Guaycura territory was assured of a poor economic base and the necessity to reconcile age-old enemies.

The Pericú differed in many ways from the Guaycura, but also presented difficult problems for missionaries. Their numbers totaled about three thousand and they spoke a common language. Their bands were far less antagonistic than those of the Guaycura. Nevertheless, they were accustomed to a great deal of personal, family, and small-group autonomy. Even when they consented to attending the affairs at a mission, they retained their independent nature and resisted the authority of the missionary as well as that of the governors selected from their ranks by their missionary. They continued to come and go as their spirits moved them. That independence was enhanced by mobility, for their skills as boatmen and swimmers were unmatched by other peninsular peoples. All missionaries who attempted Pericú conversion commented at length on that group's independence—although it was usually described in terms such as stubbornness, fickleness, impertinence, and ingratitude.

A Haven at Last for Manila Galleons

January 1734 seemed to mark the successful culmination of thirty years of royal and viceregal demands and a great deal of hard work and sacrifice by California Jesuits and their helpers. A Manila galleon put in at the cape, the first since the establishment of local missions. When it anchored at San Bernabé hoping to find relief at

Mission San José del Cabo, its crew and passengers were suffering the usual scurvy and shortages of food and water. Padre Tamaral rounded up and delivered the needed aid in a short time, and most of the afflicted were soon cured by eating fresh meat and the fruit of the prickly pear cactus.

However, the galleon's captain and the recently retired head of the Augustinian missionaries in the Philippines were seriously ill. They remained under Tamaral's care for two months after the galleon had sailed on to Acapulco. The peninsular missionaries used this entire affair to demonstrate the importance of their efforts to develop the cape region. They had resupplied the galleon and then provided well for their important visitors. And when the two stricken travelers had sufficiently recovered, Padre Jaime Bravo, then head of the California Jesuits, sent a ship to carry them to the mainland and a soldier escort to accompany and assist them all the way to Mexico City. There, they and others who had been on the ship gave grateful testimony to a newly installed viceroy, Archbishop Juan Antonio de Vizarrón y Eguiarreta.

Encouraged by these reports from the galleon's passengers, the viceroy sent orders to Manila that all returning ships should regard San Bernabé as a port of refuge after their debilitating Pacific crossings. It then appeared that Padre Juan de Ugarte's campaign to settle the South had borne fruit and that one of Kino and Salvatierra's original pledges was being fulfilled at last.

The Native Peoples of the Cape Resist Changes Imposed by Missionaries

Late in 1734 a neophyte insurrection at the four missions from La Paz south proved too large and violent to be handled by the twenty-five soldiers of the Presidio of Loreto. By October of that year, the padres at the missions of San José del Cabo and Santiago, plus two servants and a mission guard soldier, had been killed by rebels. Loyal neophytes who fled these rampages brought stories to Todos Santos of how the padres had been clubbed to death and their bodies mutilated and burned. The missionary at Todos Santos narrowly escaped the same fate when his three soldiers virtually dragged him away from his mission. The presidio was mobilized, but California missionaries and soldiers soon realized that the entire South was involved in the uprising. Traditional enemies had unified in opposition to Jesuit rule. Loreto's few soldiers could not possibly pacify or even resist an insurrection that included so many people and covered so great an area.

The Jesuits' frantic appeal for royal aid had the unwelcome consequence of bringing in the governor of relatively nearby Sinaloa at the head of forty of his presidial soldiers. The governor infuriated the Jesuits by carrying on an extended series of meetings with representatives of the rebels, meanwhile exploring much of Jesuit California seeking the kinds of information never released by the Jesuits themselves. After over a year with little military action, a neophyte rebellion in Sinaloa forced that state's governor to carry out a swift campaign that brought the California insurgents to their knees. Order was restored, but the Sinaloan governor's reports to the viceroy soon resulted in orders that he establish a second presidio located in El Sur and not under Jesuit control. Wrangling over that decision persisted for a number of years. It ended around 1741, when the Crown granted the California Jesuits full control over their soldiery, north and south. The high Spanish officials were not, however, prepared to rescind recently granted orders that private property be allotted to established peninsular gente de razón. Land grants were soon forthcoming along with the rights to raise animals, plant crops, and engage in pearling and mining.

The South in Transition

As a result of the rebellion in the south, men from the mainland—strangers with civil and military powers—had come and ranged over the land. They brought to the cloistered little Loreto colony ideas about individual rights and privileges that had scarcely been imagined before. As those and other controversial issues were aired, California's people—gente de razón and converts as well—were shown the spectacle of men who argued with the Jesuits and acted independently of them. The protracted rebellion also ended the ultraprovincialism of the cape peoples. Their isolation was lost as all resisted the common enemy, became refugees, and shared the same retreats.

Also, as an aftermath of the rebellion, the south was opened up and proved attractive to the peninsular Hispanic population. Land and water were there for the taking, and economic opportunity beckoned to soldiers and their families. A few had the temerity to take steps that would have been suppressed before. Now the padres failed to react. Gente de razón, after decades of obedient service to missionaries, were about to become a major factor in changing California.

The first California soldier to seize such opportunities was a Spaniard, Manuel de Ocio, a son-in-law of Captain Esteban Rodríguez. Ocio was the first man who boldly seized the opportunities made possible by the new laws. On his own initiative, Ocio soon made a modest fortune in pearls and established banking and political ties in Guadalajara. By 1760, Ocio had mines, ranches, and personal cattle numbering hundreds. In addition to making himself California's first wealthy man, Ocio was also responsible for bringing an entirely new group of settlers to California. To pursue his quest for silver, he hired miners, perhaps as many as forty or fifty, many from the interior of Mexico. However, mining never really prospered, as was reported in a Jesuit's account of the affairs of Manuel de Ocio.

> His wealth is derived more from pearl fishing, his butcher shop, his general store, and his unbelievable thrift from his mine. He alone sells all the meat to his fellow men and their helpers, and also all the cloth, linen, tobacco, rags, and so on, which they and their families wear and which they use to pay their workers. He is the only man who is in a position to buy merchandise and to bring it from Guadalajara over land and sea; also he was the first man to take possession of the land over which his cows were grazing.[2]

---

2. Ibid., 46.

2.2. The ruins of Santa Ana, the first secular settlement in California.

Before the end of the Jesuit era, a few other ex-soldiers had taken steps to claim land. This gradual breaching of Jesuit dominance launched the slow expansion of private ranching and allowed retirees from the Presidio of Loreto and their sons to begin creating a civilian economy.

Jesuit Control of California Becomes Less Absolute

In 1746 the illness and death of King Felipe V caused new alignments in the Spanish power structure. The old threat of Bourbon economic reforms was becoming more real and more imminent. Royal orders flew. Some were sharply critical of California practices, particularly the Jesuit resistance to a civil colony and economic development. As enthusiasm and cupidity grew, the Jesuits were painted in ever-darker terms as obstructionists with a stranglehold on the economic potential of the region. There was also growing dissatisfaction with California's static northern frontier. Royal officials increasingly complained that California Jesuits had not established a new mission to the north since dedicating Mission San Ignacio in 1728.

In response, the California missionaries quickly founded Mission Santa Gertrudis in 1751. In addition, the Jesuits in New Spain, from the Provincial down to the missionaries of California and Sonora began to plan related actions, to search for available land and sea routes to areas and ports long ago reported by sea explorers and Manila ships. The outcomes were frustrating. Land explorations in Sonora were limited by encounters with warlike unconverted tribes. Also, the California Jesuits' report of the first successful exploration by water to the mouth of the Colorado River was utterly rejected in Madrid. High-ranking marine officials were not prepared to give up the two-hundred-year-old belief that California was an island.

In this spotlight of attention and growing disapproval, California missionaries gave up a right they had cherished since their founding of the California colony. They had become convinced that their military had to be more independent if they were to expect Bourbon cooperation. The California Jesuits reluctantly renounced their absolute control of the presidio and the soldiers who had served them. When Bernardo Rodríguez succeeded his aged and blind father in 1744, he had been appointed by the viceroy of New Spain, not by a Jesuit. Within a year or two, California Jesuits also renounced the right to specify the soldiers to be hired for service in their region. The captain thereafter made his own choices.

New Orders for California

The first major change in the governance of all California people, neophytes and gente de razón alike, came in 1767, seventy years after the founding of the Jesuit colony. Carlos III, the third Bourbon king of Spain, decided to expel Jesuits from his entire empire. This stroke ended two centuries of complex religious, political, and economic developments in which Jesuits had taken part. Most

2.3. José de Gálvez was one of the most important Spanish colonial officials of the late eighteenth century. He served as Visitor General of New Spain (1764–72) and Minister of the Indies (1775–87).
Private collection. Courtesy of Dr. Iris Engstrand, University of San Diego.

Jesuit enterprises had prospered, but usually at the expense of creating opponents whose numbers and influence eventually overwhelmed support for the once-powerful teaching and missionary order. Its members were accused of intrigue and finally of plotting against the king. The Jesuit downfall was not directly related to their California venture. The king ousted them from all missions in all lands under Spanish control, and other orders of missionary priests were chosen and directed to carry on their work. The king of Spain also approved a plan to explore and colonize his California claims north of the peninsula. These moves soon changed the lives of everyone in California.

The principal author of change on the ground was José de Gálvez, the king's *visitador*, or special envoy, the first royal official ever to visit California. Gálvez was empowered to make sweeping rearrangements of local priorities. He not only substituted Franciscan missionaries for the Jesuits, but also determined not to allow the new order to assume the temporal powers of the former. He did not charter the substitute Franciscans to control business or govern gente de razón as the Jesuits had.

Gálvez brought innovations that had even more initial impact than the new order of priests. With him came the greatest wave of new faces ever seen by most inhabitants of the peninsula. In a few months he exposed California's estimated four hundred gente de razón to many dozens of Spaniards—soldiers, officials, scientists, and others—people whose educations, experiences, activities, and ideas opened some new horizons to such a sheltered population. The new arrivals created need for a term that was soon in wide use: Californio. The term was applied to local gente de razón to distinguish them from their mainland counterparts brought in by Gálvez.

By the 1760s, Spain had felt threatened in western North America. For two decades the Russians had been exploring down the coasts, and Madrid heard reports of a string of manned and fortified bases. French and English trappers and traders were rumored to be pushing overland into the north coastal areas. It was deemed imperative to establish an effective Spanish presence in the huge area claimed by the Crown. Thus the greatest of José de Gálvez's responsibilities was to create an expeditionary force that would open a road and prepare to occupy and defend coastal lands as far north as Monterey Bay, nearly a thousand miles beyond the edge of the previously explored California.

The expedition bound for Monterey consisted of two parts, one to go by sea and the other by land, and the naval group involved few Californios. But after Gálvez had appointed a Spanish Army officer, Gaspar de Portolá, as governor of California and leader of the land forces, Portolá enlisted dozens of Californio men. Those who eventually went north under him shared an epochal experience with men from Old and New Spain, an event referred to in many subsequent service records, pension claims, land grants, and assorted correspondences. Several Californios, as a result of participation in this expedition, or the several that followed in its support, would become pioneer settlers in this new territory, then called Nueva California, or New California. To make a further distinction, the original was then called Antigua California, Old California. In 1804, the Spanish government would make the names Alta California and Baja California official.

Ironically, by this process of acquiring this new adjacent area, the influence of the Jesuits did touch the California that their missions had never reached. Men whom they had selected and retained, in some cases men born and reared in Jesuit California, went on to have early and lasting influences from San Diego northward. A list of their family names is evocative of the early history of what nearly eighty years later would become American California: Acevedo, Alvarado, Amador, Arce, Camacho, Carrillo, Castro, Cota, Góngora, Higuera, López, Lugo, Olivera, Ortega, Osuna, Peña, Romero, Verdugo, and Villavicencio.

More important to the Baja California story were the men from the Presidio of Loreto who served in Nueva California and then returned to continue their lives on the peninsula. Service in strange lands under officers and alongside troops from the mother country left them much less provincial than they had been before.

2.4. Around 1760 the village of Santa Ana housed workers for Manuel de Ocio's mines and cattle ranches, the first California-based commercial activities. Descendants of Ocio's miners and cattle still occupy the region.

José de Gálvez busied himself with much beside Monterey. He found the peninsula an underused and underdeveloped place, one that he judged he could revolutionize in short order. Dozens of edicts flew from his pen as he planned to convert backward Baja California into a great jewel for the king's crown. His plans often involved local people, for he needed their special skills or often only their manpower. Gálvez also hoped to establish Californios as a nucleus for the expanding civilian population that would be necessary to sustain projected national offices, warehouses, and shipyards. He envisioned their role in growing mining and agricultural pursuits that would yield taxes.

Writing in 1769 to a colleague in the capital of New Spain to explain his ideas and enlist support, Gálvez enumerated concentrations of civilians with whom he was personally familiar. He noted that there was not a single pueblo outside mission centers, but he probably was using a Spanish yardstick to define the term *pueblo*. He said that there were groups of civilized men at the Port of La Paz, at Cabo San Lucas, and at Santa Ana. He added that near Santa Ana there were several ranches dedicated to caring for and milking cows, making cheese, and breeding cattle. He went on to describe the miserable status of the people at these ranches who were devoid of agricultural land, water, and adequate sources of labor. He remarked that these poor people provided many of the soldiers who opened Alta California and continued to serve there.

Gálvez's report confirms a picture of civilian life that had grown, stunted and misshapen, in the shadow of the missions. It is the first direct notice of those conditions that are hinted at or indirectly revealed in many documents from Jesuit times. Because the king's visitor was determined to do more than merely report on sorrowful conditions, he resorted to an old Spanish custom that had proved to be an effective stimulus to the people and that cost nothing directly from royal coffers. Guided by the advice of Fernando de Rivera y Moncada, who had been *capitán-gobernador* of California under the Jesuits and knew most of the gente de razón personally, Gálvez instituted grants of land to worthy applicants. About a dozen titles to watered land once held by southern missions were given or authorized by Gálvez himself. No doubt he intended this as a precedent that would influence events after his departure from California.

José de Gálvez, with his authority, energy, and ideas, left the scene in mid-1769, but he left Baja California missions in the hands of Franciscan missionaries, and the governance of gente de razón to a few of his Spanish subordinates. After that latter group discovered how little revenue the place could be expected to yield, its members began to request transfers or retirements, and the men who took their places were poorly prepared for significant command posts. It was not until José Joaquín de Arrillaga became governor in 1783 that the peninsular Californios had a sympathetic leader interested in their welfare.

CHAPTER 3

The Contest for Land

The brief span of six years between late 1767 and fall 1773 brought a series of profound changes to Californio life. The first shock came with the expulsion of the pioneer missionary order. The Californios had known personally many of the Jesuit priests who had created and controlled most of the conditions under which all people—priests, Indians, and gente de razón—had lived. Suddenly they were gone and Franciscan missionaries with different ways took their place. José de Gálvez, the king's envoy, had come to the peninsula as by far the most powerful royal official ever to visit the California colony. Gálvez had conscripted men, commandeered supplies and animals, and put Fernando de Rivera y Moncada, longtime captain of the Presidio of Loreto in charge of the march to Monterey. He chose the best of the Californio soldiers for the northern venture. Many never really returned; instead they collected their families and made homes in the new area.

Baja California's struggling mission and mining economy could ill afford this great loss of men, equipment, and livestock. Conditions became desperate in 1771 and 1772 when the area was subjected to a severe, extended drought accompanied by plagues of locusts. In addition, the Franciscans, lured by richer lands and greater numbers of unconverted Indians in the north, willingly relinquished Baja California to missionaries of the Dominican order. In 1773, peninsular Indians and gente de razón again experienced a difficult change as the entire mission system passed into a third set of hands in just over five years.

These were the major events, but the whole climate of the times prevented major progress in Baja California. Because of the fancied strategic importance of Monterey, royal energies and expenditures were largely channeled northward. The Dominicans soon discovered the sad, declining condition of the old Jesuit establishments, and they too turned their attentions and efforts northward into new missions among the unconverted native people of northern Baja California.

Opening and maintaining new presidios and new missions not only diverted attention and material that once would have gone to Baja California, but also bled the place dry of its small wealth. By royal or religious directives, large parts of the stores at peninsular missions were taken, used, and never returned. The missions' herds were diminished, and the best of their vaqueros, their animal herders, were sent north to serve. The private ranches and mines of Manuel de Ocio and the few other entrepreneurs also had to give up cattle, mules, and men.

The loss of mules and skilled *arrieros* to Alta California was a more serious blow to Baja California life than might be imagined. The peninsula had been opened to Spanish rule and the Christian faith by a handful of missionaries and their servants and soldiers, a group that never could have mastered such an area or its people working only on foot. The Hispanic men, always few in number, had to move rapidly over the unremittingly rocky, mountainous terrain in order to explore the new land, contact the native people, supply the growing chain of missions, or respond to attacks or other emergencies wherever they might occur. The first missionary group anticipated these needs by bringing riding animals. Comparisons between horses and mules were inevitable and swift. Horses fared so poorly that some of the earliest letters

3.1. An elderly vaquero in the traditional peninsular all-leather trappings that are used to ward off omnipresent branches, thorns, and spines.

from the California colony contained requests for more mules as replacements. These requirements grew as did the number of missions and men who had to supply them and communicate for them.

Mule breeding is a slow, painstaking art, and as years passed no substitute for mules was found. Sailing northward was slow and dangerous because of almost constantly adverse winds and currents. In Alta California, broad alluvial plains lent themselves to road building and, a few decades after its occupation, wagons and carriages served the area's freight and passenger needs. But in Baja California, broken, rocky terrain did not allow such luxuries even a century after colonization. Mission and military transport and communication continued to move on mules and burros. Ironically, the Camino Real, the peninsular artery to the new establishments in Alta California, would remain a trail for mounted or laden beasts until it was abandoned. When the peninsula was stripped of so many mules and muleteers after 1769, all commerce

3.2. Mules, the favored riding and pack animals in the opening of California, remain vital to Baja California's sierra people. Each ranch's herd runs loose until needed animals are rounded up, roped, and saddled.

was slowed, and hundreds of private and mission cattle strayed and created wild herds that were to remain a feature of the peninsula for more than half a century.

The Californio society continued to center around missions, but those missions were stagnating as their Indian population declined under the impact of introduced diseases to which they had little resistance. Measles, smallpox, and syphilis can be identified from contemporary accounts. On the peninsula that served as a highway to Alta California, only Loreto, its capital and port, had any continuous activity. As the years passed, most mission centers became quieter and less meaningful places. Neither priests nor their helpers nor their guardsmen were stimulated by any sense of progress or even status quo. A melancholy is evident in many documents. Priests bickered among themselves and with the gente de razón—the Californios. The lives of soldiers and civilians alike continued to be severely regimented, but without the purpose that must have been sensed in the days of the founders.

An Old Soldier Recollects

A remarkable memoir preserves the atmosphere and the emotions of those slow and somber times. Around 1850, a Peruvian journalist, Manuel Clemente Rojo, arrived and began to collect data on Baja California people, a group that obviously stirred admiration in his egalitarian breast. One of his informants was the aged Simón Avilés, who had served as a presidial soldier before 1800. Thanks to Rojo, we have an old man's vision of mid-Dominican years, a perspective seen through the eyes of Californios that contrasts strongly with those occasionally reported during Jesuit times.

> No one was allowed to get drunk in public or cause scandal, and there were no gambling houses where they have so many quarrels because they lose or win their bets. We lived under such subjugation that pity the man who was awake after the troop called for silence at night. This was only tolerated in homes where there was a sick person to watch over or some other just reason which the missionary Father and the commandant of the escort were supposed to know in advance. When we least expected,

the judge would come with people at midnight or in the early morning to our homes, and they would order us to open the door for them. They did this when the law suspected that there was a man in the house living in an illicit relationship with some woman, and thus they obliged any man to get married by force when they surprised him in his house together with the woman that they had been suspicious of.[1]

Simón Avilés remembered that any sort of private party—even a *fiesta*, a celebration of a marriage, or the birth of a child—required the consent of a priest and a military officer. He also recalled the spartan living conditions of soldiers and their families while stationed at peninsular missions:

> We lived in great discomfort in little, low houses with palm or earth roofs, very tiny and with cowhide doors for lack of boards. The entire furnishings of a house consisted of a bad cot or a wattle bed, a rough table and chairs made out of sticks crossed over two little adobe posts. At that time there wasn't even one man in the whole country, with the exception of Don Manuel de Ozio, who could be called rich or moderately well off. We were entirely dependent upon the missions. Since labors and adversities were common and the families in each mission very few, there was a good deal of brotherhood and union among them. They would give and lend each other everything, even their clothes. The same thing could be seen regarding those persons who came from the other missions. There were no strangers then, everyone knew each other and the majority were related by marriage or by blood. Only the missionary fathers kept their things for themselves and lived like strangers to our customs.... No one was allowed to cut any fruit from the mission gardens, not even the commandants of their own escorts. We paid cash for everything, and when we were given something on credit we would pay for it the first chance we had. The fathers kept these accounts well, and had an understanding with the troop paymaster to deduct from our salaries the amounts that we were advanced in this way.[2]

This veteran soldier's mention of clothing worn by Californios is particularly welcome today in the total absence of pictures or other descriptive accounts.

> We wore no underwear except shirts and shorts, and on the outside, pants and jackets made from cured deer hide; we wore our shoes next

---

1. Rojo, *Historical Notes on Lower California*, 73.
2. Ibid., 74–75.

to our skin; we didn't wear stockings or undershirts or cloaks in winter; then we wore some serapes from Durango over our clothes and that was our entire overcoat in the house or in the field; generally in the very cold seasons we warmed ourselves with fire; for that reason wood was never lacking in the house and was left in the middle of the rooms we lived in. I know all the parts which were populated in former times, from the Cape of San Lucas to the Port of San Diego in Upper California, and in none of these places have I seen that anyone was given any better treatment than this (I am speaking about the troop and its discharged soldiers). The fathers and the commandants enjoyed more comforts, but not many.[3]

No wonder the people increasingly voted with their feet, and it was in this period that significant numbers of Baja California's old families began to disperse from mission centers, a process that came to characterize the remainder of the mission period.

In Alta California social development followed a more cheerful and secular course. Soldiers and priests opened the new area more nearly as equals, and the Church never had an opportunity to rule and to claim all the land as it had in Jesuit California. Even though in 1790 Alta California also would face half a century of wrangling over lands held or claimed by missions, the new establishments of the north had vastly greater grazing lands for governors to parcel out. As a result, some retiring soldiers were pensioned off with sizable grants of land. Civilian settlers were encouraged to come to Alta California and were given title to garden plots when they arrived. In the last quarter of the eighteenth century, the pueblos of Los Ángeles and San José came into being. They were populated by civilians whose daily lives were not entirely dominated by either missionaries or military men. The presidios at San Diego, Santa Bárbara, Monterey, and San Francisco housed not only soldiers but also their families, servants, and assorted tradespeople, the flower of early California society. By the early nineteenth century all presidios afforded a degree of gracious if simple social life, and the population of Monterey, the capital, was ready and able to produce rustic galas with music, dance, displays of horsemanship, and generous hospitality. As the area developed, these events became more lavish and the wealth that made them possible was largely

---

3. Ibid., 75.

3.3. "This is the way a California mayordomo catches a bull. He follows it on horseback, grasps its tail and twists it around so that the bull falls down," ca. 1770 by Fr. Ignacio Tirsch, SJ. *Courtesy of the National Library of the Czech Republic, XVI B18 2050 EX0034R.*

derived from private use of land, chiefly held by active or retired military personnel or their heirs.

Baja California, by contrast, had no pueblos other than Loreto, the home of the peninsula's only presidio. That place probably did provide some amenities for its Californios, but their economic base was so limited that they never were able to afford any semblance of their northern cousins' more bountiful displays.

Private Land: The Role of the Mayordomos

No peninsular mission had ever been able to support all its Indian converts in one place. During the early years, bands of eighty to two hundred Indians were brought in periodically for indoctrination and then sent out to support themselves from their ancestral foraging areas. As neophytes gained agricultural skills, missionaries began to locate groups of them at ranches distant from missions but having agricultural potential. Each such ranch was run by a mission servant, usually an ex-soldier or a son or son-in-law of the mission's mayordomo, the foreman who supervised all activities that employed neophyte labor. Mayordomos were nearly all ex-soldiers themselves. They were men who had found favor with the missionaries while acting as their guards. They were then hired after they finished their periods of military service. Naturally, these men were in good positions to place kin on mission payrolls and locate them at the best ranches.

Those who went as foremen to mission ranches took their wives and children and, as time went on, those oases scattered in the wilderness became their homes. In 1768 and 1795, when declining populations forced abandonment of two missions, two well-placed ex-mayordomos and their families claimed titles or got uncontested squatters' rights to the best of those missions' former ranches as well as lands at the ex-missions themselves.

The word "ranch" has been used to describe stock farms in both Californias, but the implied similarity could be misleading: there were large differences in the landscapes of the "ranches" in the two areas. In Alta California, vast grasslands made cattle raising a relatively simple and profitable business. Marketing was, and would remain, the greatest limitation on ranch development. By contrast, in Baja California a ranch was created on whatever land happened to lie around any permanent source of water. Most such places consisted of a narrow wash in the bottom of a mountain watercourse, a place usable for small gardens and groves but likely to be devastated by runoff from any sizable storm. Herds had to feed off the growth on adjacent slopes so precipitous and rocky that it defies the imagination of an outsider to believe that cattle, in particular, could subsist on such unpromising terrain. Furthermore, in the central and southern parts of the peninsula, grass is virtually nonexistent, so cattle must browse on herbs, cacti, shrubs, and branches of certain leguminous trees. Few areas, previously or now, could support large numbers of animals. No large ranches, by Alta California standards, would ever be practical in the southern two-thirds of Baja California.

If the last third of the eighteenth century saw the scant beginnings of private land tenancy in both Californias, the first quarter of the nineteenth century witnessed its rapid increase. Between 1810 and 1821, the war for Mexican independence created hardships for all classes of Californios. The military received intermittent pay during the first two or three years and then no pay at all as Spain's hold weakened and finally ended. When soldiers had no money and few supplies, their superiors had to commandeer every resource at hand. Several accounts indicate that soldiers became farmers, herders, and hunters to keep themselves and their families alive. Mission ranches and mission herds contributed during this crisis. Tradition and their vital interests were involved.

Spain had always expected the Church outposts to complement and assist the military wherever possible. This had been one of the unique features of Spanish colonialism. And for missions on the Indian frontier this was not simply a duty but a matter of survival. Troops had to be maintained in the Fronteras region, the name for the gap between El Rosario in the Dominican north and San Diego, the first of the Franciscan establishments in Alta California. Not only were there large groups of unpacified native people in that mountainous Fronteras area, but there were also more warlike desert tribes to the east who constantly threatened and attempted to invade and pillage the region.

In order to perform their minimum functions, both missions and presidios had invariably required considerable contributions from Spain's government and Church. In addition to money, this assistance had always included some food and all necessary manufactured items. When revolutionary turmoil in New Spain diverted Spain's attention, drained its coffers, and cut its supply lines, both Californias developed long backlogs of necessities. Whenever possible, they found new sources.

Peninsular assets were extremely limited. As the people cast about for solutions to their problems, the only promising sources

The Contest for Land

3.4. Here a cattle gate is opened between ranches in the Arroyo San Pablo, Sierra de San Francisco. Few of the world's cattle are run on such rugged terrain or must subsist on such desert plant life.

of food or media of exchange were farming plots, orchards, and cattle ranches. Baja California's excellent dried fruits, chiefly figs and dates, could be stored for local distribution in time of need or exchanged advantageously for goods brought by trading ships or whalers. However, the dried fruit industry could not be expanded readily due to the lack of land and water. These necessities were controlled by missions, which therefore remained the only substantial producers.

Cattle raising was another matter. Herds did not require arable land or the elaborate waterworks needed by orchards. Even a small permanent water source could be used to support some cattle. As food needs increased during the trying revolutionary years, men ventured farther and farther afield to herd cattle in the vicinities of most known springs in the area south and west of La Paz and as far as the tip of the peninsula. In those years a few ships began to put

3.5. Dates are grown and harvested at many sierra ranches. Jesuit-introduced date palms flourish in peninsular lowlands wherever the subsoil contains permanent water.

in at Todos Santos and Cabo San Lucas to replenish their stores of meat and water as well as to take on cargoes of hides and tallow.

The concept of direct trade was new to California. In fact, it was still illegal without elaborate paperwork leading to permits and taxation. But in this respect, the weakened hold of the mother country helped the beleaguered Californios. The same turmoil that had cut off Spanish pay, goods, and services had also so impoverished New Spain that it could not support the forces needed to regulate or prevent trade with passing ships. The few authorized merchantmen, mostly Peruvians, who sailed these coasts soon had competition from clandestine American traders. All through the revolutionary decade, a contraband trade grew that involved ranchers, missionaries, and even the reluctant complicity of military governors. Alta California, with its great herds of cattle, more prosperous mission groves, and such exotic offerings as sea otter pelts, was able to engage in significant commerce. Baja California had much less to offer and consequently a greater need to change its ways.

Since most of the peninsular missions south of El Rosario had small and declining Indian populations, their productiveness and use of land had also declined. Some of these centers—Todos Santos, Comondú, La Purísima, Mulegé and San Ignacio—were especially valued by the Dominicans as their residences and as places to concentrate remaining Indians. The missionaries exerted themselves to make these centers as productive and self-sufficient as possible. That left several dwindling missions farther south no longer able to tend to more than their immediate lands, thus their outlying ranches lay idle. During this period a number of ex-soldiers claimed or simply occupied such ranches. The Dominicans must have agreed at least tacitly to give them up because there is no evidence that they opposed the squatters' claims. This forbearance seems remarkable and very much at odds with the usual policies and actions of missionaries.

Dire necessity provoked this apparent paradox because the Church could not let people starve. In addition, there is evidence to show that this process of relinquishing mission ranches was not

3.6. Antonio Ríos, a Cochimí Indian, is descended from neophytes of the missions at San Ignacio, Santa Gertrudis, and San Borja. Very few peninsular Indians survive.

entirely impersonal. Almost all the men who claimed ranches had been mayordomos with long service at the mission or missions in the area of their claim. The churchmen must have agreed to allow these men to revitalize abandoned ranches knowing that at the same time they were acquiring familiar and potentially useful neighbors. Ample evidence is provided by contemporary mission books of baptisms and weddings. The ex-mayordomos and their wives, now called *vecinos* (neighbors), frequently appear as godparents to neophyte children or witnesses at neophyte weddings.

The lands that passed into private hands and the men who claimed those lands are vital ingredients in the story of the Baja California mountains. Most of the sierra ranchers from then until now have descended from one or more of those ex-mayordomos, whose offspring spread from the original ranches to other sites scattered to a greater or lesser extent through all the midpeninsular mountains. These early private landholders were thereby set apart from their fellows and from the decades of Baja California land controversies that were to follow. Having seized unusual opportunities, they found themselves settled in remote places and, as a result, were little supervised and economically independent.

The mayordomos' active occupation of unused land and the success of their ranches probably created a trend. After them, a small but steady stream of hardy individuals who were tired of waiting for land in the favored centers struck out to pioneer entirely new sites for themselves. Taken together, these fugitives changed Baja California life. First, the Indians had lived off all the land. Missionaries then put them into more or less fixed residences, and Californios clustered in the same places. Now the Indians were less present and the Californios were spreading out, nearly completing the cycle.

Since this division of society came at about the time of independence from Spain, it created endless problems for the new and inexperienced governments of all Mexico's states and territories. Before long, half of Baja California's people were dispersed and difficult to contact. This resulted in frustration for any representative of government, whether he was interested in collecting taxes, educating people, taking a census, tallying a vote, or simply proclaiming laws or edicts. But the split would remain. If half the population continued to live around the ports and missions, subject to the attentions and quarrels of religious and government officials, the remainder had taken matters into their own hands. Divided into little groups of one to three families, they lived quietly at remote springs of water, often in foothills or mountains. Soon they had formed a kitchen garden and stock-raising society, far-flung and loosely organized. Only during the latter part of the twentieth century did major outside influences largely alter the customs and practices that had developed during that formative era in Baja California history.

Stepchild of the Republic

The independence from Spain that Mexico achieved in 1821 brought little but confusion to distant Baja California. More than ten years of isolation and neglect during the throes of a complex revolution had been trial enough, but during that time of privations and self-help, the character of the mother government, while resented for its indifference, was known and could be accommodated. Independence proved bewildering. First came two years of an abortive monarchy, a government that managed, through an envoy, to upset what had been left workable in the mission system. Powers of missionaries were reduced and Indians were given more freedom, along with such rights as pay for services rendered and individual ownership of mission lands. The short-lived monarchy sent no money to implement any of its dictates, and its authority was soon deposed, but not before its orders had created much mischief. Many Indians ceased working, sold their rights to land, and became vagrants. Many died in the plains and hills in which they no longer knew how to subsist.

When a republic was declared in Mexico, its manifestos and proclamations were strewn with the rhetoric of the French Revolution. Ironically, the egalitarianism thus expressed was more natural in Baja California than perhaps any other sector of Mexico. Jealous missionaries and limited resources had always prevented such phenomena as great estates, peons, and absentee landlords. Baja California had long been a place of remarkably independent individuals, a fact little noted because of the area's isolation and few visitors. This independence of character was soon to impress most of the travelers who described peninsular people.

Independence, whatever the central government, meant less paternalism in the Californias. Spain was gone, the power of the missionaries was vastly reduced, and Mexico was too poor and preoccupied to govern effectively. Somehow Californios had to help themselves governmentally and economically.

In Alta California, men and means were at hand to create a viable economy and hence a base to support taxation and local government. The Franciscan missions had great herds, broad fields to plant and harvest, and many hands to do the necessary work. A few large, private cattle ranches had grown up, demonstrated their potential, and trained men in the needed skills. As many as a dozen foreign ships a year, mostly English and American, came as trading vessels to Alta California ports and the products of both missions and ranchos were in high demand. A solution to many problems was obvious. Between 1823 and 1825, new Alta California governor Luis Antonio Argüello granted nine extensive ranchos to as many influential men. Such moves launched Alta California into its famous era of cattle barons and the hide-and-tallow trade, which brought prosperity to the region's elite.

It was Baja California's bad fortune to have been divided governmentally from Alta California by the Spanish at the beginning of the nineteenth century. This separation was retained by independent Mexico, and it doomed the people of the peninsula to very inferior prospects. That area's surviving missions were poverty-stricken. Each required an annual infusion of outside funds, and none created surplus wealth. Most ranches were operating at the subsistence level. They supported their people but provided little excess for selling or trading. No industries flourished, and few raw materials promised to create demands for trade.

Without national help and with little prospect for collecting significant local taxes, peninsular government was chaotic for years. In this, peninsular California's largely religious history also played a part. During the first seventy years, the Jesuits bought all of the goods needed by most of the colony's people, delivered them, distributed them, and did the bookkeeping. Even in the fifty years after the Jesuit expulsion, Franciscans and Dominicans managed to work out informal governing partnerships with military commanders. Together they discouraged private enterprise. And by handling all forms of government and all money matters themselves, they helped to create a society poorly prepared to deal with the requirements for independent modern life.

Unpublished letters provide many insights into conditions

during the first years of the Republic of Mexico. The new nation had just taken steps to create representative government. A touching 1824 report from the newly elected town council of Loreto was directed to an unnamed functionary of the central government. Regulations of the time made the councilmen of Loreto, collectively, the executive head of the whole peninsula during any absence of a duly appointed political chief (the new government's title for a governor). Thus the councilmen of Loreto became responsible during the resignation, removal, or even the absence of that principal executive. In fact, the council's power was nonexistent. It had no funds, no troops or even policemen, and therefore no ability to hire or deputize anyone to do anything. Since the very few prosperous, practical, well-informed people could see the folly of serving on the council, most avoided election or appointment, and those honors went to simple, well-meaning citizens who were overwhelmed by the resultant tasks. The following plea for federal help in coping with a sea of troubles is taken from their report. Implicit is an argument for some secularization of missions lands.

> It is a shocking thing, Señor, but at the same time not to be doubted, that in the vast extent of more than five hundred leagues which this Province has from south to north there should be found not one town that has brought its citizens together. The cause is not hard to find. This council attributes it to this: that the Missions having taken over all of the land that can be cultivated by irrigation, and because to till the unwatered land is to lose time and labor on account of the notorious aridity of the country and the rains so unreliable, it comes about that the greater part of the inhabitants of this Province live in miserable shacks five or more leagues apart and some more than forty (and none less than fifteen from this Capital or any other parish), compelled to support themselves on the milk and meat from a small herd of horned cattle which they keep for this end, their only resource in their need. For this reason, well-ordered towns are not being formed, nor can Christian instruction, or agriculture, nor intellectual nor political culture, make progress.[4]

The second letter is from a more experienced and knowledgeable source. Its author, José Manuel Ruiz, who was born on the peninsula

---
4. Rudkin, "Conditions in Baja California, 1824–25," 110–11.

and had been a soldier there for nearly fifty years, is a prototypical Californio of his time. His ancestors came from El Fuerte in Sinaloa. His father, Juan María Ruiz, served as a soldier in California as early as 1750, and he, in turn, was probably a son of the Manuel Ruiz listed on California's military muster in 1718. Juan María Ruiz married Isabel Carrillo, of the Carrillo family, which became prominent in Alta California. Juan María Ruiz was attacked by a mountain lion and died of his wounds in 1765, when José Manuel was ten years of age. The boy, his brother, and three sisters were raised by their mother with the help of their Carrillo uncles.

What was distinctly unusual about the children of Juan María Ruiz and Isabel Carrillo was that each achieved a degree of prominence in one of the Californias. Francisco María Ruiz enlisted as a soldier and after a long and colorful career rose to be captain of the Presidio of San Diego. Even after his retirement in 1827 at the age of seventy-three, he added to San Diego history by building the first substantial house outside the presidio walls in the area later known as Old Town.

José Manuel Ruiz also enlisted and worked his way to a captaincy at Loreto. His longest service was as sergeant in command of troops defending Dominican missions and the Camino Real in the Fronteras region south of San Diego. Here his small force repelled many Indian attacks and earned Ruiz a fine reputation as a leader.

Captain Ruiz's greatest challenge came, as it did to most peninsular officials, during Mexico's struggle for independence. Ruiz kept his troops together and worked valiantly to help them subsist at a time in which pay was intermittent and then absent and even the source of authority was in doubt. After rising to the captaincy of the Presidio of Loreto, he retired. However, his grateful neighbors had further need for his services. In 1822, he accepted the new Baja California office of political chief and attempted to organize a workable government to replace the deposed Spanish system. It was in the course of these efforts that he penned this 1825 report to Mexico City, the truly faraway federal capital.

> Internal government is disorganized. The activity, zeal, and energy with which it is carried on have been insufficient for two reasons. First, lack of pay or even of regular subsistence for the military and naval forces in my charge. They have suffered to the point of having no bread. In such poor circumstances each body has become insubordinate enough. Secondly, on the civilian side, people are almost universally ignorant, municipal authorities are apathetic and remiss in carrying out duties beyond those they are forced to do.
>
> Part of the problem is that people are preoccupied by published notices that lands held by missions will be distributed to Indians and citizens, preoccupied in spite of the fact that they do not know how to claim them or whether they will be worth working.
>
> Meanwhile they hardly know how to subsist unless they are given their back pay earned in the time they served as soldiers and sailors. There is unequivocal evidence that the greater part, perhaps all, of the population is in the pauper class.
>
> Public treasuries and excise taxes are not established. Only missions hold community property and have management of it. Their missionaries answer only to their bishop, since the local government has no connection with or official knowledge of them.[5]

Ruiz described the low estate of missions, which were without income because the dislocation with Spain had upset normal channels of support. He noted that since 1810 the missions had fed and supplied troops at the frontier at an accrued cost of forty-seven thousand pesos, a debt that would never be repaid. Ruiz's description is eloquent: "Missions have fallen away so much that it may be said that those of Baja California are only phantoms, what with their few laborers, their buildings and fields almost destroyed for lack of funds and tools."[6]

Ruiz remarked on the low level of trade, the lack of capital investment, and, again, on the unpreparedness of the people to live an independent life. Much of this he blamed on an almost universal lack of education.

> Enlightenment has no hold in the territory, nor will it make progress, because... young people have failed to get the first principles of letters

---
5. Ibid., 113–14.
6. Ibid., 114.

or arts. Of a surety, there is not to be found a teacher of elementary reading or of the common mechanical arts, much less the liberal.... Children grow up in this ignorant condition, live scattered throughout the desert and vegetate until old age without understanding the moral or political cause of their bad education. Municipalities have no funds for education. For this reason, as much as for the lack of capable persons and necessary equipment, it has not been possible to sustain a single school.... In truth, those who know how to read and write correctly are extremely rare (I refer to the native born of the country).[7]

The old leader was seventy years of age when he wrote this report, which he finished with a plea for his land and his people. This plea reflected the hope held out for the new republican form of government. He asked for federal aid for Baja California "because it has passed over to another system of government, with new institutions to govern us, and only so will it be able to progress, taking into consideration that something new is going to be created for the inhabitants and for their posterity, that they may know what civilized life is, of which they now have only a very imperfect notion. This is as much as the undersigned can report from the practical and extensive knowledge that he has of the country of his birth, as the record of his long continued service shows."[8]

The Issue of Mission Lands

Mexico City was unable to fulfill any of the dreams of Ruiz or the councilmen of Loreto. The new central government was besieged by other claims, nearly all closer and more persuasive. The Church still clung doggedly to its mission holdings, which now really held the attention of Baja California's chronically land-poor society. Land was the central issue in the turmoil wrought by independence. Obtaining federal money seemed reasonable to leaders who had at least seen or handled considerable sums, but the idea must have seemed a meaningless will-of-the-wisp to the common man, for he did not miss what he had never known. Land was different.

---
7. Ibid., 115.
8. Ibid., 117.

People knew its potential and it lay before their eyes, announced as part of their legacy, but was tantalizingly denied to them by the slow working of procedures they did not understand.

The crux of the matter was the status of missions that held much of the useful land. If missions continued to serve their original purpose, the Church still had the right to hold them as an estate in trust for neophyte Indians until they had developed to a point where they could administer their own affairs. However, the logic and justice of these provisions of the original license granted to Jesuits over a century before had long since been obscured by practical politics. The Church had succeeded in retaining its hold as long as the semblance of a mission could be demonstrated—a priest, some buildings, and at least a few communicants of mostly Indian origin. Therefore, the mission depended on the survival of peoples whose population was declining. Locally, everyone knew that their numbers were falling to very low levels. These facts were also known abroad. For example, José Longinos Martínez, a Spanish naturalist who conducted a peninsula-long survey as early as 1791, wrote that there were "hardly any Indians from Cabo San Lucas to San Ignacio."[9]

At first the Church faced no real challenge. Its authority came from an accord between the Church and the Spanish Crown. But after 1810 or so, that firm footing began to tremble. Spain was out of the picture, her involvement terminated by the successful rebellion of her Mexican colony. After that, maneuvering and bitterness grew apace. Increasingly, missionaries had to hold their phantom missions by politics and intrigue and to depend less on a clear right. In this climate the last three or four Father Presidents of California Dominicans, powerful men among the ignorant and backward frontiersmen, used their influence and that of the Church to resist the enforcement of laws that would have broken up the very estates they had been appointed to administer. In this resistance they were greatly aided by the political power of their superiors in Mexico City and, after independence, by political cross-fire that could be manipulated to their advantage.

---

9. Longinos Martínez, *Journal of José Longinos Martínez*, 14.

By 1823, two factions, one liberal, anticlerical, and federalist, the other conservative, clerical, and centralist, contended for supremacy over the new central government. Liberals would obtain power and order emancipation of Indians and private ownership of mission lands. By the time these orders were being executed, a coup would install a conservative government that listened sympathetically to clerical appeals. Secularization would be shelved until liberals arose in their turn to begin the process again.

Baja California suffered from one attitude—contempt—that was shared by all the forces contending for central power. All viewed the peninsula as the nearly worthless home of a mere handful of people, and they treated it accordingly. The clearest proof of this contempt was the deplorable quality of most representatives sent by both religious and secular powers during the first forty years of Mexican independence. The religious group was assailed both from within and without by accusations of every sort of wrongdoing imaginable. With one or two notable exceptions, political figures in Baja California were a succession of incompetents that included drunks, murderers, strutting colonels, and traitors in time of war. Such a sorry combination of spiritual and temporal authorities militated strongly against any progress or stability on the peninsula.

A dismal pattern can be traced in the aftermath of each well-publicized decree of secularization and land distribution. Each began with fanfare and high resolve that raised the expectations of the people. Each resulted in granting to individuals the use of a few parcels of onetime mission lands, and each encountered stubborn resistance from the religious sector and was subsequently impeded or shelved for years.

Governors were seldom high-minded champions of the people. Secularization of land was occasionally part of a scheme by which a governor or his cronies planned to profit. Some secularization edicts appeared to favor Indians' claims over those of priests or Californios. As a result, it was not unusual to find that at least part of the peninsular population fell in behind the clergy to oppose a change of land status that they feared or did not understand. The bewilderment and disillusionment resulting from this prolonged struggle shaped peninsular attitudes through many generations.

The travail around mission centers must have strengthened the resolve of the more independent men who had taken to the mountains. Had it not been for the land battles, these people, who had sacrificed their social lives to gain property, might have gravitated home to claim mission lands. As it was, disputes around missions persisted so long that the exiles adapted to their isolated environments. Thus they were inspired to retain their relative freedom and rejoice in the tranquility of their lives. Others must have been encouraged to join them.

Old California Lives On

From 1821 to 1846, most visitors to Mexican Alta California were so struck by the great ranchos that they described little else. In fact, the really large ranches of the north, with their dozens of Indian laborers, were exceptional, as was the grandness of their owners' lives. Although the great landholders dominated society and politics, they were far outnumbered by poor relatives with modest ranches, especially in the southern parts of the province between Santa Bárbara and San Diego. The more typical holdings were family-run, with few if any employees, and yielded not great profits but a hard-bitten subsistence. Even at the level of the poorer ranchers there were regional distinctions based largely on differences in soil and climate. But the basic practices, like the culture and bloodlines, were similar at smaller ranches throughout both Californias.

All during the Mexican period, Alta California was being quietly invaded by growing numbers of foreigners, chiefly Americans. A few were deserters from ships. Others who arrived by sea were merchants or traders. By overland routes came trappers, prospectors, fur traders, and, finally, would-be farmers. These people soon came to dominate commercial activity. In that manner, as well as by marriage, they infiltrated Californio society. After 1836, when the United States recognized the independence of Texas, some Californios and some officials in the central government of Mexico actively feared a similar American takeover of Alta California. Subsequently, despite various Mexican plans and precautions, the alarm proved to have been justified. During the early part of the Mexican War (1846–48) Alta California fell into American hands.

With the Americanization of Alta California, Californio control of grazing and agricultural land was doomed. Those with small plots near the gold country were the first to lose their land, since they were least likely to be able to produce the kind of official grants for their ranches that American courts or commissions would recognize. Also, they had fewer social or financial connections with the new rulers of their land. Over time, ranches north of the new international border acquired a markedly American stamp and tended to progress and change as part of nineteenth-century American culture. Californios themselves became a humble element in the new society: laborers using the tools and practices of their new employers. Ironically, in this democracy many of them were virtual peons, a fate that their frontiersmen ancestors had managed to avoid even in royalist New Spain.

In Baja California the situation was totally different. Although parts of the southern peninsula were occupied by American forces during the 1846–48 conflict, there was no population invasion or significant political or social changes. Ranches continued to be run as before, particularly those that were isolated in the mid-peninsular mountains. Their people were quite unaware that they were the only Californios living in ways once characteristic of both Hispanic Californias.

CHAPTER 4

Picturing the Californios

Baja California's remote ranchers were never able to attend schools. While a few became semiliterate, none left accounts of their thoughts or actions. Spanish California had few visitors, and its Hispanic settlers probably interested those few as little as anything they saw. Their references to common people are scarce, oblique, and brief. What is known of the Californios of those times must for the greater part be pieced together from enlistment and discharge papers, muster rolls, pay records, supply orders, baptismal and marriage and death records, and other paperwork routinely generated as military or Church documentation. The commonplace activities of daily life must be inferred because seldom does any chronicle provide details. Priests were in the best position to do so, since they were educated, wrote letters and reports, and worked with and ministered to soldiers, mission servants, and their families throughout their peninsular service. With few exceptions, however, they took their soldier helpers for granted and made few reports of their many services.

Padre Baegert's years on the peninsula were from 1750 to 1768. Most of the gente de razón he described in his book were products of mainland upbringing. Only a few youths as yet were true Californios. But during the remainder of the eighteenth century, increasing numbers were native born, especially those who took to isolated ranching. Regionalism blossomed during this time as a result of the particular nature of Californio heritage and experiences. Originally, California's Hispanic people were selected as servants for the Jesuit missionaries. They were not a random group of volunteer colonists in a new land. In isolated California they were little exposed to the changing styles and practices found in larger centers closer to the mother culture. Even the poverty of their barren peninsular homeland made a positive contribution to their distinctive regional character. Since their area offered no opportunities for great or profitable landholdings, no ranches or farms were developed in the same way that they were in most other parts of New Spain. As a result, there were no grandees and no peons. Their class system did not encompass that great gulf between master and servant. By the time Mexico had liberated itself from Spain, most Californios were what we would call "lower middle class"—they were poor but independent, a combination not common elsewhere in their new nation. Baja Californians were developing a sense of pride and dignity that would distinguish them for more than a century to come.

There are no direct accounts of the steps by which the peninsula's people acquired their characteristic attitudes and mannerisms. This blank in the record makes it clear that few observers were interested in "the common person," and Californios were about as rustic a group as could be imagined. The concept of these people displaying a "culture" would have amused the largely European padres and escaped the understanding of the occasional visitors from the mainland. The latter seldom remained long enough to notice the phenomenon of adaptation that was taking place. The nineteenth century would change all that. The Age of Independence also saw the world shrink, travelers multiply, and intellectual curiosity expand apace.

The first decades of Mexican independence, 1820 to 1840, brought Baja California more than the struggle for mission lands. Many policies of the new governments in Mexico City were very different from those of Spain and its viceroys. For centuries, Spain had closed all of California to foreign commerce. Mexican independence had opened the area to commercial interests, especially whalers and traders who could disembark, view the country, mingle with the people, and, in a few cases, go home and write about what they had seen. These writings do not give direct views of many mountain ranchers. Few visitors reached the sierras, and none left illuminating descriptions. However, some of these travelers did describe the people they met in other relatively isolated places, and those descriptions are especially valuable. In those early times, mountaineers and lowlanders, ranchers and townsfolk had not yet diverged sufficiently in appearances, practices, or traditions to allow visitors to distinguish one group from the other. After all, until the late nineteenth century, all of Baja California, except perhaps La Paz and two or three mining centers, was so remote from the greater world and so relatively untouched by progress that most of the folkways observed by outsiders in the ports and lowlands were probably current in the sierras.

A French Trader in 1830

In 1830, Cyprien Combier, a French skipper of a trading schooner out of Le Havre, spent some months touching at various ports around the Gulf of California—Mazatlán, Guaymas, Loreto, and La Paz. At La Paz, Combier was shrewd enough to see potential profit in huge mounds of discarded oyster shells. He exchanged his conventional stone ballast for the exotic material, which he rightly guessed could be sold in Europe for the manufacture of buttons, inlays, and the like. During the many days it took to load the shells onto his schooner, he was free to visit the area and meet the people. His experiences around Loreto were the most important in forming the impressions that he was to record in a book. His task at the old peninsular capital was to obtain a cargo of eight thousand cowhides, but since the tiny port had no dealers or agents, Combier had to travel from ranch to ranch arranging the slaughter of cattle and the preparation and delivery of hides. After these visits, Combier wrote of the inhabitants of Baja California, "I could not fail to recognize in their physical appearances, as in their moral dispositions, an immense difference from Mexicans of the continent. They do not seem to belong to the same origin and, on their faces, tanned as much by the excessive heat of the climate as by mixed blood, you notice a striking variety of features and of expressions. The men, preserving the complexion of their mother stock, are generally above average in stature, strong and robust and inclined to stoutness."[1]

The Frenchman went on, like José de Gálvez sixty years earlier, to note the peninsular dependence on beef cattle for sustenance and economic gain. In the intervening years, the pursuit of wild cattle had further sharpened Californios' skills as vaqueros. It was an accomplishment that drew comment from nearly every visitor to both Californias between the 1770s and the 1850s. Combier also anticipated the thoughts of many others when he remarked on Californio pride and independence:

> Most of the people live on little ranchos, or farms. The ranchers' occupations consist of riding horseback from early morn to overlook their herds, break horses and mules, slaughter the animals whose meat nourishes the family and serves in bartering, and, finally, in drying and preparing the meat, the hides and tallow that may be sold as excess.
>
> It is without doubt to this kind of life as much as to their origin that we must attribute their independent nature and a noble pride which strikes us at first sight. They are generally good, obliging, and energetic, but their imperturbable dignity would never stoop to render a service which would have an appearance of domesticity or servitude.
>
> Their clothes consist of a cotton shirt, breeches, and an overcoat of deerskin tanned and prepared by themselves and decorated in different ways by the women.[2]

Cyprien Combier apparently had a keen eye for family life and some of its implications. He was one of the first to remark on the vitality of the people and the size of their families. His description

---
1. Combier, *Voyage au Golfe de Californie*, 334.
2. Ibid., 334–35.

of the trend that was populating the midpeninsular sierras was only slightly exaggerated.

> Women dress themselves properly and even with a certain coquetry. Preserving the complexion of their father race, they are, in general, much whiter than the men. Their features are more delicate, their manners sweeter and more engaging. The cares of the household, the education of the little children, milking cows, and making cheese are their exclusive functions. Their incomparable fecundity is due, without doubt, to a strong constitution maintained by coarse and simple but abundant food. It is not rare to find among them mothers in their forties having families of fifteen or even twenty children in good health. It is rare to see any of this age who have less than a dozen. One is surprised everywhere at the prodigious number of children who multiply in the thatched cottages and amid the brushwoods that surround them. This spectacle impresses the mind with an idea of the great growth of population, growth which manifests itself by the incessant establishment of new ranchos in places previously uninhabited.[3]

An American Traveler in 1843

James Hunter Bull, an American from Pennsylvania, visited Mexico in 1843 and decided to go to California as well. When he got to Sonora, he found the Yuma region in the middle of an Indian war. Following local advice, he chose Baja California as his route to Monterey and sailed over to Mulegé. After his experiences with peninsular people, Bull wrote, "I was struck immediately with the difference of manner, a greater freedom of thought and expression, none of that servile politeness in these people which everyone who glances at the manners of the Mexicans must necessarily observe. The haughty and proud Spaniard compelled from the Mexican a servile obedience. The same character is stamped deep into the manners of their descendants. The Californian boasts of California. He claims no kindred with the Mexican."[4]

The American obtained a guide and mules and headed northward to reach Alta California by following the old Camino Real.

---
3. Ibid., 335.
4. Bull, *Journey of James H. Bull, Baja California, October 1843 to January 1844*, 20–21.

Three days of riding in barren surroundings magnified the joy of encountering the first village:

> We arrived in San Ignacio about 9 o'clock in the evening after a hard day's travel over the most desolate country I had yet seen. It was a welcome sight to see the lights glimmering in the distance, and a welcome sound to hear joyous merriment as we came nearer to the mission. . . . It was a Sunday night and the people were dancing the fandango . . . which I learned was given by the Padre as a farewell treat to his parishioners on the eve of his starting for the upper country. I entered the long hall where all was boisterous merriment. The Padre came up and welcomed me, inviting me to use everything as my own—occasionally using a word of English by way of compliment.[5]

In San Ignacio's fandango, James Hunter Bull had stumbled upon a rustic example of an extravaganza that astonished and fascinated nearly every American who visited Mexican California. Dancing has always been a part of Spanish national life. Its antiquity may be traced back with hardly a break to performances in Imperial Rome by the famous dancing girls of Cádiz. During the eighteenth century, the fandango, a lively dance in triple time, had a great vogue in the mother country and soon spread to the colonies. In the 1840s, Bull could have encountered similar but grander affairs in San Diego, Los Ángeles, Monterey, or San José and might have described those affairs in the same fashion.

> The fandango is an exceedingly lascivious dance, or rather a number of dances. Even in the most indelicate dances the women perform their parts without a blush. The music was rather inferior, but what it lacked in harmony was made up by the lungs of the musicians. In these dances the musicians always sing as well as play upon the guitar. The verses are almost always bawdy and when the singer adds something to their lewdness he is greeted by shouts of applausive laughter. The women were not dressed with so much taste as we would find displayed in a ballroom at home, but I think they moved with more ease and grace. It is true their bodies were not confined by stays and tortured into less than their natural size, but their limbs were free and moved easily and gracefully in the figures of the dance of their country. And I am not Platonist enough to deny that they often appeared bewitching to my

---

5. Ibid., 29–30.

Picturing the Californios

4.1. *Trajes mexicanos—un fandango* (1851) by Casimiro Castro. This mid-nineteenth-century painter caught the spirit of the fandango, a popular dance extravaganza in California and other Mexican frontier regions. From *México y sus alrededores: Colección de vistas monumentales, paisajes y trajes del país* (1869).
Courtesy of General Research Division, The New York Public Library, Astor, Lenox, and Tilden Foundations.

sight as they whirled through some of the intricate figures of the Jota or passing by me in the less interesting but no less graceful Jarave. Many of the dances are derived from the Indians, as the Venado and Coyote (The Deer and Little Wolf), and Burro (or Ass), and numerous others. In one dance the performer goes through a number of difficult figures bearing upon his head a goblet filled with wine or liquid, and if he should be so unfortunate as to spill it, he is ridiculed by all the company. But if he succeeds, he meets with great applause. It was late when I retired from the scene of amusement, but when I arose in the morning, they were still dancing and did not cease till about 9 o'clock.[6]

---

6. Ibid., 30–31.

The fandango, in California at least, became something more than a particular dance form—it was an immensely popular and elegantly bawdy social event. Men who attended were from all classes, but were expected to be well dressed. Women who aspired to any social standing, or who expected to be considered virtuous, came to fandangos only as spectators and then properly chaperoned. Girls and women who came to dance were from the lower classes and unmarried—or had very tolerant husbands! Women who excelled at the fandango had no trouble obtaining suitable finery. Lovers and other admirers saw to it that milkmaids, shopgirls, and harlots, if they could dance, wore the extravagant and daring garb that so dazzled visitors from the more staid United States.

The fandango had a considerable history at San Ignacio before James Hunter Bull's visit. As early as 1803, California missionaries were scandalized because one of their number, Fray Rafael Arviña, the padre at San Ignacio, "attended fandangos," jesting with women his critics knew to be favorites of his. In context, it is clear that the priests who wrote the complaint and the superior who eventually received it well understood a fandango's barely covert sexual adventurism.[7]

An English Naturalist in 1835

Cabo San Lucas had been a landmark and stopping point for mariners since the dawn of the Manila-Mexico trade in the late sixteenth century. Its relatively sheltered harbor, water, and wood were always in demand. During the centuries of the Manila galleons and the privateers who preyed on them, the cape region was populated only by mobile bands of Pericú Indians. But by 1800, the needs of a new stamp of mariners—whalers, traders, and sea otter hunters—encouraged gente de razón to live at the harbor of Cabo San Lucas and engage in raising cattle that could be sold to nearly every ship that put in. Because the tiny settlement was so

---

7. Letter of a group of Dominicans to Rafael Arviña, January 12, 1803, cited in Engelhardt, *The Missions and Missionaries of California*, 1:743.

essential and accessible to foreigners, it is no wonder that several early descriptions found their way into print.

In 1833, English commercial interests sent surgeon-naturalist Frederick Debell Bennett out on a whaler to determine the best ways of conducting a sperm whale fishing industry. His globe-circling three-year cruise resulted in a book that Herman Melville considered one of the best works on whaling. Bennett's description of Cabo San Lucas in 1835 reveals both his sociological interests and his recent exposure to the ways of Polynesians. His picture of Baja California life probably would have fit most of the peninsula's isolated cattle ranches.

> The village or settlement consists of about eight dwellings, erected at a distance from the sea, beneath the shade of some mimosa trees. They are small, built of adobes (or unburnt bricks) and thatched with flags (rushes) obtained from the neighbouring town of St. José [del Cabo]. Each hut usually contains one or never more than two apartments and is faced with a portico, which affords a favorite lounge for the resident family. Their furniture is scanty, and rather more useful than ornamental. The hairy surface of a dried bullock's hide, spread on the hard earthen floor, is the usual bed. The tables and benches are very rudely constructed. Beneath the portico are deposited dried or tanned hides. The horse furniture of the farmers includes the cumbrous but luxurious saddles, saddle-bags capable in themselves of containing a horse-load, and spurs of murderous length. On lines passing across the roof are suspended large pieces of beef undergoing the process of jerking. Some sheds, distinct from the dwellings, are used for cooking, or preparing cheese. An extensive range of corrals, or cattle-pens, contain at night the milchkine and goats.[8]

Bennett found about thirty persons in residence and went on to describe them as ranging from European to Indian types. He noted their custom of separate dining times for men and women, which remains standard practice in Baja California's mountain ranches.

> The women are notable and modest. The men are expert equestrians, and excel in the use of the lasso. It is a curious fact, that the women, whether

---

8. Bennett, *Narrative of a Whaling Voyage Round the Globe*, 2:5–6.

creole Spaniards or half-caste, cannot be prevailed upon to eat with the men: a prejudice which must be regarded as of native or Indian origin, and one which coincides in a remarkable manner with the primitive custom of the Polynesian tribes.

The costume of the women is neat, and as light as the climate demands. It is comprised of a chemise garment of white cotton, and a short striped-cotton petticoat. Their hair is simply parted on the forehead, and descends over the shoulders, braided in an elaborate and becoming manner. The men wear a cotton shirt, open at the neck, breeches loose at the knees to facilitate equestrian exercises, a broad-brimmed straw hat, and shoes and buskins of rudely-tanned leather, well adapted to protect their legs from the thorny plants of the country. Some of the men wear their hair short while others have it braided into a queue and pendant over the shoulders, after the manner of the women. A large woollen rug, white striped with blue, worn over the shoulders or enveloping the entire person, they more capriciously assume, and chiefly when on their journeys.

Since the character of the soil offers no inducement to agricultural pursuits, these people confine their attention to rearing cattle, which, together with the cheese they prepare from the milk of their herds, form the staple commodities of the settlement. As we had been accustomed among the Polynesian islands to notice a race of people living almost solely on a vegetable diet, so here we found another subsisting entirely upon animal food: the only vegetables they consume being maize, which they procure from a distant part of the country, and a few small and indifferent sweet potatoes, which they rack their own soil to produce.

The sale and use of ardent spirits is interdicted by their social laws. But they nevertheless indulge occasionally in a kind of rum or *aguardiente*, distilled from sugar-cane, grown in the inland parts of the country. Notwithstanding their monotonous and highly animalized diet, these people are healthy, active, and robust. Their only endemic diseases are agues, which they contract from the malaria arising from the jungle, soon after the termination of the rainy season. They live contented, and consequently happy; and their conduct towards each other, as well as to ourselves, was equally courteous and hospitable.[9]

A Japanese Castaway in 1842

The most exotic of all accounts of Californio life is also one of the very few with pertinent illustrations. Hatsutarō was a sailor

---

9. Ibid., 2:6–9.

on the *Eiju Maru*, a shipping vessel working the coasts of Japan. He and the twelve other members of the crew were blown out to sea in 1841. After drifting for four months in their disabled craft, they were rescued by a Spanish ship that brought them to Baja California. All thirteen survived the rigorous crossing, and nine, at least, were put ashore. Two of these, Zensuke, the master of the *Eiju Maru*, and Hatsutarō, the supercargo, made their way back to Japan in 1844. Hatsutarō wrote down his adventures and worked with an artist to create the pictures he felt were needed to supplement the words. His narrative is unique in its basic perspective. All other descriptions of Californio life were written by men born in societies grounded in European culture. However odd, regional, and specialized California life seemed to all these other observers, it was at its roots a Western culture. As a result, factors common to the experience of observers and observed alike were omitted as matters of little interest to American or European readers.

To the Japanese, by contrast, every detail in a report from Baja California was a novelty. It was a rare view of an alien culture. Hatsutarō returned from his adventures several years before Admiral Perry "opened" Japan. Until 1868, the ruling Tokugawa Shogunate imposed a death sentence on any Japanese who attempted to emigrate. To satisfy some of his countrymen's curiosity, Hatsutarō, in words and pictures, tells more about Baja California people's appearances and social customs, clothing, houses, and the shapes of things in general than all the American and European writers combined. Furthermore, this Japanese sailor was unique among the visitors because he lived and worked among Californios for nearly seven months. He wore their clothes and cut his hair as they did. He experienced their climatic changes and, most important, came to have personal relationships with them. No other traveler prior to the twentieth century had so many insights to impart or left such a complete and satisfying tale of his encounter with peninsular life.

The Japanese sailors' Baja California adventure began just after the rescued mariners were rowed ashore and left alone near the small settlement at Cabo San Lucas. This was the same place visited by Frederick Bennett only six years before. Below are somewhat abridged selections from Hatsutarō's colorful report. In the manner of the Japanese at that time, he wrote in the third person.

> The people seemed quite surprised to see men approaching in the moonlight, but they took the Japanese with them for another hundred yards to a place where there were two houses. On the outsides there were structures like broad platforms on which were gathered some twenty persons dressed like Dutchmen.[10]
>
> All of the people were astonished and tried to ask questions, but the Japanese could not speak their language. The castaways managed by gestures to tell of their sufferings, and the people seemed to understand, for they first gave each of the men a cupful of water to drink. Then when they seemed to be asking where the men had come from, the Japanese said "Nippon" several times, which they apparently understood because they then said "Japón, Japón."
>
> All the Japanese soon lay down for the night on two cowhides which were spread at a large tree nearby. Although it was then the middle of May, the heat was intense and the weather was like that of August in Japan, but there were very few mosquitos.
>
> At daybreak two or three women came from the two houses and welcomed the Japanese to come to their homes, where each was served a drink called "café," which is something like tea with sugar in it. The seamen were then divided into two groups of three and four men, and on a cowhide spread beneath a sunshade made of something like thatching, which hung down from the eaves outside the house, they were served a meal of corncake, preserved meat, and bananas.
>
> One of the two houses was built in the style of a warehouse, with walls some three feet high. A doorway faced the east, and the roof was thatched. The thatching material resembled iris plants. The thatch was made of thin stalks in bundles of about twenty pieces, each bundle being about ten feet long and eight inches thick.[11]
>
> The inside of the house had an earthen floor, and on it there were spread mattresses covered with cotton print, which served as beds. The

---

10. Europeans. The Dutch were the first to visit Japan, and the name applied to them was transferred to all Europeans.
11. The plant used for this thatching was *carrizo*, a giant grass or false cane, dense stands of which grow to heights of fifteen or more feet in swampy lowlands or wherever there is standing or running subsoil water. In the mountains, where carrizo was rare, leaves of the common fan palms were used for thatch. The practice spread and palm eventually supplanted carrizo for all peninsular thatching.

cookhouse was built separately and had an oven made of clay. They cooked with iron pots and pans.

The second house was a cabin with walls and roof built like the first house. More than twenty persons lived together in these two houses. The people were fair of complexion, their hair was black, and the color of their eyes was the same as that of Japanese people. But there was one man who was apparently the master of the larger house, and he looked just like the Europeans.[12]

This place was called Cape San Lucas, in Baja California, on the American continent. It seemed to be a narrow place on the seashore at the base of the mountains.

The two households raised several kinds of livestock—swine, deer,[13] and sheep—which they sold in other more populated places. Meanwhile the animals were kept in the many pens they had built.

The Japanese seamen stayed at this place for two days, and during that time they drank tea with sugar in it in the morning, and ate meals each day at noon and evening. On the third day the Japanese were taken, together with a cargo of dried meat and lard, on board a ship of about thirty or forty tons capacity, and apparently they were being sent somewhere else. Although it was a small vessel, its hull was sheathed with copper on the bottom, and in other respects also it was like the Western ships. The ship had two masts and there were four sailors on board.

On this ship they sailed to the east. At about 10 a.m. on that third day they arrived at a beach after having traveled fifteen or twenty miles. White sands extended off to the left, and the mountains seemed to be ranged in a row.

Presently some people of this place led twelve or thirteen saddle-horses to the seashore. Just as in the former stopping place, the horses' saddles were quite similar to those used in Japan. (However, these saddles were made of plain wood, with silver fittings attached.) They had each of the castaways mount a horse and one of them led each horse by the mouth. Some of them had to ride on the rear end of the horses because more men, evidently some sailors, also rode along with them to the north. A man who lived in the two dwellings which the Japanese had first visited sailed with them on the same ship, and he mounted a horse and raced off somewhere in a hurry. It seemed as though he was probably going ahead to report to some government office.

---

12. This was Thomas Ritchie, an English whaler who jumped ship around 1830 and lived for about forty years at the tip of the peninsula.
13. Actually cattle, a distinction apparently not made by some Japanese.

After they had ridden for a little over a mile, they came to a place where there were seventy or eighty dwellings. This place is called San José, in Baja California, and it is under the government of the capital city, called Mexico, on the North American continent.

When they came to a house at the head of the street, the Japanese dismounted from their horses and bowed, because there were three men there who seemed to be officials.

However, while the castaways were talking over the events that had occurred, some twenty men who looked like merchants came up and took each of the nine men off to separate homes. When Hatsutarō was the only one left, a man who seemed to be fifty years old came up to take him away.

His house was approximately thirty feet in length and eighteen feet in width, and was built like a cabin with white walls and a thatched roof. Ten members of the family, both men and women, dwelt there, with one male and two female servants. Inside the house the floor was entirely earthen, and each person had a bed on which a mattress was laid.

The people here looked the same as at the previous place, both the men and women being handsome with light complexions and black hair. Their clothing and food were also the same as those at the other settlement. Maize, wheat, and meat formed their diet. When they got up in the morning, they drank their tea with sugar in it and ate pan. (Pan is made by kneading wheat flour with eggs and baking it like a sponge-cake.)

The men and women all wore shoes. The men's were made of tanned cowhide, and the soles were built in three layers. The soles were made so thick because the sandy soil there was burning hot when the heat became severe. The uppers were made from the hides of deer or sheep.

In the prevailing hot weather of this land, which lay at about twenty-five degrees north latitude, the sand was baked until it was dark red in color, and to walk barefoot even a couple of hundred yards was difficult. However, every day at about 10 in the morning, a cool breeze blew up from the south, and so the people fortunately could endure it. This seemed to be the natural pattern here.

Every four or five days the men and women went together to the bank of the river where they bathed in the water. No one exposed his body, and the women covered themselves most modestly. All of the nine men—Hatsutarō was the first—had their hair cut in the fashion of that country. Their clothing too was made in the native style.

The master of the house where Hatsutarō was lodged was named Miguel Choza. (Miguel was his given name and Choza was his family name. It is the custom of foreigners to say the given name first.) His wife was named Ignacia, and they had two sons and three daughters. The elder son was Blas, the eldest daughter was Antonia, the second daughter was Ascensión, the youngest daughter was Jesús, and the younger son was Agustín.

By some lucky chance, Miguel Choza took pity on Hatsutarō, and even gave him all new clothing to wear. When Hatsutarō first went out on the street wearing his new clothes, everyone he met was surprised and envious. The man who took Zensuke to his house was also generous and sympathetic, but as there were no women in his home, Zensuke was not cared for as well as was Hatsutarō. Neither of the two had any housework duties, and their health was better than ever as they passed the time in ease. The other seven men were employed in gathering firewood on the mountains, tilling the fields, drawing water, or tending the gardens. Whenever they had spare time, the nine men would meet together to talk about their native land.

The master changed his clothing every other day and had Hatsutarō do the same, and the latter's meals were the same as his master's. Hatsutarō was taken everywhere with him. The reason he treated Hatsutarō so well was that he intended to marry the Japanese to his daughter. On one occasion the girl and Hatsutarō were given instruction together in the details of the wedding ceremony. There would sometimes be expeditions with the master to shoot rabbits.

Early in September, the master, Miguel Choza, received a letter from the capital of Mexico directing him to go on business to a place called Mazatlán. He sought out a ship that was bound for Mazatlán and hurried away, after telling his family that he would entrust his affairs to Hatsutarō, rather than burden his wife.

Thereafter Hatsutarō lived with Miguel Choza's family, taking good care of things in his absence. From the middle of May to the end of November—about two hundred days altogether—the men stayed in San José. During that time very little rain fell. There were sudden showers with a little thunder twice in July, and in September there was a rainstorm only once.

There was a sailor from La Paz named Beron who now and then came to San José. Since he was a good friend of Miguel Choza, he came to know Hatsutarō quite well also. Early in November of 1842, Hatsutarō happened to see Beron at his inn, and he asked Hatsutarō if he intended to return to Japan. Hatsutarō said that he could not for a moment forget his feelings for his native land and his aging parents.

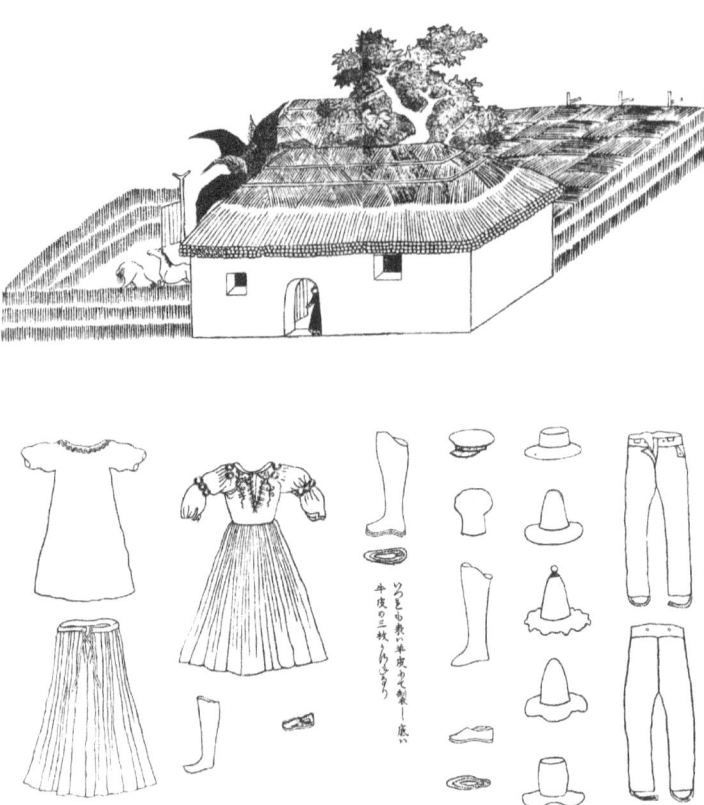

"If that is so," Beron said, "perhaps I could arrange matters for you. Miguel Choza is very kind to you and intends for you to be his son-in-law, and in that case you will never have a chance to return home. Now, I am always going back and forth on the ship to Mazatlán and I know my way around that place quite well. Dutch ships come there occasionally, in fact, I have heard that one arrived just recently. Since the Hollanders trade with Japan, it should be an easy matter to get you back home if we would go and appeal to the Dutch ship."

Hatsutarō took Zensuke to the master's house and told the family that they had to go to Mazatlán on business. Miguel Choza's family

Picturing the Californios 111

Opposite: 4.2. A few examples of the drawings created by an artist under the direction of Hatsutarō, who intended to show Japanese readers the exotic nature of Baja California people, buildings, implements, and clothing. From Maekawa, Sakai, and Hatsutarō, *Kaigai Ibun: A Strange Tale from Overseas, or, A New Account of America*. Miguel Choza's house is shown at the top. Hatsutarō provided careful descriptions of the house and other items: "The length is about five *ken* and the depth is about three *ken*. The roof is thatched with what seem to be iris stalks. It is covered on the lower part with bundles of some twenty stalks each, and about one *jo* (put long *o* sign of this letter) in length. On the upper part there are also thatches hanging from the ridge, folding over onto both sides and held in place by bamboos. Center posts are set in the ground, and their forked tops support crossbeams. The walls, both inside and out, are plastered with lime" (96–97).

Clothing on far left: "'Camisón,' a woman's undershirt made of white cotton. It is closely sewn all around and has an opening through which the head is put. The upper garment has a single layer, but the garment worn below the waist has three layers. 'Naguas,' a garment tied around a woman's waist. It has pleats like a monk's skirt" (119).

The back of a dress, showing the silk flower-shaped bindings at places on the arms and shoulders. The dress is put on over the head as far as the neck. A woman's shoe: the upper is made of cotton and the sole of a single layer of leather. A woman's stocking, made of "melania" (122).

Clothing on the right: "Hats of various kinds. 'Sombrero.' 'Cachucha,' a hat usually worn by soldiers. 'Zapato.' A stocking made of a knitted fabric. A shoe and its sole. High boot and its sole. The upper surfaces are made of sheepskin, and the soles are three thicknesses of cowhide" (118).

asked why they were going, and Hatsutarō said that they wanted to see the place and that they also hoped to meet the master. At that, the family could not restrain the men, but for the next three days made many new garments so they would not look shabby in such a grand place as Mazatlán, and fixed various treats for them to eat from morning to night. Zensuke continued to stay at this house.

When it was learned, on about November 30 or December 1, that Beron's ship was ready to sail, the mother and children seemed to guess the men's purpose, and they all parted mournfully, never knowing whether the two men would ever return. They took Hatsutarō by the hand and embraced him, and sorrowfully bade farewell. In that country when anyone, whether man or woman, young or old, rich or poor, would part from his close friends, they would clasp hands and embrace him in this way. Miguel Choza's children, riding on horses, came down to the shore with the seven remaining castaways to see the men off.

Hatsutarō and Zensuke boarded Beron's ship, which they saw was a two-masted vessel of about 80 tons capacity, with a crew of seven. That same day they put out from San José and sailed towards the southeast. They had good sailing weather and a strong wind, so they arrived at Mazatlán on the fifth day.

Meanwhile, Miguel Choza, the master from San José, who was still in this town on business, heard about what was happening and came to see them. "If you will stay at my house rather than return to your home country," he said to Hatsutarō, "I shall some day give you my daughter in marriage together with a dowry of ten thousand silver coins. If you go into business you should make a good living, so don't you think you should stay?"

"During the last several months," Hatsutarō told him, "I have incurred a great obligation to you, as deep as the ocean, and now again you honor me by asking me to remain. Although I am truly grateful for your understanding, I have left my aging parents behind in Japan and I feel that I should return to serve them, and so I must respectfully decline your offer."

Beron, who was also present, added his views, recommending that they return to their own country, and Miguel Choza finally consented. Just before he took ship for home, the master and Hatsutarō embraced each other and parted with sad farewells.

Hatsutarō felt a great debt of gratitude to Miguel Choza, who had cared for him as for his own son, and to Beron also, who aided their return to their homeland and sincerely tried to help them in so many ways. It was certainly divine providence that the castaways should meet such men of good will. Thus their minds were more at ease about enduring the ten thousand miles of rough seas on the return voyage to Japan.[14]

The United States Invades Baja California

By a curious stroke of fortune, the same Miguel Choza was soon to play a part in a larger-scale encounter with foreign seamen. In

---

14. Maekawa, Sakai, and Hatsutarō, *Kaigai Ibun*, 36–49.

early 1847, ships of the United States Navy, engaged in the war with Mexico, touched at La Paz and San José del Cabo, and their commander requested the cooperation of municipal authorities in a peaceful takeover under the American flag. In exchange for nonbelligerency, the citizens were promised that they could continue to run their own affairs under their own officials and civil laws. Since Miguel Choza was appointed by the Americans to act as port captain and customs collector, it is reasonable to assume that he already held a similar position. His service as some sort of official earlier was suggested by Hatsutarō's statement that "Miguel Choza received a letter from the capital of Mexico directing him to go on business to a place called Mazatlán."

Many records indicate that Baja California had been particularly neglected during the two or three years prior to this incident. Local officials, businessmen, and landowners were especially apprehensive because there were no units of the Mexican army or navy to protect them or to enforce laws. At the same time, unofficial bands both of patriots and of insurgents roved along the gulf's mainland coast, looting towns and ranches. Reports of these affairs had made the residents of the peninsula very nervous, and many of them naively supposed that the Americans could protect them and their property. As a result, the U.S. forces found themselves remarkably welcome. Since top American officers understood that the peninsula was to be annexed, they made grand promises to Baja Californians from the governor down. Before long, most of the more prosperous citizens were convinced that their land, like Alta California, was to be part of the United States and that their cooperation with the Americans was the only sensible course.

The Americans were few and not every Baja Californian welcomed their presence. Patriots organized guerrilla forces and gathered stores. Yaqui Indian mercenaries were imported from Sonora. Skirmishes were fought, and the small U.S. forces holding both La Paz and San José del Cabo were besieged and nearly overrun. American forces finally prevailed, but at great cost to property, much of it belonging to those who cooperated with the invaders.

The Treaty of Guadalupe Hidalgo, which ended the Mexican War in 1848, shocked American commanders in the area and, more deeply, all those who had allied with them. Under its terms, the United States did not annex Baja California, and all promises to that effect were nullified. The Americans in Baja California were embarrassed, and the local people who had received their assurance were devastated. Lieutenant Colonel Henry S. Burton, in charge of U.S. Army units at La Paz, summed up the situation in a letter to Richard B. Mason, military governor of Alta California:

> I request instructions ... respecting those inhabitants of Lower California who have taken up arms in our favor during the late disturbances in the country, relying upon the assurances that Lower California would never revert to the Republic of Mexico, made to them by Commodore Shubrick, in his proclamation issued at San José, November, 1847, and contained in the statement of the President of the United States, in his annual message of 1847, that it should never be given up to Mexico.
>
> These assurances were received in good faith. And among the better class of the population in the country, great pleasure was evinced at the prospect of receiving, in Lower California, a just and permanent government.
>
> As nothing is said, in this treaty of peace, respecting persons in the situations of these inhabitants of Lower California, they are left to the mercy of Mexico. Many have appealed most earnestly to the agents of the United States in the country for protection, saying their property will be confiscated, their lives and those of their families endangered, if they remain in the country after the American troops leave, and requesting that means of transportation may be furnished them for removal of their families and effects to Upper California, Oregon, or such other of the United States as they may select for their future residence.[15]

Having thus compromised the Baja Californians, American military leaders accepted their responsibility. Three hundred and fifty men, women, and children were taken aboard U.S. ships bound for Monterey. On board were Miguel Choza and presumably his family. He was also one of sixty-four people who received cash payments for goods or services rendered. The amount was $1,032, the tenth largest settlement on the list.

---

15. Henry S. Burton to Richard B. Mason, June 27, 1848, in Henry Stanton Burton Diary and Letter Book, 1846–1848, The Bancroft Library, C-B 440.

Colonel Burton, who requested the transfer, apparently had more than compassion and national honor on his mind. Shortly after reaching Monterey he married María Amparo Ruiz, one of the refugees and a relative of an old soldier and past governor of Baja California, José Manuel Ruiz.

The Mexican War in Baja California brought in unprecedented numbers of foreign visitors as troops, and it was inevitable that some of them left records of their adventures and observations. Most had also visited Alta California, which gave them grounds for comparisons. For example, Lieutenant Edward Gould Buffum of the New York Volunteers wrote: "The people of Lower California are a curious race of beings, isolated from their mother country and neglected by her, they have assumed a sort of independence of thought and action which I never found in Upper California. But a kinder-hearted, more hospitable class of people never lived."[16]

William Redmond Ryan, an English adventurer, also took part in the American military occupation. His experiences were published in London, accompanied by several of the author's sketches.

> The inhabitants of La Paz are more intelligent than the people of Monterey, whilst the habits of the lower classes were even more simple and primitive. The chief articles of food amongst the latter are beef, tortillas, and penoche. These tortillas are a kind of cake made of ground Indian corn, and the penoche is a mixture of coarse flour and sugar, made up into very hard square or round pieces. I have frequently seen an Indian, or a Californian of the lower class, breakfast off a couple of these tortillas, weighing together no more than two ounces and a half, and a piece of this sugar and flour, previous to undergoing the most severe physical labour.[17]

The Englishman's "penoche" was actually called *panocha* and contained raw sugar, but no flour. This staple food item is still made in quantity at scattered ranches and villages throughout the southern half of the peninsula, and its formula is ancient. Local sugarcane is squeezed between the rollers of a mule- or burro-powered press and the juice conducted to a copper cauldron, which acts as a cap on a hardwood-fired furnace. The raw sugar squeezings are

---

16. Buffum, *Six Months in the Gold Mines*, 135.
17. Ryan, *Personal Adventures in Upper and Lower California, in 1848–1849*, 1:119–20.

4.3. Mule- or burro-powered sugarcane presses were hewn locally from mesquite wood and were used at mountain ranches as recently as 1930. *Courtesy Harry Crosby.*

4.4. A brass cauldron used in making panocha by boiling down cane pressings. Hundreds of pounds of this sugar cake accompanied Portolá and Serra to San Diego in 1769.

boiled down to a molasses-like consistency and then poured into molds in which the liquid solidifies to form little cakes or blocks, often with the elaborate shapes of stars, pyramids, cones, crescents, and the like. Bits of citrus rind may be added just before molding and help to make the product even more of a confection. Very bad teeth are observed at most ranches where people have had access to unlimited sugarcane and panocha since childhood.

Leaving La Paz for sorties into the deep countryside, Ryan visited several isolated ranches whose primitive way of life interested him, and his eyes caught many details rarely reported by others. Despite its brevity, Ryan's account is notable for such diverse elements as his observations of the behavior of horses and mules, the craft which underlay Baja California irrigation methods, and the preparation and utility of beef jerky. On another level, the Englishman was aware of less mundane matters. He sensed the ranch families' pride and appreciated both the difficulties overcome and the rustic graces that the folk in each ranch oasis evidenced.

Every image in William Redmond Ryan's mid-nineteenth-century verbal picture could be found intact at isolated sierra ranches more than a hundred years later.

> These ranches generally occupied some picturesque spot, and the sight of them infused new life into the whole party, man and beast. The latter especially, whose instinct seemed to be even superior to the intelligence of our guide, the animals being always first to give us due intimation that we were approaching quarters, by pricking up their ears, pawing and snorting, and increasing their pace. Many of these ranches were built of adobe, plastered over and whitewashed, and had good cavallards,[18] and well-cultivated gardens, irrigated with much ingenuity. Indeed, it was impossible to contemplate them, contrasting as they did so singularly with the wild scenery around, without astonishment and even admiration at the enterprise which had erected, in regions so repulsive and ungrateful, these domestic memorials of a tolerably advanced civilization....[19]
>
> I had occasion to visit a ranch in search of salt, and, taking advantage of the opportunity, made acquaintance with several ingenious native

---

18. Strings of riding and pack animals.
19. Ibid., 1:142–43.

118 *Californio Portraits*

Above and opposite: 4.5 and 4.6. William Ryan's 1847 sketch
of a Baja California homestead as compared to Pie de la Cuesta,
a mid-twentieth-century Guadalupe ranch. The similarity emphasizes
the traditional character of mountain life. From Ryan,
*Personal Adventures in Upper and Lower
California in 1848–49,* 139.

contrivances adapted to the exigencies of their domestic economy. To preserve that scarce article, water, cool and clean, a great desideratum in a torrid climate, and in a country abounding with vermin, and the atmosphere of which is charged with minute particles of sand, the natives select from a tree a branch having three forks, the ends of which they trim to the convenient length, and, fastening the trimmed branch horizontally to a stout upright cane, slip into this triangular basket the brown clay pitcher containing the water reserved for culinary purposes, the top of which they cover with a piece of wood fitted to it. The whole apparatus is usually placed beneath the overhanging foliage of a tree, or under the shade of a projecting crag. The drinking-cups, or bowls, are formed of the shell or husk of a yellow tropical fruit,[20] scooped out and carefully scraped. The cooking utensils are made of clay, and are of all dimensions. The Indian corn for making their tortillas is ground under a flat stone of

---

20. The common gourd.

about eight inches long by three broad, this being worked upon a stone table, averaging in length some eighteen inches by twelve in breadth, and standing upon four stone legs, the hindermost being quite two inches higher than the foremost so that the surface of the table forms a pretty steep inclined plane, and facilitates the process of grinding, as well as that of separating, the bran from the flour. I observed several raw hides stretched upon the ground, shaded by a screen of bamboo-cane and leaves; on these the natives indulge in their siesta. I also noticed a number of long switches, similarly protected, on which were suspended as many strips of beef as they could hold. When this beef is thoroughly salted and dried, it will keep for a very considerable time, and is admirably adapted for the long journeys which the traveler is frequently obliged to take between one ranch and another, when to procure fresh meat is impossible.[21]

---

21. Ibid., 1:136–38.

Forty-Niners in Baja California

The U.S. occupation forces left Baja California in 1848, but soon another historical upheaval threw Americans and peninsular Californios back into uneasy contact. Overnight, the great Gold Rush created more change in northern Alta California than all the years of gradual American infiltration. It also impacted Baja California to a degree—a matter that has never been much discussed or widely recognized.

The forty-niners came from every point of the compass, and some of their routes were so well traveled that many accounts fill the literature. Tales have been collected about rounding the Horn, or going from sea to sea across Mexico, Nicaragua, or the Isthmus of Panama. Other volumes assemble the stories of parties that left the eastern United States and crossed plains and mountains to reach California gold. By comparison, few bands of men approached by way of Baja California, and most of those did so because other plans were changed or abandoned. Nevertheless, approximately a dozen parties did make the arduous peninsular trek. Members of some of those parties kept journals from which details can be gathered.

A typical forty-niner was not an ideal reporter of contemporary life in Baja California. He was generally preoccupied with his adventures and the hardships he faced. He was also perhaps more impressed by the strange, harsh landscape than by its people. The obvious value of these accounts is to reveal a little-known chapter in the saga of men converging on California for its gold. But such writers also left observations of deeper significance. Unlike the foreign soldiers or seamen who visited Baja California, these forty-niners followed the historic Camino Real to Alta California and thereby traversed at least the foothills of the midpeninsular sierras. There they met and dealt with the children and grandchildren of the pioneer settlers of those sierras.

The earliest extant journal by a forty-niner in Baja California is a good example of this type of writing. It was composed by W. C. S. Smith, who later became a newspaper editor in Napa, California. Smith joined a party of gold-seekers that left New York by ship on January 15, 1849. In fifteen days they landed at Vera Cruz,

Mexico. Then they crossed overland headed for San Blas. They arrived on March 14 and took passage for California on a broken down ex-whaler. The ship was so crowded and the conditions so miserable that Smith and three companions went ashore at San José del Cabo determined to traverse the entire peninsula by land.

The adventurers bought horses, saddles, bridles, and food and were able to leave San José by April 10. They did not have the slightest idea of the difficulties they would face. Nevertheless, the party of four made its way safely to San Diego in sixty-two harrowing days. Along the way, encounters with Californios produced descriptions and comments such as the following from April 18, at a ranch on the western slopes of the Sierra de la Giganta:

> Laid by all day ... buying horses and making provisions for prosecuting our journey. People very kind. My new horse is a beauty, but wild like the Californians themselves. Much interested by their wonderful performances with the lasso. This seems a good specimen of a California ranch ... a fine vineyard and fruit trees in a valley back in the mountains. The old proprietor is one of the ancient Patriarchs. They are better people than the Mexicans.... The people live almost entirely on beef cooked every way except any mode we were accustomed to, but they never fail to add chili pepper enough to bring tears from the eyes of a dried codfish. We bought a steer and had the men dress and jerk the meat for us. They roasted the head, hair, horns, and all with hot stones in a hole in the ground. They politely invited us to share. We were not fastidious and laid hold. We found it perfectly delicious.[22]

On April 25, at Mission San Javier in the Sierra de la Giganta, Smith reported, "My San José horse gave out ... met a man and gave him the horse to guide us to Comondú." And the following day: "I forgot my gun and sent the guide back for it. The boys said I would never see my gun or guide again, but he disappointed them."[23]

W. C. S. Smith's journal continues, recounting a bone-racking series of adventures, threatened disasters, and hair-breadth escapes. However, a single vignette gives a sense of the country's impact on these eastern Americans and also the oasis character of the Californio settlements:

---
22. Crosby, "The 1849 Journal of W. C. S. Smith," 133.
23. Ibid., 135–35.

> April 27—All day, the so-called road was over a table mountain. The most barren region imaginable. The earth or rather the rocks have been convulsed in a singular manner and piled fantastically one on another. They could not be more rugged. Over such a country we picked a difficult way, depressed by the suffering of our poor horses and the utter desolation around us. Unexpectedly we came to the margin of a great chasm. Someone said, "See, there is Comondú." Looking down there lay, some 200 feet below us, a perfect picture. A beautiful little valley green as an emerald, while the sunlight glancing from water fairly made the very horses laugh. Impulsively we scrambled down the barranca side at a breakneck pace and soon arrived to the satisfaction of man and beast. We were tired out but here we now are enjoying plenty of good food and sweet water, and our poor horses are revelling up to their knees in green grass.
>
> ... A place could not be more secluded than this. Yet the people appear happy. They are quite civilized and a large proportion are part blood Castilian. The valley is about two miles long and 200 or 300 yards wide. Plenty of running water which they say never fails. The products are corn, grass, sugar cane, oranges, olives, figs, bananas, pomegranates and grapes. From the latter they make an astringent wine, like a bad port.... The valley is all closely intersected with small irrigating canals, and all cultivated. We feasted on strawberries.[24]

Smith and his companions had come upon a village in which the old peninsular dream had come true. Twenty years before, the mission was abandoned and Californios in the area had quietly moved in and utilized its developed fields, groves, and waterworks. In its isolation, Comondú grew slowly and remained rather simple and idyllic until recent times. Even with recent changes, it is the best-preserved example of an old Baja California settlement.

When the gold rush subsided, the peninsula became quieter than ever. The American annexation of Alta California meant that the previous small amount of traffic between that area and the peninsula nearly stopped. By then the missions had truly died, and within a decade their lands were finally parceled out. A century and a half after its founding, Baja California's economy was secular at last.

After 1850 the central government of Mexico took a more consistent stand in favor of peninsular colonization. Lands were granted

---

24. Ibid., 135.

4.7. Thirsty and exhausted forty-niners were delighted to stumble upon such a well-stocked haven as Arroyo Comondú, parts of which have changed little since their day.

and titles upheld. The desire to settle the land and derive taxes from it moved federal authorities to grant large land concessions to American and English companies promising immigration and development. All such ventures proved to be either poorly conceived or downright fraudulent. The few that were actively undertaken soon failed. The peninsula did receive erratic spurts of immigration throughout the second half of the nineteenth century. The chief stimuli were mining booms at widely separated points such as El Triunfo in the south; Santa Rosalía, Las Flores, and Calmallí in the center; and Real del Castillo and El Álamo in the north. These bursts of activity attracted miners and quickened trade. The gulf coast ports flourished modestly and became the permanent homes of most newcomers to the southern half of the peninsula.

In their isolation, mountain ranchers were little affected by changes on the lowlands. Since they were neither miners nor traders, they had scant interest in the mineral booms. They continued to raise animals and fruit wherever conditions permitted. Prosperity in nearby low country probably meant that they profited from brisk sales of meat, cheese, and fruit. When mines failed and mining camps that had housed hundreds stood empty, the mountaineers seem to have been philosophical. "We ate as well as before," old-timers say, "we just had farther to go to market and got less for our produce."

Peninsular people who went to the mountains and lived as isolated ranchers changed less than those who populated ports, mining camps, or the pueblos that grew up in the wake of certain missions. In the latter places, new immigrants were common. They soon became neighbors of old families and then relatives by marriage. Sierra people were less affected. A few later immigrants, both foreign and Mexican, did intermarry with the descendants of gente de razón. They settled in the various populated mountains and adopted the local ways. However, such cases were rare. Research on sierra surnames shows that a great majority of the progenitors were on the peninsula by 1800. Most later immigrants remained near the coasts and married women of the towns. It was no wonder. Even those relatively tame parts of the peninsula must have seemed terribly primitive, because only those born to the task could survive and flourish in the remote and forbidding mountains.

The sierra folk remind us of the past and preserve old ways for the best of reasons. The challenges they face are similar to those of their ancestors, and the means with which they meet them have changed very little. The term *gente de razón* has disappeared from the dialect, but the people who bore it live on. The mountain people not only perpetuate the culture of their ancestors; they also bear their names and faces.

CHAPTER 5

The Sierra de Guadalupe

Any view of Baja California's mountain societies eventually leads to the Sierra de Guadalupe. There, on the ground, are the clearest traces of the mission past, the secular colonization, and the little-diluted descent of today's people from the settlers of over two centuries ago. Archives in La Paz, Mexico City, and American California contain documents that reveal more completely than for other regions the succession of events—social, economic, and genetic—that resulted in the creation and survival of such a showcase of the past.

Descendants of California's eighteenth-century Hispanic settlers still can be found in nearly all of the peninsular mountains, but their numbers and their adherence to old customs vary greatly from place to place. The high Cape Sierra, due south of La Paz, has been ranched only in the twentieth century, and then by a few people whose ancestral homes in the foothills below had close ties to relatively active and populous centers at La Paz and San José del Cabo. Ranches in the foothills and mountains of the northern part of the peninsula are of comparatively recent origin, and their people have been greatly influenced by proximity to the U.S.–Mexico frontier area, with its large population of Mexicans with nonpeninsular origins.

5.1. The Guadalupe uplands remain relatively unscarred by human occupation. Vistas are much like those that greeted the first Spaniards to cross this pass about 1712.

The best examples of the old culture described in this work are found in three ranges of midpeninsular mountains: the Sierras of La Giganta, Guadalupe, and San Francisco. Rancho San Gregorio, the mountain homestead described earlier, is located in the San Francisco range, a small sierra with relatively few families, few permanent springs, and few ranches with one or more huertas. Most of its inhabitants herd goats and move as their water catchments are drained. By contrast, both the sierras of La Giganta and Guadalupe harbor many people and have more water and more permanent ranch sites. However, they also differ from each other in history and topography. Guadalupe is higher, more broken, more difficult to approach, farther from any sizable population centers and therefore less affected by the external influences that have gradually modernized the lives of all people on the peninsula. No part of Baja California today offers as rich and little changed a view of the area's past. And no part has a history as simply and purely derived from mission origins.

Geology and History

California's Jesuit missionaries came to the midpeninsular mountains early in their seventy-year regime, and Mission Nuestra Señora de Guadalupe was founded in 1720 at a place that local Indians, the Cochimí, called Huasinapí. These missionaries never ceased to wonder at the difficulties presented by peninsular sierras, their unremittingly harsh aspects characterized by steepness, rocks, heat, and dryness. After some Jesuits had returned to Europe—and after the passage of several years—they wrote accounts that showed how their struggles with this terrain had scarred their memories. Today a visitor who contemplates sierra life has similar reactions. Much of the land does not seem fit for human habitation. One can get the impression that it is largely vertical and all rock.

The Sierra de Guadalupe, like its neighbors, is the eroded remains of a volcano roughly 20 to 50 million years old. Its flows of lava thrust upward through ocean-bottom sediments and spread out. In a geologically rapid sequence, other eruptions of ash, lava, and assorted pyroclastic fragments built up the mountains like pancakes successively added to the stack. Then the rains of millions of years began their work. Runoff waters etched gullies into the cap materials, and then seasonal rain runoffs and the deluges from epic summer storms began to slice down through layer after layer. The originally simple, mounded form of the sierra was cut more and more deeply by arroyos that began in Guadalupe's central highlands and radiated outward in all directions. By the time the Europeans came, the cutting process had become more evident than the original form. The sierra seemed to be a maze of peaks, ridges, and gullies—all rock, solid, or tumbled.

Nevertheless, these forbidding mountains did contain water in small springs and deep plunge pools, and did support plant and animal life. As recounted in chapter 1, early human inhabitants made the sierra part of their annual rounds of hunting and gathering. They returned for such long periods that their stone artifacts and now-famous paintings on rock walls are found at every level.

After establishing Mission Santa Rosalía de Mulegé in late 1705, the Jesuits and their soldier escorts began to explore the region, including the approaches to the wall-like sierra that rose fifteen miles to the west. The foreigners gradually came to know the mountains. In 1709 they crossed over for the first time, out of the huge, amphitheater-shaped arroyo of Mulegé and into the long, south-flowing arroyo of Guajademí, which finally empties into the Pacific. In the sierra, the Jesuits and their soldiers discovered California's first real timber trees—the giant poplar, called *güéribo*—and in 1720 they cut them to obtain the timbers for the first ship built on California soil.

The new mission in the heart of the sierra, Nuestra Señora de Guadalupe, suffered cruelly from plagues of locusts and epidemics that soon decimated its neophytes, but it also became noted for the success of its cattle ranches. At its height, about 1760, Mission Guadalupe, with its various ranches, was reported to have between five and six hundred head of cattle. A decade later, the Jesuits were

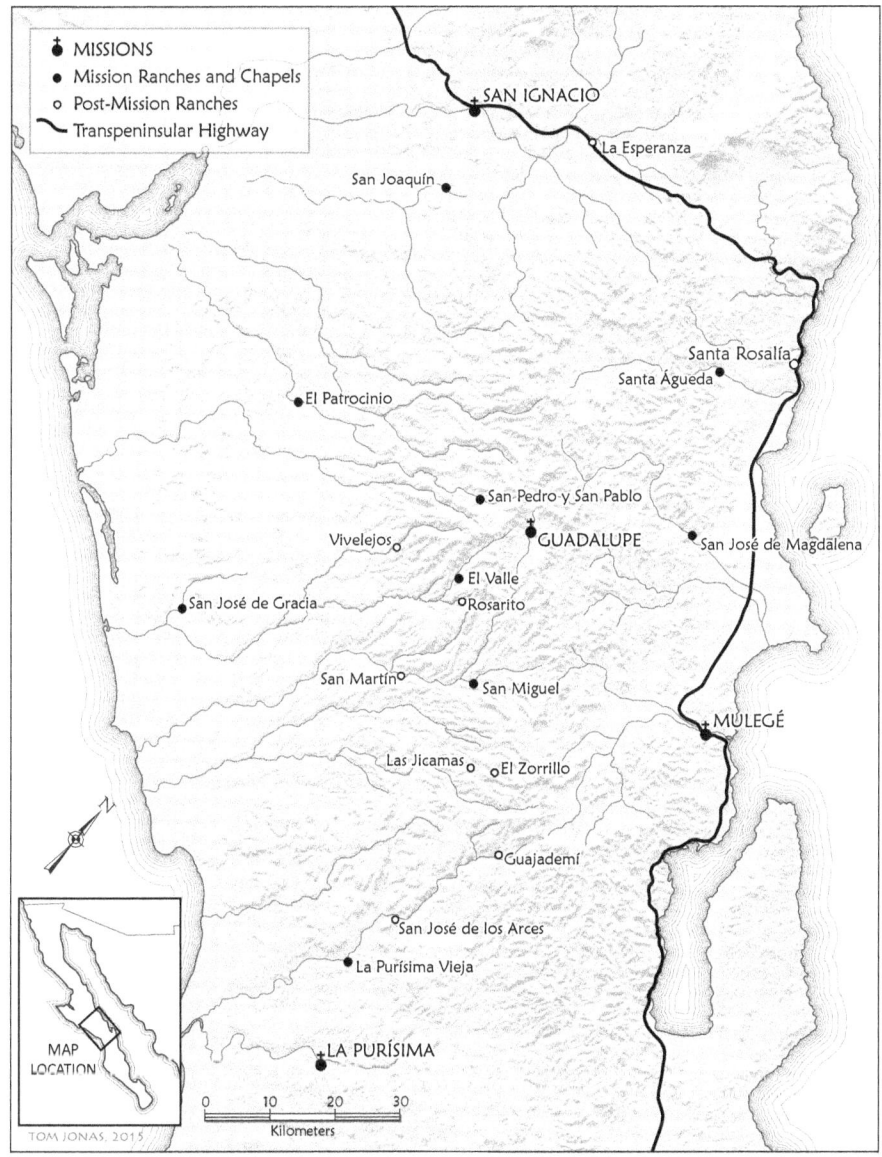

Map 4. Missions, mission ranches and chapels, post-mission ranches.
Map by Tom Jonas. Copyright © 2015 by the University of Oklahoma Press.

expelled and diseases continued to ravage the Indian converts. No wonder the place did not appeal to either the Franciscan missionaries or their Dominican successors.

In 1795 Mission Guadalupe was closed and its people dispersed. A few went to Mulegé and San Ignacio, but most went to La Purísima, some forty miles to the south. The ostensible reason for closure was a lack of converts. Superiors in the religious order and officials in Spain's colonial government begrudged support for such clearly struggling establishments. In addition, there is little doubt that the missionaries' convenience was also a factor. Guadalupe was one of several missions that were remote, difficult to supply, and unpopular with priests, who were becoming more and more isolated as their congregations decreased. In 1795 Mission Santa Rosalía de Mulegé had fewer neophytes than Guadalupe, yet it remained open for many additional years because Mulegé was a port that received visits and supplies from ships. It also had the social life provided by a small but growing community of non-Indian people.

Cattle in Californio Life

With its mission closed and its Indian population moved out to other places, the Sierra de Guadalupe might seem to have been abandoned by humans. Such was not the case and the reason was cattle. The Guadalupe area had demonstrated its ability to support large numbers of cattle and it is probable that by 1795 many cattle had gone wild in the area.

During the latter years of the eighteenth century cattle were the basis of the slowly growing secular life throughout peninsular California. The first significant private property on the peninsula were the cattle that Captain Esteban Rodríguez was allowed to raise for his own use as early as the 1720s. Rodríguez's son-in-law, Manuel de Ocio, created great herds and contended with the Jesuits over his right to the lands on which they browsed. By 1768, when Gálvez, Portolá, and Serra came to Baja California, cattle provided most of the food on which gente de razón subsisted. Their dependence on herds was so complete that the relationship was a matter of wonder to the newcomers and cause for much written comment. Missions and missionaries dominated the few acres of potential agricultural land, so the Californios took the only avenue open to them and herded cattle on any unused land that had enough water for a few animals to drink.

Cattle became synonymous with survival, independence, and any hope of wealth. As soon as private land was available in Alta California, transplanted peninsular Californios and others with cattle-raising experience brought the industry to the new area, where better conditions allowed it to prosper immensely. But even men who remained in Baja California were aware of the opportunity. Cattle had proved amazingly capable of living off cactus, leguminous trees, and seasonal herbs. All that was needed for economic independence was the use of a large tract of land that got annual rains and retained some water in springs and catchments. Guadalupe had proved to be such a place, and one group of men knew all about it.

The Will of the Mayordomos

Each mission had a foreman of the works, usually a retired soldier who planned and supervised labor; stored, guarded, and dispensed mission supplies; and oversaw the management of herds and satellite farms or ranches. In the last decade or two of its poorly documented operation, Mission Guadalupe had at least three such supervisors or mayordomos. These men must have been acutely aware of the sierra's assets and its promise for the future. Each was to play a part in the quiet but effective homesteading that soon transformed the area into a secluded enclave of independent Californio life.

Luis Ignacio Aguilar, born in Loreto in 1742 and a veteran of the opening of Alta California, was mayordomo at Guadalupe in 1795 when the mission was closed. Probably because of his service record and his presence on the scene, Aguilar was able to

5.2. Rancho Vivelejos, one of the most remote of Guadalupe's many isolated homesteads.

persuade the governor to make him and his heirs the custodians of the ex-mission's lands and properties. Soon his sons Pedro and Buenaventura received titles or recognition of their rights to hold, respectively, Rancho El Patrocinio and the lands that had comprised Mission Guadalupe itself.

The Aguilar claims were the first step in the secularization of the Sierra de Guadalupe. The next man to receive a title was a retired soldier, José Julián Murillo, an old crony of Aguilar's, who had served briefly as mayordomo at Mulegé in 1806 and 1807. Murillo and his family first settled at El Patrocinio with some other longtime Aguilar adherents, but in 1813 he received a grant for the ex-mission rancho called San José de Gracia. José Julián Murillo's influence on Guadalupe's future population not only came through his own children, but was also magnified by the fact that he was joined by several nephews and nieces from Loreto.

5.3. Casimiro Aguilar, right, descendant of Luis Aguilar and other mission mayordomos.

The parceling out of Sierra de Guadalupe lands had only begun. The struggle for independence in Mexico between 1810 and 1821 cut off almost all outside aid—money or supplies—previously sent to California. The people of that large, poorly organized region were forced as never before to depend on their own products and ingenuity. At the same time, the century-long decline in Indian population had reduced all of the Baja California missions' labor forces to a point where their numbers were not sufficient to plant, tend, and harvest crops, or run herds properly at all ex-mission holdings. The general need provided an opportunity long sought by gente de razón to claim or at least to work unused lands. The Guadalupe area soon attracted their attention. The Aguilar family and its adherents were not yet numerous enough to work or even occupy all the former mission lands, yet those lands had proved that they could support large herds of cattle. A delegation of prominent men persuaded Governor José Darío Argüello to assert the government's rights to unused Guadalupe lands. As a result, in 1816 nineteen applicants rented various-sized plots of ground for nominal fees. The group included José Manuel Ruiz, then commander of troops at the peninsula's northern frontier; Fernando de la Toba, a Spanish officer at Loreto's presidio; and Fray José Viéytez, a Dominican missionary acting in his own interest. No records survive that show how many of the nineteen actually developed herds of cattle or in any way exercised their options. Nevertheless, the event was significant because its list of renters provides the earliest connection between the Sierra de Guadalupe and several families that were to become prominent settlers and ancestors of its present population.

One who rented land in 1816 was Salvador Mayoral, son of a Filipino sailor and father of Raymundo and Pedro Mayoral, pioneer ranchers in the southern reaches of the sierra. José Ignacio Romero and José María Romero, probably brothers, brought their already-old California name to the Guadalupe area. That year José María Murillo's name appeared there for the first time. He was a man destined to live long and be recognized as the patriarch of the old Murillo clan that took root and multiplied here as nowhere else on the peninsula. José Rosas Villavicencio was also listed as one who rented land.

The most important result of those 1816 land rentals seems to have been that they legally located in the area various Romeros and Mayorals, as well as a Murillo and a Villavicencio. In a few years, when Mexico became independent, these families were placed so that they could make claims for permanent titles to lands that they occupied and that were not claimed by the Church. As explained previously, the opportunity to make any sort of an effective claim to watered land was rare as early as 1816. The men, mostly mayordomos, who seized this opportunity thereby put their stamp on the area for a century and more to come.

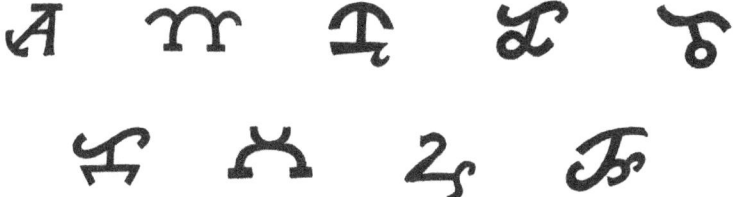

5.4. Cattle brands in use before 1850.
Top left, a brand registered at Comondú by
Juan Bautista Smith-Aguilar. Top right, a brand used by
the family of Luis Aguilar at El Patrocinio and ex–Mission Guadalupe.
From Ryan, *Personal Adventures in Upper and
Lower California in 1848–49*, 140.

The third actual title to Guadalupe property had its origins even before Luis Aguilar moved to the region and became the first successful claimant. The previous mayordomo at Mission Guadalupe was Juan Miguel López, a man who, though born at Ahome in Sinaloa just across the Sea of Cortez, became a career California mission servant and married a peninsular woman who was the daughter of a mayordomo. After Guadalupe was closed, Juan Miguel López finished his stint as mayordomo at Mission San Fernando de Velicatá, far to the north. He then moved his family to San José de Magdalena, one of Guadalupe's ex-visiting stations, located in a large arroyo called Rondín that lies northeast of the suppressed mission. In 1818, his son, Domingo López, born at Guadalupe in 1787, made a formal application and received a land title to San José de Magdalena in the name of his descendants. The value of that title is clear when one learns that today San José de Magdalena is a small town with many dozens if not hundreds of inhabitants.

A third longtime mayordomo who had served extensively in this area was Sebastián Arce, who, with his brother José Gabriel, brought the Arce name to California. Sebastián had served at Mission San Ignacio as early as 1764, and he had been mayordomo at Mulegé from 1784 to 1788. Between 1789 and 1795, old Sebastián closed out his career as a mayordomo at La Purísima. He died there in 1795 just as Mission Guadalupe was being closed. His widow and several of their children stayed on at La Purísima. His son Manuel became mayordomo by 1800. Both Manuel Arce and his brother, Juan Bautista Ignacio Arce, stayed in the area, and their sons settled around the old mission centers of Comondú and La Purísima. They also occupied San José, which once was a satellite ranch of La Purísima. Indeed, this place is still called San José de los Arces as a reminder of past and present inhabitants, and also as a means of distinguishing it from San José de Gracia and San José de Magdalena within the same sierra.

Yet another mayordomo was to have a great influence on Guadalupe's population. Old soldier José Urbano Villavicencio, born in 1745, retired as a sergeant and became mayordomo at Mulegé about 1807 or 1808. The history of his family epitomizes the close relationship between serving as mayordomo and acquiring land, and, even more, the close relationships that developed between these several families founded by mayordomos. José Urbano Villavicencio married Josefa Arce, a daughter of Sebastián Arce's brother, José Gabriel Arce, a retired sergeant and longtime mayordomo in missions to the north. José Urbano Villavicencio's daughter Rafaela married Domingo López, thus becoming the mistress of San José de Magdalena and the mother of its inheritors. Another of José Urbano Villavicencio's daughters, Dolores, married José María Aguilar, son of Luis Aguilar, and settled at El Patrocinio.

Two sons of José Urbano Villavicencio moved into the Sierra de Guadalupe. They contributed greatly to developing its ranches and left immense families that spread their surname throughout the area. José Urbano's eldest son, José Rosas Villavicencio, first served as a soldier for some ten years and then became mayordomo at San Ignacio around 1814. Before long, he moved to Santa Águeda, a well-watered, broad valley that once had been dependent on Mission Santa Rosalía de Mulegé. From this base, José Rosas raised large herds of cattle and opened additional ranches with foremen who worked for shares.

An old soldier and interim political chief of the peninsula, José Manuel Ruiz wrote reports concerning the poverty and frustration of his people and their confusion over the distribution of mission lands. Nevertheless, he did not discriminate against the few people not suffering—the relatively well-situated sons of landholding mayordomos. These men made some of the few applications for lands that were actually at the political chief's disposal. In 1823, Ruiz signed documents that gave José Rosas Villavicencio the title to Santa Águeda as well as ex–Mission Guadalupe's ranches and visiting chapels at San Miguel and El Valle. The latter two places had elaborate irrigation works, corrals, and other structures surviving from their recent mission past. In his long life, José Rosas Villavicencio became perhaps the wealthiest and most influential man between San Ignacio and Loreto.

José María Villavicencio undertook similar ranching activities but had his headquarters at Rancho San Martín in the central part of the Sierra de Guadalupe, south and west of the bailiwick of his older brother, José Rosas Villavicencio. José María and his sons established several of the most permanent and successful postmission ranches. These homesteads were noted for their extensive groves of fruit trees.

Both of these Villavicencio brothers married daughters of Anastasio Verduzco, the son of a mayordomo who once served southern missions. Such unions were common. Apparently, mayordomo status, or the landholding status so often associated with that office, created a social class, and children born to it tended to marry within it. There was nothing to discourage that practice. Most of the mayordomos were old soldiers with long years of peninsular service who at one time or another had served together and had become related by marriage or *compadrazgo*, the godparenting that was such an important part of their ritual lives.

There was an additional bond among mayordomos. Many who were more fortunate—that is, those who had risen highest in service, who had friends or relatives among the Spanish officers, or who had been sought out for service in Alta California—had

5.5. Brothers Porfirio, Francisco, and Inocencio Amador, whose ancestry traces entirely to eighteenth-century California soldiers and miners.

moved to the northern frontier with their families. Most members of the old Californio families named Carrillo, Verdugo, Alvarado, Amador, Góngora, Higuera, Lugo, and Ortega, along with some of those named Castro, Cota, and López, had emigrated to the new California and become some of its most prominent people. The old soldier mayordomos who stayed behind nevertheless did well by peninsular standards. That success must have been especially sweet to those of humbler backgrounds. Old Luis Aguilar, for example, was the son of a soldier, Juan Antonio Aguilar, who served the presidio of Loreto, and a woman named María Dolores Montaño, the daughter of a Loreto soldier from Peru, Juan Miguel Montaño, and a neophyte at Mission San Javier.

The long-range effect of those early mayordomos' efforts to acquire and work their own land can be measured today in a census of any region of the peninsula, but nowhere was their influence so predominant as in the Sierra de Guadalupe. Today, by a conservative estimate, 90 percent of those who live within the confines of the sierra are descended at least in part from men who had been mayordomos. These mayordomos, their sons-in-law and daughters-in-law, and the families of a few retired soldiers who came to live and work at their ranches, all before 1820, account for more than 80 percent of *all* the genetic inheritance in the sierra today—and a surprisingly high percentage of that in the towns of San Ignacio, Mulegé, and La Purísima as well.

The influences of Luis Aguilar, Sebastián and Gabriel Arce, and Juan Miguel López were not confined to the Guadalupe region or even to Baja California. All had children who moved north to live and who helped to populate the new establishments on both sides of today's border. Today some of their descendants live in most major cities of Alta California. Although the children of José Urbano Villavicencio did not travel as far, his brother Rafael went north with Governor Gaspar de Portolá, married an Alta California neophyte, and established the widespread Villavicencio family in that region.

Settling the Sierra

In the 1830s, Alta California began a pastoral era. This was a period during which huge private cattle ranches prospered and certain families became grandees in splendid isolation on an as yet undisturbed Hispanic frontier. In Baja California, especially in the Sierra de Guadalupe, one factor was similar. The people had come from much the same stock and cultural backgrounds, and all had waited for generations to own and occupy their own land. In both areas, descendants of soldiers and mission servants now were relatively free from military or religious regimentation and able to profit directly from their own efforts.

Geographic differences between north and south in the Californias were striking. On the peninsula, there were no rivers and few large springs. The concept of a ranch was so different in the two places that it seems strange to find the same word employed to describe them. Within a few years, owners of lands in Alta California could expand a herd of fifty cattle into thousands. While some effort was required, the basic water and grass were provided generously by nature. However, in the Sierra de Guadalupe, even at the various ancestral ranches that have been introduced—San Miguel, El Valle, San José de Gracia, El Patrocinio, San José de Magdalena—there was only enough water to irrigate half a dozen acres and support a few hundred head of cattle at best. As a result, by 1840 these ranches as well as others developed by the heirs of the mayordomos could no longer support additional generations. This necessitated the development of new practices that have characterized the settlement of the sierra. Since that time, every generation at each ranch has had to send some of its young men out to found new ranches or to leave the sierra altogether.

Customs that controlled inheritance of land were not basic to the problems. A ranch could only be expected to support two or three married couples and their children. However, a ranch owner might have five or six sons. The inheritor often was the eldest son. But just as often, for one reason or another, the inheritor proved to be the son best able to care for his parents during their declining years. By mutual agreement the heir-apparent would indicate the brother or brothers who best fit in at the ranch, and the others then had to make their own ways in other places. In most cases, this difficult transition was apparently carried out without acrimony and often as a welcome adventure. Traditionally, those who stayed behind shared their livestock and the goods of the ranch with departing brothers. They also often went out to help

5.6. The long Arroyo de Rosarito, typical of the west-flowing watercourses, supports several ranches. One is visible at the lower right.

build the homes, corrals, and retaining walls at the new sites. In a similar cooperation, scattered families rejoined at their mother ranches for such seasonal chores as cattle roundups, where every hand was needed.

As a matter of fact, cattle raising, the magnet that first attracted Hispanic settlers to Guadalupe, greatly influenced the pattern by which the sierra was settled as its population had to spread out. In order to get maximum use of plant growth and naturally retained waters, ranchers discovered that they must drive their cattle down to the lowlands soon after the onset of rains so they could graze off the herbage of the flat country. Then, when the lowlands dried up, the ranchers had to bring them up arroyos. As a herd retreated into the mountains, it could browse on the slopes and drink from *tinajas*—the catchment pools in the bedrock bottoms of the watercourses. Finally, the cattle would spread out on the higher mesas

5.7. A tinaja or natural water catchment, in this case a plunge pool worn into volcanic bedrock. Such water supplies are the basis of many ranches' existence.

and drink from permanent springs when all standing water was used or evaporated.

This annual movement of cattle generally took place in one drainage basin, that is, within the confines of one arroyo and its tributary cañadas. Therefore, as any family grew and spread out to find additional ranches, the tendency was to remain in the same arroyo either up- or downstream from the pioneer ranch. Another family might occupy an adjacent arroyo, and it, too, would tend to utilize watered sites located all the way from the mouth of the arroyo back to its headwaters in the heights of the sierra. In this way, each family made its annual roundups and drives in concert over the land of relatives and with their help. Strayed animals would be spotted by close kin and their locations reported. All these activities were facilitated by the cattle's tendency to remain in a given drainage basin and not to cross the dry crests into another.

More as a result of cattle raising than any other factor, the Sierra de Guadalupe today presents a striking pattern of human occupation: a great wheel with arroyos radiating out as spokes and each arroyo lined with ranches occupied by people bearing the same one or two family names.

Climate and Calamities

Another profound difference between Alta and Baja California ranching was the greater frequency and severity of natural disasters on the peninsula. People on its tiny, poor ranches had to endure more furious storms and more severe droughts than their cousins to the north did. Chubascos, with their high winds and torrential rains, strike locally on the peninsula and at erratic intervals. One region of a few hundred square miles may be devastated and an adjacent area little affected. A specific ranch may be hit twice in ten years or not once in thirty, but the average for peninsular ranches seems to have been one rampaging storm for each generation of people, that is, about one per twenty years.

Chubasco winds may tear the roofs off houses, flatten crops, and whip fruit trees bare, but they are rarely the major cause of damage to ranches or the land. Animals, whether domestic or wild, find adequate shelter in caves or in the lees of steep cliffs. Native plants, even trees, have adapted so well that they usually resist these gales without serious damage. But the *trombas*, huge localized cloudbursts, are another matter. When these torrential rains fall on the nearly bare rock surfaces of the uplands, little is absorbed. Instead, the deluge is channeled into deep cañadas. Beginning as an intricate net of capillaries, these naturally eroded watercourses grow into a system of open veins directing greater and greater volumes of water to a tumultuous union in the arroyos below. When all converge and roar toward the sea, the flood, locked between high walls, may be fifty to a hundred yards wide and twenty or more feet deep. Nothing movable can resist it. Trees are torn out of their root holds in crevices of solid rock, and boulders half the size of a boxcar are rolled hundreds of feet, stopping only when jammed together at turns in the arroyo or when the great rush of water subsides. Finally the flood reaches the edge of the sierra and spreads out like a giant fan onto the alluvial plain below. There, in spite of its spread and shallower waters, it continues to devastate all life it encounters on its way to the sea.

Ranchers receive little or no warning of these storms, but in a sense they are never taken by surprise. There is no loss of human life. People in the mountains know how to avoid danger during the chubasco season, from July to October. Homes are usually placed above flood paths, and if not, the occupants withdraw to higher ground before they are threatened. However, there is no way to protect huertas or the waterworks that support them. These must be near the bottom of arroyos in order to take advantage of the only available level ground to which water can be conducted. As a result, even a modest summer storm can cause great damage. And a direct hit by a large storm means that a rancher essentially has to rebuild his entire establishment. Today in various parts of the peninsula one hears stories about labors in the wakes of the storms of 1919, 1931, and 1959—the legendary chubascos of the twentieth century. As the waters subsided, families huddled on slopes looking down at homesites that had been blown away or swept clean of houses, corrals, garden plots, and any canals or piping they might have had. In some cases, problems were compounded when wells filled up with sand and rocks or when springs were buried by the same debris. As cattle and goats straggled back, ranchers desperately worked to reach and clear out their water sources. Fortunately, temporary pools of water would sustain men and beasts for a few days. Then there was everything else to rebuild.

In contrast to storms, droughts come on slowly and affect livestock more than they do orchards or gardens. It is curious that as skimpy as each sierra spring is inclined to be, its sources are so deep in the mountain that it now varies little from season to season or even after several consecutive rainless years. The effect of a drought is to retard the growth of plants on which cattle or goats browse. An equally important result of scant or absent rainfall is the drying up of tinajas, the water catchments on which the animals depend when venturing more than a day's journey from a spring. When tinajas give out, domestic animals cannot range over large areas that could still yield food. Such circumstances seriously complicate drought problems. After a second dry year, most ranchers must kill off or sell animals in order to avoid losing them altogether. After three or four dry years, everyone in a region is poverty-stricken and reduced to the most desperate measures in order to survive.

Several remedies are recalled by those who have had to cope with the ordeals of drought. One was a general return to ancestral ranches where larger springs still supported gardens. Greater numbers of hands allowed more planting, tending, and harvesting. In such times, it was not unusual to expand the huertas, build new walls, pack in soil, and attempt to use all the water in a gainful fashion.

As a second remedy the sierra inhabitants gathered wild food. These resources had always been used to some extent, but when people were faced with starvation, all lore gained from the peninsular natives and all experiences passed along from their forefathers were put to maximum use. From mesas they collected tuberous roots of *zayas* and hearts of large green agaves—a variety of mezcal, but not the small, glaucous type from which liquor is derived. The roots of zayas resemble small, misshapen parsnips and were prepared like that vegetable. Hearts of mezcal were roasted in a heated pit as if to begin the liquor process but then were removed and eaten like giant artichoke hearts. A rarer native of the mesas

5.8. On the trail, branches are cut to feed mules and burros during any break in their labors. *Dipugo* and mesquite are leguminous trees that have provided this fodder since the times of California's earliest chroniclers.

5.9. Kodalith of an agave.
Courtesy Harry Crosby.

was harvested in the southern Sierra de Guadalupe: certain low spots or sinks supported the growth of jícama, the large white-fleshed tuber common on the Mexican mainland.

The edible fruit of various cacti has served admirably in warding off starvation after storms. *Pitahaya dulce*, in particular, bears in the fall after most chubasco activity is past and provides a heavy crop of sweet, juicy fruit. But no cactus fruits are produced during a drought—a further hardship that was even more keenly felt during Indian times, when vastly greater numbers of people had to live off the same land.

By tightening already taut belts, by helping each other, and by utilizing every known natural resource, the superbly acclimatized Guadalupe ranchers lived through their trials and held on to their claims, a fact that adds a footnote to the comparison of their legacy with that of their cousin ranchers north of San Diego.

5.10. Switchback trails, laboriously built and maintained, link mountain homesteads to each other and to the outside world. Note Rancho Las Jícamas at lower right.

5.11. For 150 years peninsular ranchers have made difficult, time-consuming journeys to sell their produce or to obtain supplies, aid, or companionship.

Soon after Spain's dominion ended, Alta California's prospects began to attract foreigners, who came as prospectors, on business, or out of curiosity, and stayed on to further their fortunes. This foreign colony, chiefly Americans, grew and began to acquire land. At the beginning of the Mexican War, the colony helped the United States annex the region.

Baja California was also known to a few foreigners, including some Americans, but its attractions and its promise were considered insignificant by most, and it was bypassed at a time when U.S. military forces and a national sense of Manifest Destiny would have made its acquisition very simple.

By 1860, tables had turned to a remarkable degree. The once relatively wealthy and carefree Hispanic landowners of Alta California were being dispossessed in a land where their language and culture had been reduced to an inferior status. Their landholding cousins in the Sierra de Guadalupe were free to live on in the old ways, and especially free to take land as they needed it. Benito Juárez, a friend of small landholders, was in power in Mexico. At his suggestion, many titles that dated all the way back to Spanish grants were submitted for registration and official recognition. New titles signed by Juárez himself were returned and held by the sons and grandsons of Luis Aguilar, José Urbano Villavicencio, Buenaventura Arce, and Juan Miguel López. These pieces of paper are still treasured in many a sierra ranch.

The proliferation of Guadalupe's ranches has never really stopped. As population grew, new homesteads spread out from each old center. By 1900 they had reached the most remote and inaccessible watered places. At about that time, a new practice grew out of experience gained while coping with the old problem of persistent droughts. In such times some people had had to return to those older ranches with larger water supplies and usable gardens. When no more springs were available, this once-desperate retrenching was adopted as a mode of life. People built ranches wherever large catchment pools of water remained after rains. They built small dams to enlarge these tinajas or even to

5.12. A represa or artificial catchment traps enough water for small-scale seasonal cattle herding in the dry uplands of the Sierra de Guadalupe.

create artificial ones called *represas*. Herds, usually of goats, were run at such ranches as long as water was available. Then, when a tinaja went dry, the ranch family and its herd went to another or back to a base ranch. These people became known as *cambiaderos*, "movers" or "changers," because they expected to change locations at least once a year.

With the advent of cambiadero ranches, the sierra reached the zenith of its population. Throughout the nineteenth century a few young men in each generation drifted away from mountain life. Some simply wanted other things, but most sought places where ranching was not so restricted and difficult. A number migrated northward and settled around Ensenada or old mission centers between El Rosario and the international frontier. After 1920 this exodus increased. Large, healthy sierra families began exporting people because they could not offer more opportunity in their own

5.13. Seasonal or cambiadero goat ranches are simple in construction and spartan in furnishings, as shown at top in the kitchen at Rancho El Cerro.

5.14. Rancho El Zorrillo displays another common practice: a cave is used to house the kitchen.

environs. That pattern has accelerated, and sierra families now are heavily represented in all peninsular towns, fishing camps, and major cities along the border between the United States and Mexico.

These pages, in brief, named the early settlers and told how they claimed the sierra and made it their own. Now it is time to look at the people themselves, outline their lives and customs, and follow them through a few more of the daily routines by which they derive their living from an environment so apparently sterile and hostile as the canyons and mesas of the Guadalupe mountains.

CHAPTER 6

New Lamps for Old

The people of Guadalupe, like most other isolated agrarian folk, are close to their roots. Their hours are filled with meeting the demands of subsistence, their minds preoccupied with thoughts relating to tangible, practical matters. Their ability to learn and to reason is excellent, but the cycles of their lives do not lead them to juggle many hypothetical problems or to involve themselves deeply in matters that lie beyond their immediate experience. The lack of formal schooling, books, or other stimulating outside influences has challenged them to derive mental satisfaction from familiar companionship and a never-ending contest with their environment.

Work and the sum of each person's life are perceived by sierra folk as more indivisible and intertwined entities than is common among people in more complex societies. Most mountaineers, the men in particular, have very complicated occupations. Unlike most employees in the modern world, a sierra man must cope with dozens of widely different problems during the course of a year. He is both foreman and principal laborer of an enterprise that may demand some of the skills of a farmer, livestock rancher, veterinarian, hunter, carpenter, mason, leather worker, repairman, doctor, counselor, drover, barterer, and so on. His wife copes with

6.1. Portrait of a Californio couple painted at a mountain ranch in the 1890s by an itinerant artist.

a corresponding range of maternal and domestic requirements. All of their varied occasional pursuits were familiar to their parents and will be known to their children.

Together, daily needs and the means by which they are met form a large part of the subject matter of everyone's social interaction because everyone in the sierra beyond early childhood is employed. Needs are immediate and apparent. Work is an anticipated part of everyone's life. Children contribute as early as they can and shoulder a growing share of family burdens. As a result, few think of time as divided between a job and home life or between private time and an employer's time. Furthermore, the beneficial result of most work is easily seen. Necessary drudgery is accepted in a lighthearted fashion and shared wherever possible. Few fail to do their part, because the economic system is so simple and each person's contribution is so obvious.

In affluent societies children have a great deal of time to themselves. In one familiar pastime, these youngsters pretend to be adults engaged in attractive occupations—they play at being doctors, nurses, astronauts, cowboys, and so forth. Sierra children engage in much less of this. They seldom have access to many playmates of similar age, so they begin socializing with older children or adults, usually tagging along with them as they do their chores. A little girl may be given a few simple or discarded household utensils to use as toys, but very soon she is busy drying dishes and getting out or putting away real objects in daily use. Similarly, a boy following his father or older brother soon learns to open gates, pull weeds, milk goats, or perform any of a dozen other simple acts that allow him to share in the family's daily life rather than just playing around it.

The great growth of goat ranching in the twentieth century seems to have given further impetus to the old practice of allowing or encouraging young children to work. Goats are small, very docile animals. Two children as young as eight to ten years of age, perhaps assisted by an experienced dog, can herd one hundred or more goats from a mesa, pen them up, and help to milk them. When cattle raising was the only major industry at most ranches, young boys had to wait longer before they could play major roles because cattle are too large, powerful, unpredictable, and wide-ranging to be handled by novices.

The partial shift from cattle to goats was inevitable. Guadalupe can support no more cattle today than it did a hundred years ago—fewer if, as many believe, rainfall has diminished in that period. But people have multiplied tenfold, and a large proportion of their ever-increasing needs has been met by ranging herds of goats over uplands that formerly supported few or no cattle. Goats have usurped the traditional role of cattle and have become the basis of the sierra's small cash economy.

Not all goat herds are handled alike. Schedules depend on the season, local geography, water locations, and the habits or convictions of individual proprietors. Some pen their goats at night and milk them in the morning; some rise before dawn, hike out to find the herd, drive it back to its pen, and then milk. The former practice is gaining favor as mountain lions increase in number and claim larger shares of the herds. Herds brought in at night naturally suffer fewer losses.

Fortunately for the sierrans, they are able to make a goat cheese that is long-lived and easy to transport and has found a receptive market. Cheese buyers export most of this goat cheese to mainland Mexico, where it is dried and grated. This particular cheese provides the familiar, pungent, slightly salty topping for tacos, enchiladas, and other dishes. For several months after the end of the summer rains, this cheese is made in most sierra ranches every day. It is an undertaking that involves everyone for a span of three or four hours.

Milking is a lively and colorful activity. One or two large wash boilers are placed outside the pen and covered with damp cloth to keep out dust. Each milker, and they often number five or six in a single pen, has a pail and carries it around from animal to animal. The actual milking requires only a minute or so per nanny, and each nanny appears to yield a quart or more. As the pails are filled, they are carried to the edge of the pen and handed to a man or boy who raises the cloth and empties the bucket into the wash boiler. In less than an hour, one hundred or more goats are milked of some thirty or forty gallons. Then the goats are released and the milk is carried carefully over the always-rough ground back to the shade of the ranch kitchen.

The kitchen area has been tidied to allow adequate space, and all the utensils to be used are freshly washed. If the cheesemaker has just engaged in milking, he or she changes clothes, combs or brushes his or her hair, and then scrubs up thoroughly. Clean cheese is a matter of pride and economics. The surroundings are primitive, but under the circumstances the general cleanliness is impressive.

Traditionally the cheesemaking process began by adding rennet, or scrapings from the dried after-stomach of a deer or cow, to the

6.2. A young sierra man is instructed about a ranch's needs as he prepares to make the long ride to a town.

6.3. Young people learn adult roles and accept responsibility early in life. Each mountaineer, to the best of his capacity, learns the skills and lore of his father or mother, as well as knowledge of special interest acquired from other relatives or neighbors.

fresh milk. Rennet contains the enzyme rennin that curdles milk. However, in many ranches today, a purer tinned product is used for convenience as well as a more uniform result.

The milk curdles very rapidly, and in less than ten minutes the cheesemaker begins to use a large strainer to lift out semi-solid curds, which are placed gently in a V-shaped wooden trough with a crack at the bottom to allow the liquid whey to drain into a pan below. After a half hour or so, the curd in the trough solidifies to the point that it can be sliced. The slices are salted and then crumbled by hand as the salt is kneaded in. At this point the cheese acquires its characteristic form—a somewhat flattened rectangular block or loaf.

Each rancher has constructed a dozen or more stout little baskets, about fifteen inches long by ten inches wide and five inches high, from the straight stalks of an arroyo bush called *guatamote*. These are bound together in log cabin fashion using rawhide lashing at the corners and edges. Each container is lined with clean cloth and then packed with firm but still viscous milk curd. When a basket is full, the cloth is folded neatly over the top and then covered by a piece of wood that just fits into the basket-form. A rock weighing fifteen or twenty pounds is set on top of the cover board to squeeze the cheese inside the cloth and press it tightly to the form. Larger cheeses require so much pressure that those who make them have constructed ingenious presses capable of exerting a hundred pounds or more.

After a few hours, or a day at most, the cheeses are removed from both the forms and their wrappings and placed on racks suspended up out of the way in the high gable of the kitchen or a storeroom. There they will cure and dry for a few days, until the rind is tough enough to undergo the strenuous trip to market.

In a good year, cheesemaking continues from October through April and provides each family with the cash and credit needed for its growing list of purchased items. And the herd of goats contributes more than cheese and the resulting money: the family drinks the milk, eats the cheese and goat meat, and uses and sells goatskins as well.

6.4. The economic basis of goat ranching is the sale of cheese. Activity is constant: goats are driven in daily, corralled, and milked, and the milk is converted to cheese.

Extended families dominate all aspects of sierra life. These days the parents of a child born there are probably cousins. The godparents are often an uncle and aunt, or cousins once removed. As the child grows, playmates will be brothers and sisters or first cousins residing at the same ranch or an adjacent one. Every neighbor up and down the arroyo—and in nearby arroyos as well—is a close enough relative that all can trace the connections. None are likely to be more distant than third cousins. When the time comes, the sierra youth probably will marry one of those cousins. Frequently the spouse is a second cousin on both sides of his family—that is, equally related to both fathers and mothers.

Throughout sierra history most children have been christened with traditional names drawn from a small group regularly bestowed since mission times. The most frequently used can be

6.5. A woman milking a goat.

determined from nineteenth-century baptismal records. Foremost among men's names was José, and for every child called by this name alone, another was addressed by some combined form such as José María, José Rosas, José de Jesús, Juan José, and so on. In order of their decreasing usage, the most common men's names were José, Juan, Francisco, Manuel, Antonio, Ignacio, Loreto, Vicente, Tomás, Anastasio, Domingo, and Ramón.

More than one-third of all women were named with some combined form of María: María del Rosario, María de los Dolores,

María Luisa, and so on. But unlike the combined forms of José, these in daily use were often shortened (by dropping María) to Rosario, Dolores, Luisa, and so forth. The most common women's names were María, Juana, Josefa, Dolores, Rosalía (or Rosa), Francisca, Loreto, Antonia, Ramona, Rosario, Luisa, and Gertrudis.

People with these men's and women's names made up over half of all those baptized in the entire nineteenth century. Most of these are common Hispanic names, peculiar neither to California nor to Mexico. The high frequency of three of them, however, can only be explained through California history. Ignacio, Loreto (on both lists), and Gertrudis all owe their popularity to the peninsula's Jesuit past. San Ignacio de Loyola was the founder of that religious order, and Nuestra Señora de Loreto was the patron saint of the Jesuit mission enterprise in California. Baja California's many German and Bohemian Jesuits left their special marks by encouraging the use of such saints' names as Gertrudis, Wenceslao, Estanislao, and Juan Nepomuceno. These saints were all well known on the peninsula, but this was not the case elsewhere in Mexico or in the rest of the Hispanic world.

Sierra families are usually large. In the nineteenth century the average couple raised about six or seven children to adulthood. This figure still applies. Families are also large in a different sense, since most consist of three or more generations. Thus a typical ranch, physically made up of a few structures of adobe and others of tree trunks and thatch, will house a colony of ten to fifteen people ranging in age from infancy to dotage, with no intermediate generations omitted. Compared to the average child in the United States, a sierra child is raised in more numerous and varied company and thus receives a greater diversity of experiences and role models. The child also is provided with generous amounts of daily affection and attention.

People living at a typically isolated ranch do not experience much entertainment obtained from outside their group. They read little for pleasure, have no television, and find radio expensive and much

6.6. Tacho hanging goat meat to dry as it is made into jerky.

6.7. Domestic chores.

6.8. A girl grinding the salt needed to make cheese.

of it unrewarding. Other than near neighbors, visitors are infrequent. Family members therefore entertain themselves or more often entertain each other. In this quasi theater-in-the-round, no characters are more central or vital than the children.

Any child, from the cradle up, is everyone's toy, pet, doll, playmate, apprentice, audience, and friend. They are looked after not only by their parents, but also by loving aunts, uncles, grandparents, and great-grandparents. Early in life children learn to toddle up to any larger person whom they can count on to feed them, clean them up, comfort them, or entertain them. This arrangement does not solely benefit the child; everyone takes pleasure in the interplay.

One outgrowth of this communal interest in children comes as a surprise to Americans who are not accustomed to seeing this practice in the United States. Some sierra parents have more children than they can afford or properly care for. Under these circumstances, children are frequently given to childless relatives to raise. Those who accept this responsibility of being foster parents view it as a favor that has been conferred on them, since children are such integral members of every family. The youngsters who are placed with relatives seem to accept these arrangements without great difficulty and adjust well to their new and usually permanent homes. Visits with their biological parents and siblings are frequent unless the child has moved far away, which is not a common circumstance.

Everyone's broad, family-centered rearing produces a social pattern very different from that found in most large urban areas. In the sierra no one generation takes real precedence over another. There are no clearly defined peer or age groups. Naturally, there are activities confined to groupings of children, unmarried youths, or the less active elderly. But these separate activities do not really divide anyone from the family, since they are necessary and traditional interludes of relief from the communal atmosphere.

This very old social pattern, which has evolved on nearly every frontier, solves many problems for its people. No babysitters or daycare centers are needed for children. No hired hands are needed in kitchens, milking pens, gardens, or animal herding pursuits. No special institutions are needed for the elderly or the dying. Each extended family provides its own social welfare program without bureaucracy. Medical services are primitive and inadequate by American standards, but the psychological benefits of living in these family communities are obvious when compared to those of most modern urban cultures. The daily routines of elderly people, most of whom are active to the limit of their strengths and desires, include necessary tasks that contribute to the common good. Humanity and continuity accompany even the end of life, as illustrated in this common vignette: a great-grandmother is so frail and crippled that she is confined to her bed, which has been placed to one side in the kitchen. In order to sit up, she must be bolstered with pillows and folded blankets, but she does sit and work away at stringing beads while listening to relatives as they go about their chores. A tiny boy crawls up on the bed and soon has wheedled a favorite story from great-grandmama. Before long he takes his nap at her feet.

In a few months or a year, the old woman will die. All of her people, including the smallest children, will follow her coffin as it is carried up the slope from the ranch to a burial plot where she is lowered to rest alongside her husband and among the previous generations. Everyone experiences the reality of all life's events, and that, too, contributes to the closeness and tenderness of family ties.

It would be difficult to find a cultural group that has been and is still so free from ancestral fears and has been subjected very little to belief in the supernatural. There is no fear of black cats or walking under ladders. The dark of night harbors no ghosts, and no one dreads unlucky days or dates. The mountain people of Baja California are not and apparently never were ridden by superstitious folklore. But this absence comes with a cost. Their culture lacks some of the colorful verbal traditions of societies that have made fantasies and romances from the elements of their superstitions.

6.9. Pulverized rock salt is worked into cheese curd just before it is molded into its final form. The salt preserves and helps to impart the characteristic tang of sierra goat cheese.

6.10. A goat is slaughtered. Male goats provide most of the meat in typical ranch diets, either eaten fresh or salted and then dried in jerked strips for future use.

The grist of verbal exchange in the peninsular sierras concerns real people and real events. Every mountaineer who travels as far as a neighboring ranch is part of a grapevine that transmits news and gossip with remarkable speed to all corners of the sierra. Most of this flow is made up of simple, homey fare. These isolated people have little interest in or understanding of the torrent of affairs and catastrophes in the outside world, and their own society is notably

6.11. Life in the mountains is segregated by family groups,
not by age groups as is common in urban living in developed nations.

nonviolent and stable. Novelties are generally small things and occur infrequently.

A fiesta serves to break the monotony of mountain society in two important ways. The event itself is a diversion, especially for women who travel to them but otherwise seldom get far from home. Then, at the fiesta, people get together in fairly large groups and share a conversational exchange of greater breadth than they will know until another fiesta, which might be months or years away.

Before roads and ferries and mainland people had so much impact, major religious fiestas were much greater events than any seen today—greater and apparently more colorful. Elías Villavicencio, a grandson of Guadalupe pioneer José María Villavicencio, was born in 1886 and lived all his life at Rosarito, a large orange ranch in the heart of the sierra. With the fruit from over two

6.12. Portrait of a mountain ranch family.

hundred large orange trees, Elías had an economic motive for attending the large fiestas that were still flourishing well after the turn of the century. In the late 1970s, the old man remembered how it was in those days:

> I had fruit to sell, but I also was looking for excuses to travel about and meet people—besides, we mountain people seldom got to church. Attending a fiesta in the right spirit performed a religious duty.
>
> I visited La Purísima, also Comondú, also San Javier, but no farther—never have I been to Loreto. I used to take oranges to festivals in all those other places. Mulegé had great fiestas—the streets were full of people—but the finest and largest fiesta of all was at San Javier on the third of December, the name day of the patron saint, San Francisco Javier. We went to many of those in spite of the great distance—four or five days with pack animals.
>
> Our first duty when we finally reached San Javier was to pay our respects at the beautiful *templo*. People had walked there from as far as Mulegé. They came on foot to make good on vows to San Francisco.

6.13. Most sierra adults help to raise generations of children, and nearly all children have generations of "parents" ranging from older brothers and sisters to great-grandparents.

6.14 and 6.15. Older people work and take active parts in family life as long as they are able.

Everyone crowded into the church—no one visited any other part of the festival until he had thanked the saint. Even men who drank, who would be drunk all the days of the fiesta, came to church first without drinking.

Afterward, there were grand dances at a house across from the church, the one with olive trees. There was music from many men, but, most of all, violin music. The greatest master of the violin was Teódolo Bastida. He came from Comondú and lived also in Santa Rosalía, but he was born in San Javier and he was a great favorite there.

People from the towns would come in fine clothes. Gentlemen wore wide sash belts with big buckles. Their sombreros had dangling fringes and embroidered chin straps. I remember that *lechuzas* were popular, cloth pouches of fine silken material that held tobacco and papers in little compartments. Gentlemen had them tied in fancy ribbons and carried them in hidden pockets of their coats.

Ladies rode to fiestas on sidesaddles with red velvet fringe. They wore Spanish combs in their hair and mantillas with borders of silken thread. Some of them had their names or mottos worked into the lace of a mantilla. We saw things at the fiestas that were told all over the sierra for long after.

I went to those dances at the home of Don Santa María de Castro, but I did not know how to dance. We men from the sierra were very backward and wild, not knowing the ways of the pueblos. We were *muy bronco*, like young mules not yet broken. Two sisters from Loreto helped me. They had ribbons braided into their hair and embroidered dresses. I was afraid to touch them, but they taught me to dance. That was a very long time ago.

Such grand occasions in the sierra were few, in earlier times or today, but sierra society does not need elaborate or imaginative material with which to entertain itself. In the seclusion of their quiet valleys everyone and their every move is news. The most minute attention is paid to individual thoughts and acts, and they are recounted with humor and concern. A pervasive preoccupation with family and individual identity is raised to an art. Endless anecdotes draw their points and their flavor from each person's uniqueness, often gently caricatured, or a whole family's real or imagined traits, broadly satirized.

The mountaineers are essentially optimistic about each other. Most of the storytelling has some positive twist where people are concerned. The prosperous and able may be singled out for a little more attention and sharper barbs, but they get due recognition in the folklore of their times. The less fortunate are not slighted. In fact, fortunes are usually not the point; personalities are. For example, a stranger spending a few weeks in the sierra may hear many stories about two men, contemporaries, whose exploits have attracted wide admiration. The two are usually mentioned in the same breath or compared, as to certain skills, in a close contest. After a time, the stranger may learn, quite incidentally, that one of these men is a well-to-do rancher with groves and herds, while the other is an old cowhand retained on a ranch as a sort of informal pensioner. Those facts had no place in the anecdotes passed around campfires. Those stories were spun from the lore of men's hunting skills, touch in breaking mules, and knowledge of regional trails, as well as traditions, honor, and loyalty to friends.

Every person has a unique identity. If someone is an apparent nonentity, that trait is not overlooked: that very inconspicuousness will be made conspicuous and will become a widely known trademark. Personal identity is an instant and lifelong possession of everyone born to this sierra world. One leaps onto its stage with one's first steps and speaks lines as soon as he or she is able to form words. This sense of having a close and devoted audience exerts a powerful influence as long as one lives. Even those who move far from the sierras or from the peninsula itself tend to conduct themselves as if their family were close by and could follow every step of their lives.

Men and women in the sierras of Baja California are only beginning to encounter the problems of the greater world. Taxes, inflation, pollution, crime, and the threat of war, to name a few, are as yet small factors in their collective consciousness. Outsiders faced with all those ominous realities might tend to view mountain life as a near-Arcadian escape, a simple, blissful existence isolated from the great burdens of the world and devoted to the virtues of family, harmony, and hard work. That view would be far too simplistic—the old sierra way of life does not work perfectly, by any means.

6.16 and 6.17. Until recently, sierra ranch buildings and their furnishings were constructed at the sites from local materials. A traditional bed and chairs of güéribo wood were covered, respectively, with rawhide strips and tanned leather.

6.18. Elías Villavicencio, born in 1886 at Rancho Rosarito, with his wife, Juana Aguilar. Both are descendants of some of Guadalupe's earliest settlers.

Isolation helped to create this culture and to preserve it. Isolation has also taken its toll. Sierra ranches were not only far from larger lowland communities but also far from each other. Women, in particular, lived entire lives during which their social contacts seldom included more than the members of their immediate family. Loneliness and a desire for some novelty and a few fresh faces and ideas must have been the common lot of most sierra women.

6.19. Mules are usually broken by recognized experts—
men in demand all over the sierra.

Women also suffered disproportionately in the ritual of finding spouses. Immobilized as they were, young women were in a poor position to make acquaintances or even to be known to more than the few families in their part of the sierra. Of necessity, most had to marry men who were both their neighbors and relatives. In every generation some mountain girls were doomed to remain single, partly because some of the more mobile sierra men left altogether, or returned having met and married girls from the towns or lowlands. Few male suitors from below "came a-courting" to the upland ranches.

This inequity in marriage opportunity led to another unfortunate aspect of sierra life: illegitimacy. In the mountains, few unwed mothers have been young. Sadly, most have been women who lost hope of marriage altogether. Mountain women were trained from

6.20 and 6.21. Conversation, the exchange of stories and ideas, is the mountaineers' fundamental entertainment whether it involves family, visitors, or a potential suitor for whom a sierra girl has donned her little-used finery.

childhood to love children, to cope with all that their presence implied, and to expect and need their company and support. They also were conditioned to live in family units headed by couples, men and women depending on each other for physical and emotional stability, that is, the conjugal knot. Not surprisingly, many women who never were asked to marry fell into less formal, often transient relationships with men. When babies resulted, they were accepted with little prejudice by their mothers' child-oriented families. Illegitimate children would know the love of a mother, grandparents, and uncles and aunts, but their mothers had no husbands. The already isolated life of a woman in the sierra must have seemed especially bitter with this additional deprivation.

Isolation has affected men as well. While most coped successfully with the challenges of their relatively difficult and solitary lives, some could not and therefore ran away. A number of men in each generation left the sierra forever. A number of others left periodically to wander around the low country, often drinking to excess, until they had no money or the means to earn more. Many men had the habit of drinking and womanizing whenever they came to town to buy or trade.

For the most part, however, life in the sierra was strong and stable. Most of its people were survivors, most of the time. But the system had its strains and cracks, and its people were human. Knowing some of these things makes it easier to understand why the mountain people are gradually giving up their individuality and accepting new ways even when these also have apparent flaws. "The old order changeth and passeth away" because its heirs are bored with the products of two centuries of isolation and are ready to experiment once again.

7.1. Eustacio (Tacho) Arce at seventy—a mountain man and scion of the old Californios.

CHAPTER 7

A Man of the Mountains

It is evening at Rancho San Pedro, high in the San Francisco range. Nearly all daylight has faded from the sky. The ranch men are in from their labors, cleaned up, lounging on the porch, and waiting for dinner. All attention is turned to Tacho Arce, a quiet-spoken, white-haired visitor, a cousin to all. Tacho has forever "recently returned" from far places. His stories are eagerly awaited and not long in coming.

> You will all be relieved to hear that Ramón Ávila—the one who owns Rancho San Marcos and not much else but a poor little appetite—that same Ramón is still managing to fend off starvation. Last month he bought cheese all over the sierra and took it to sell at Santa Rosalía—though God only knows how much of it gave force to Ramón and never came to market! When he had made his sales he headed home and, above Santa Cruz, met some cowherds who were low on supplies. These men soon spied three large cheeses, five kilos apiece, peeking through the slats of one of Ramón's pack-crates. They tried to buy them on the spot. "Never," cried poor Ramón, "those are my lunch!"

This tale finds a ready and appreciative audience even though it is set in the next sierra to the south. Partly through Tacho's past efforts, Ramón Ávila is known far and wide as a great eater. Indeed, his reputation is proverbial. Tacho has merely to mention his name and his listeners begin to smile, settle down, and anticipate the latest account of his prodigious appetite. Moreover, Tacho is too consummate a storyteller to waste an audience warmed by a successful opening. Invariably he is prepared with a follow-up.

> Ramón Ávila came down to Santa Águeda, three days' ride from his home across the mountains, to buy provisions at the little store where he always trades. Before even mentioning necessities, Ramón did not fail to ask the storekeeper for a supply of her famous homemade *colache*.[1] To Ramón's dismay, he found that her stock was reduced to what she had to show on the counter, a big glass jar holding about six or seven pounds. No other container was at hand, and she had no wish to give up the jar. Finally, knowing Ávila's appetite and moved by his well-known devotion to her colache, the woman found a way around the problem. Ramón would pass San Fernando on the second day of his ride home. The rancher at San Fernando was coming to Santa Águeda soon after. "Give him the jar as you pass by." Ávila promised to do this, finished his purchases, and left. Three hours later, Anastasio Villavicencio, from up the valley, came into the little store saying, "I ran into Ramón Ávila this side of El Bule. He asked me to bring this back to you." And he handed the jar back to the colache maker. It had been scraped clean!

Some men are born and raised in a sierra and spend all their lives on ancestral ranches or new ones developed just a few miles away. Others move out permanently and go to work in nearby towns, coastal fish camps, or move far away to Ensenada or border cities. A few remain attached to mountain ways but move around, scratching out a living here and there, restless but not wanting to lose their ties with their past. These are called *andariegos*—rovers—and their comings and goings add color and excitement to sierra life. A few seem to find ways to make livelihoods while traveling all over the mountains. They are the couriers of a remarkable grapevine that carries news and lore between relatives, particularly women who seldom meet face-to-face. Among these perambulatory types are skilled raconteurs carrying not just headlines, but detailed anecdotal accounts that are eagerly awaited whenever such an andariego appears in a remote place.

---

1. A syrupy preserve of any soft fruit, such as peaches, guavas, or papayas.

Around the Sierra de San Francisco, the dean of itinerant storytellers was Eustacio ("Tacho") Arce, long a mounted trader, scout for hunters, or guide to anyone who wished to visit "his" sierras. This man brought pleasure to all who crowded around their isolated hearths, awaiting his latest collection of anecdotes. Certainly, he was worth knowing for himself, but, more than that, the stories of his lineage and his life contributed to the intimate and characteristic history of the area.

The first Arce in California was an English-born presidial soldier, Juan de Arce, who came to Loreto in 1698, the second year of the "conquest." This well-documented fact has led some to the easy conclusion that he was the forebear of thousands of Californios with his surname. At this time, no one really knows. Juan de Arce came to Loreto from Villa de Sinaloa and may well have returned there when he quit California around 1701. The next Arces on the peninsula were the brothers José Gabriel de Arce and Sebastián Constantino de Arce, who came in 1751 and before 1764, respectively. They were born and raised in Villa de Sinaloa, but as yet no proof has been obtained that they were descended from Juan.

Sebastián Arce's earliest known documentary appearance in California is an entry in Mission San Ignacio's baptismal record dated September 13, 1764, to record the birth of his son Ignacio María Arce, who was only the fourth child born to gente de razón at the nearly forty-year-old mission. The baby's godparents were his uncle and aunt, José Gabriel de Arce and his wife, Ana Gertrudis Velasco.

Ignacio María Arce grew to manhood on the peninsula. Somehow he acquired literacy and learned to write a fine hand. He enlisted as a presidial soldier and had a long and honorable career, culminating in his promotion to sergeant in 1814. In 1789, while serving as part of the escort on guard at Mission Santo Domingo, he married María Mónica Aguilar, daughter of the mayordomo, Luis Aguilar. The following year, still at Santo Domingo, a son was born to this couple and christened Ignacio Buenaventura Arce. The day after giving birth, María Mónica died, but the infant survived

and apparently became very close to a subsequent stepmother, María de Jesús Romero.

Little is known of Buenaventura Arce's youth. As an adult he carelessly referred to himself as "from Loreto," and he may have spent some years there while his soldier-father was stationed at headquarters or at a frontier post too hazardous for family occupation. The next clear evidence of Arce's movements appears among the baptismal records at Mission Santa Rosalía de Mulegé in 1816, where Buenaventura Arce and his wife, Romualda Murillo, were inscribed as godparents to an Indian child. Romualda's background strengthens the idea that Arce grew up in Loreto: her father, Jaime

Opposite and above: 7.2 and 7.3. Tacho Arce was one of the few men who traveled constantly and acted as vital links in the sierra grapevines carrying messages and gossip to isolated ranch families.
Here he visits his maternal aunt and brings news to others at Rancho San Nicolás in the Sierra de San Francisco.

Murillo, had served there as a ships' carpenter, and her mother, Petra Pérez, was a daughter of Diego Pérez, long a skipper of the sailing launches that worked out of Loreto to supply the northern missions.

By 1818 Buenaventura Arce and his family were established at San Ignacio, where he perhaps served as mayordomo. No documents are known that indicate his exact status in those early years at the troubled end of Spanish rule. Local lore has him making a fortune in placer gold ferreted out of the desolate Santa Clara mountains west of San Ignacio. This idea may be fanciful, but his continuing quest for real estate certainly was not.

Many records attest to his diligence in making claims to land. In 1825 he got title to San Carlos, a ranch with an *aguaje*, or water hole, located north of Las Tres Vírgenes, three clustered volcanic cones thirty miles northeast of San Ignacio. In the years between 1839 and 1854, Buenaventura Arce claimed and received titles to six other ranches, including San Francisco, Santa Marta, and San Carlos. The record of Buenaventura's title to Santa Marta bears the inscription "bought from an Indian." That footnote to history recalls a curious series of events that involved Buenaventura Arce.

After a stormy career with the frontier Indians in the northern Baja California missions, Padre Félix Caballero retired to San Ignacio, where he, too, had bought ex-mission land from an Indian. The priest had served as president of the peninsular missions and had become very wealthy by the standards of the time and place. He owned outright more than fifteen hundred cattle, thirty-three mules, and much more. Widely reputed to be a smuggler, Caballero had complicated dealings with Americans, Indians, ranchers, and soldiers assigned to guard his missions. He was embroiled in politics, as each Father President had been, in order to protect "mission" interests against waves of land reform legislation. Caballero died on August 3, 1840, apparently a victim of poisoning. The appointed *alcalde*, or justice of the peace, in San Ignacio was obliged to list and attest to all the deceased's tangible assets. The inventory covered many sheets of paper and was signed by the legally constituted justice of the peace, "Ventura" Arce. Within a month or two of Padre Caballero's death, Buenaventura Arce claimed and eventually was awarded a title to certain buildings and grounds of the former Mission San Ignacio. The priests' quarters became his home, and the adjacent storehouse became his warehouse. Both served him for nearly thirty more years and can be seen to this day standing just north of the church's great nave.

Several bits of documentary evidence suggest that Arce was the recognized leader in the village and its dependent area. This idea is strongly supported by oral history still retold in San Ignacio. Buenaventura Arce is depicted as a boss surrounded by henchmen

7.4. Filling a canteen at a pool in an arroyo.

7.5. San Ignacio at daybreak. For over two centuries, this once-isolated mission oasis has greeted travelers on the Camino Real in Baja California, a succession of churchmen, soldiers, forty-niners, and, finally, tourists.

to do his bidding and to give force to his official pronouncements and decisions. The sources of his influence are obvious. He held enough land and owned enough cattle to be an employer, perhaps the only one after Caballero's death. And as the sole government representative, Arce had prestige and some pretense to power. It is not surprising, therefore, to find that he could raise a posse on short notice, entertain people he favored, or impede those he did not.

Buenaventura Arce's original appointment as justice of the peace at San Ignacio related logically to his earlier land acquisitions and his subsequent claims to a large part of the valuable irrigated mission acreage. Governors making token efforts to distribute land probably welcomed the claims made by a few ambitious men who lived in the isolated areas and would support a government that showed them favor. Buenaventura Arce clearly played his cards shrewdly over a long lifetime to become and remain a regional strongman. This status is clearly reflected in several American accounts dating from the mid-nineteenth century.

At least two diaries written by forty-niners who made their way up the peninsula tell of encounters with inhabitants of the San Ignacio region. One was written by W. C. S. Smith, whom we have already met. The other was composed by J. D. Hawks. These two writers differed significantly in their depictions of Buenaventura Arce and other San Ignacio people. Smith misunderstood the role of the priest, mistook the people for Indians (most of them were not), and said his party was abused by the alcalde, who most certainly was don Buenaventura. Hawks described an obliging priest and a roguish but agreeable Buenaventura Arce. He was entertained in a private home. These accounts probably tell us as much about the Americans as they do about their hosts. Clearly, the Smith and Hawks parties were made up of different sorts of people. On May 6, 1849, W. C. S. Smith began the following account of his party's visit:

> The Mission of San Ignacio . . . [is] the largest and best preserved of these old establishments we have seen. About 100 half-civilized Indians live around in mud huts. . . . A priest comes once a year to marry them

and to say Mass for the dead.... We were detained in San Ignacio on the 6th purchasing a horse. Next morning our best mule, a valuable and beautiful animal, was missing. These people had tried to buy or trade us other mules for her, failing that, the cut throat villains had stolen her away in the mountains where we could not find her. They took advantage of our necessity to ask an exorbitant price for any other mule, far more than we could afford to pay. Our remaining animals had no strength to pack our scanty stock of baggage, provisions, and the water which we must carry, so we were stuck fast. All we could get to replace our pretty Jul was a miserable old horse. We went to the Indian Alcalde. He only laughed at us. The day before he could talk Spanish fast enough. Now all we could get out of him was "no entiendo" (don't understand). We were sure that he was the very thief. We could not bear to give up the only animal that we could depend upon. It seemed like risking our lives to go on without her to pack water. In our anger we almost cried.

We left the place the evening of the 7th.... We did not know the full value of our good mule until at last we started without her. After beating along the miserable old substitute for about 5 miles, we halted, and after a consultation agreed that while one kept camp the others should go back and make one more attempt to recover Jul. That failing, we would, at all hazard, seize the best mule we could find.... Three of us put our pistols in order and mounting the best horses, returned to the village. Our search and demands were of no avail, though we threatened to burn the whole place unless they produced her. So we openly took possession of the Alcalde's best mule and led it off to camp. We then packed it and started off by moonlight, traveling all night to elude the pursuit. Making a short halt the morning of the 8th we kept on over a dreadful road. About the middle of the afternoon while winding through a narrow chasm we found ourselves surrounded by an over-powering band of 100 or more black rascals, armed with escopetas.[2] We kept them at a safe distance with pointed guns, but we were out of water and it was evident they would kill the whole of us in such a place, so preferring discretion to valor we turned the mule loose, after which they did not molest us. It was well for them they did not. We were desperate and had ready in hand 40 shots.[3]

Four months later, another party of forty-niners was in San Ignacio, and Hawks, one of its members, wrote this in his journal:

2. Muzzle-loaders.
3. Crosby, "The 1849 Journal of W. C. S. Smith," 137–39.

August 18th—The church buildings of San Ignacio are in a very good state of repair, and we find the padre who has charge of the mission a very excellent man. He has been constant in his attentions to us, and has assisted us materially in making our purchases of animals, etc. He invited us into his library, where we found a fine collection of books, maps, etc. We found here a map of Mexico, including Lower California, from which we have made notes for our future guidance. The padre has kindly offered to send letters for us through Mexico, and I shall avail myself of his offer and write home. He has also given me a letter to the padre of Santo Tomás, and I think this may be of service to us as we journey through the country.

At a little distance in front of the church there is a large octagonal reservoir built of stone, with a stream of water running through it. The masonry is very good. Besides the church buildings, the town is composed of a few miserable huts.[4]

The Hawks party also had a scrape with Alcalde Arce but brought it to a much happier resolution.

The whole country appears to be under the proprietorship of a portly old Castilian, named Don Buentura, or Buenaventura. He owns all the cattle and horses, and we are endeavoring to make some purchases from him. We were obliged today to bring him to terms. One of our party had a quantity of jewelry, consisting of rings, chains, etc., and as we were trading, a Spaniard very coolly put a ring on his finger, and went off with it against the remonstrances of the owner. He appealed to Buentura to have him stop the man, but he affected indifference, and allowed the fellow to mount a horse and ride off with it. We at once determined that it would not answer to allow the matter to rest in this manner, and the whole party of six, armed with a rifle and pistols, went immediately to the house of Buentura. As he saw this formidable army approaching, he surrendered, coming forward and asking the value of the ring. I answered $10, and he said that he would settle it, and we marched back to our quarters. In about half an hour he came in and handed us the amount, and we had very little trouble in trading with him after this. He sent out for some horses, and sold us some saddles, and assisted us in various ways.

Sunday, August 19th—Not much attention is paid to Sunday here. The church was open for Mass in the morning, with an afternoon service, with a sermon. We were invited by Don Luis Argular,[5] to visit his casa, which is about a mile from the church, and at the upper end of the valley.

---

4. Browne, *Resources of the Pacific Slope*, part 2, 134.
5. Actually, Aguilar.

We found his house delightfully situated, surrounded by date and fig trees, with a fine vineyard and melon-patch. The grapes were the finest we have seen. After spending a couple of hours with Don Argular and his agreeable wife, we returned to our quarters.[6]

Both of the reported attempts on the Americans' possessions have to be viewed in context. Not only were most forty-niners woefully inept in Spanish, but they also seem to have been completely ignorant of the feelings of a people who had been invaded two years before by Americans and whose country had been plundered in an unjust war. Moreover, gold seekers, in passing through, foraged off the country, taking livestock and provisions from ranches and, in at least two well-authenticated cases, stealing church goods, including items of gold and silver. It will be recalled that another American, James Hunter Bull, passed through San Ignacio in 1844, only five years earlier than Smith and Hawks but, significantly, before either the war or the gold rush. Bull's memoirs describe an idyllic stopover with no hint of unpleasantness. Most contemporary accounts in both Alta and Baja California make it clear that forty-niners, taken as a group, were not the sort of transients that anyone would welcome.

Twenty years later, Buenaventura Arce became a minor character in the widely distributed book *Resources of the Pacific Slope*. One of the contributors was William Gabb, who had visited San Ignacio in 1867. By then the Mexican War was a generation past and Gabb pictured this genial scene.

> San Ignacio is a village with a population, including the suburbs, of about 20 families. The only buildings of any importance in the place are those belonging to the mission. The others are mere shanties. The church buildings, consisting of the church itself, and two lateral wings, one of which is prolonged into an L, are in excellent repair, and are the most imposing buildings of this class in the territory. They are very solidly built of stone with arched roofs, being out so as to be flat on top. The church is in the form of a Latin cross, and has a hemispherical dome of stone, at the intersection of the cross. There is a fine commodious gallery for the choir, also of stone, and, in fact, no wood enters into the construction of

---

6. Ibid., part 2, 134.

the building, except the doors, unless it may be some of the lintels. The ornaments which vandalism, sacrilege, and the poverty of the Government have left are still sufficient to show that neither expense nor labor was spared to make this the most elaborate church in Lower California.

The buildings all stand on a terrace, partly artificial, about four feet high in front and ten feet behind, very carefully walled up with stone.

Gabb found the place occupied by a "jolly, fat old fellow," whom he called don Ventura Arce and who lived in a truly patriarchal style surrounded by a troop of his children and grandchildren.

> The gardens are very extensive, perhaps more so than any others north of La Paz. Grain of various kinds, beans, and all sorts of vegetables are raised in abundance, while thousands of date palms, growing spontaneously, yield their proprietor a large income. Besides these, figs, olives, grapes, and pomegranates are cultivated extensively, and sugar-cane is raised to such an extent, that panoche is an important article of export. A perennial superabundance of running water relieves San Ignacio from all fear of drought, and the only labor necessary is to keep open the irrigating ditches, and collect the crops.
>
> We brought a couple of letters of introduction to Don Ventura, who received us kindly, and placed us in an unoccupied room in the mission buildings. We spent a day here, waiting for some mules to be brought in, and, as is always the case, they could not be found until the next morning. When they were brought in we made an exchange, getting a fresh animal in place of one of our pack-mules, and in the afternoon, after a promiscuous hand-shaking with nearly the whole town, sallied out, more for the purpose of getting a start than because we expected to travel any distance.[7]

With these lines, Buenaventura Arce bowed out of American letters. Coincidentally, at that time an unrelated but major element began to affect local affairs, a discovery that in one generation would be changing the lives of all who lived in the San Ignacio area.

The Boleo Mining Company

At that time, a rancher named José Rosas Villavicencio was based near the tiny village of Santa Águeda located about forty miles

---
7. Ibid., part 2, 101–102.

east of San Ignacio on a lower northeast slope of the Sierra de Guadalupe. In 1868 he had occasion to ride to the north, probably looking for strayed cattle. About ten miles out he began to notice nodules, strange ball-shaped fragments of a heavy mineral substance, eroding from the side of a cliff. He soon found others, collected a few, and took them to show others. When no one he knew recognized these curiosities, he took a few across the gulf to Guaymas, a port city in Sonora with local mining activity. There his nodules were recognized as a rich form of copper ore, and the word spread quickly.

By 1873 there were thirty-three mining entities registered in the area of their origin. Each small operation soon was setting up a camp and employing pack animals to haul its take to the nearest beach site accessible to small cargo vessels. However, their mining practices were haphazard, and the work was done almost exclusively by Yaqui Indians brought over from Sonora. In addition, the small scale and desolate locations of all these operations limited their economic success.

Around 1880, samples of that ore reached members of the mammoth Rothschild investment organization in France, which was interested because the meteoric and ongoing late nineteenth-century rise in the creation and distribution of electricity was creating a skyrocketing demand for copper. The Rothschild group determined the richness of the ore and sent agents to visit its source. The agents learned that it would be feasible to install local facilities to further enrich it and make it profitable to transport to Europe. They set up a formal business, Compagnie Du Boleo, as it was named in French. *Boleo* (ball) was the word used by the Californios familiar with those curious nodules of copper ore. By 1885, Rothschild interests had bought from the Mexican government all rights to work the area of those deposits. Soon they were shipping ore, primarily to England and Germany.

Development occurred rapidly. Within three years the company had invested $6 million in the site, quickly creating a growing community called Santa Rosalía in which they built housing for

7.6. In its heyday (1900–1940), the mining town of Santa Rosalía consumed most of the moonshine made in the nearby Sierras de San Francisco and Guadalupe.

French engineers and other management personnel, as well as additional infrastructure. Nearby they built a smelting plant and a temporary dock. By 1890 the population of the mining colony totaled more than three thousand. By the end of its first year the Boleo Mining Company was Mexico's greatest producer of copper. By the end of its first decade it was earning a healthy profit for its owners in France. By 1900 its local facility, including three different camps and Santa Rosalía, contained over six thousand people, a railroad with twenty-two miles of track, a steel church brought in pieces around Cape Horn, four schools, a hospital, several hotels, an almost completed permanent dock (built chiefly using the slag from the smelting operation), a bakery, a company store, cantinas, brothels, pawn shops, and cigar stores. All of these were entities one might expect in a booming company town.

Beyond dealing with its own internal affairs, El Boleo found it necessary to deal with the natives of the area. It needed to hire men from local families to operate the ranches the company had created to provide needed food. Beyond that, El Boleo found it necessary to buy meat, cheeses, crops, and leather goods from the Californio people of the local ranches. This practice aided those who were engaged in supplying the needs of a growing population.

A more subtle change was the fact that the long-term nearby presence of a large group of alien outsiders educated the natives of the area subconsciously in ways not found elsewhere on the peninsula. Despite having limited social contact with these outsiders, the Californios learned how foreigners behaved toward them and how they treated each other as well. From them they learned how to handle many unfamiliar tools and pieces of equipment. On a more harrowing note, as will be shown, they learned the pitfalls of contraband sales activities to employees of El Boleo and how to avoid them.

All that said, the actual relations between those groups remained surprisingly distant. It is true that over a long period of time perhaps half a dozen Frenchmen did marry local women, but in general there was little social mixing between the visitors and the locals. So when local supplies of copper ore began to diminish during the 1920s and the numbers of workers serving the Boleo began to shrink, the most tangible effect on the Californio population was a local loss of income. This hardship was handled stoically. And at least in memories, it was less trying than the aftermaths of destructive storms known to the area.

Back to the People of the Sierra de San Francisco

For some fifty years Buenaventura Arce was the personal hub and power of activities in and around San Ignacio. He died in 1870, but his local fame has not disappeared to this day. San Ignacio is sprinkled with his descendants, and most of the people in the Sierra de San Francisco trace part of their lineage back to "Tata Ventura" (Grandpa Ventura).

Buenaventura Arce (1790–1870) and Romualda Murillo (1797–1892) had at least eight children born between 1815 and 1830. The four girls and four boys who survived to adulthood married and had families. Lucas, their eldest son, born in 1817, had ten surviving children, including a boy, Cesario, born about 1852, who was not only Buenaventura's grandson but also Tacho Arce's grandfather. Cesario's son Severiano Arce (1883–1981) married Domitila Villavicencio (1885–1975). Tacho, born in 1911, was the second of their ten children.

Buenaventura Arce's wealth was primarily in land that he was able to buy, seize, or simply claim as unused. His acquisitions came at a low point in midpeninsular affairs, a time when missions were fading away and gente de razón were few in the area. He divided his holdings among his sons and sons-in-law who primarily lived on comfortable farms in and around San Ignacio. But these households produced over sixty grandchildren for Buenaventura, and the village could not maintain that increase for another generation.

7.7. Domitila Villavicencio,
mother of Tacho Arce and nine other children.

San Ignacio's excellent climate and water resources ensured reasonably good diets and health conditions. Everyone had a large family, not just Arce. Most infants became adults, and San Ignacio was soon an exporter of people. Most of Buenaventura's grandchildren and great-grandchildren had to live far from town as heirs to his scattered ranch claims. They and their relations by marriage populated the Sierra de San Francisco.

Rancho San Francisco is located in the heart of the sierra that now bears its name. When Buenaventura Arce got title to it in

7.8. Tacho Arce at the tombs of his grandparents near Rancho San Antonio.

early 1840, the site had already served as a ranch and visiting station of Mission San Ignacio. A report of 1762 shows that San Ignacio then harbored seventy-eight people in twenty-four families. Along with his land grant, Arce had acquired two buildings made of solid stone—a visiting station and its adjacent chapel in which services were held during mission times. This structure still stands, only slightly modified, and serves some of Arce's descendants as a home and storehouse.

Tacho Arce was born at San Francisco and grew up at Rancho San Antonio, also in the heights of the sierra, but about five or six miles south of San Francisco along the principal trail leading to San Ignacio. By the time Tacho was seven, he was helping his older brother Ignacio ("Nacho") herd goats. Before long, he was helping his father with the pack trips by which the family exported goat cheese and obtained provisions from San Ignacio. In a year or two Tacho had established his competence in handling animals, money, merchandise, and various transactions involving haggling, bartering, and, hence, human relations. Tacho's father, Severiano, when ninety years of age, remembered that even as a youth, Tacho had a special gift. "Nacho," he joked, "had a way with goats, so he went as a goatherd. Tacho had a way with gente, so he became a *falluquero*."

Originally, the term *falluquero* indicated a smuggler of *falluca*, contraband goods that were usually carried on the backs of mules or burros. However, since the traveling purveyors who brought dry goods into the sierras used the same animals and equipment as those real smugglers did, local traveling salesmen were soon known facetiously by the same name, as Severiano referred to Tacho. By the same token, falluca had originally been applied to smuggled goods, but soon evolved to be the general term for store-bought goods that had to be packed into the sierra. Professional falluqueros went about from ranch to ranch selling out of the packs on their strings of mules, burros, or both. And the puckish trend did not end there. Before long, the young man who took a ranch's pack animals to town to pick up monthly supplies was solemnly referred to as its falluquero.

Tacho thoroughly enjoyed both the responsibility and the freedom to move about afforded by his cheese exporting and supply runs. Soon he began to imagine this as the basis of a career, but he failed when at age sixteen or seventeen he tried to become an actual *falluquero*. These mounted merchants could make money on both legs of their trips into a sierra. They bought goods, often specifically ordered, in the nearest town and charged a higher price for them at the sierra ranches. Then, at those ranches they would buy cheese, fruit, vegetables, leather goods, or any other local products, and sell them at other ranches or back in town, making a profit on each transaction. Tacho's mountain neighbors remember that he gave this all up in a year or so because he could not bring himself to charge enough for his services. "I could not eat my own relatives,"

7.9. Tacho Arce at the ruins of
Rancho San Antonio, his childhood home.

7.10. Falluqueros, mounted merchants with strings of burros, pack dry goods and staple foods into the sierras to trade for cheese or other ranch products.

growled Tacho recollecting those times. But neither could he go back to San Antonio and its relatively sedentary life, not after he had had a taste of the outside world and of running his own affairs. Late in 1930, just before he was twenty years old, Tacho joined his cousin Leandro Arce in a ride to Calmallí, fifty miles to the north. During his travels Tacho had heard tales of placer gold being dug and separated by squatters using hand tools. He and Leandro went to make their fortunes.

Calmallí is an old place-name. The area lies in the southern foothills of the Sierra de San Borja, some sixty miles by air north of San Ignacio. Around 1882, Cayetano Mejía, a prospector from Mulegé, found placer gold in the washes below Calmallí. He and a Cochimí Indian helper named Antonio Murillo worked a few diggings profitably until their secret was discovered. At news of

7.11. On the long trips to and from market, pack and riding animals must be unloaded, fed, and rested at midday as well as at night.

their findings, a growing throng of would-be *gambusinos*, hand miners, pushed into the vicinity and prospected sands and gravels over an area of several square miles. Showings were good, but no large-scale recovery seemed possible because of the scarcity of running water, which was the usual medium for carrying off dross and concentrating gold. In desperation, the poor but resourceful gambusinos made crude, hand-cranked wind machines and used them in combination with shaker tables. The moving air carried some of the lighter tailings away from the treated material. Such practices produced only marginal profits, and activities rose and fell with the energies and persistence of the men at work. Emiliano Ibarra, a Sinaloan experienced in many other goldfields, was the most persistent. He built a real home, corrals, and a store, and also bought out others' claims or occupied them when they were abandoned. Although Ibarra never engaged in any large-scale mining, he was the local force to be reckoned with when, about 1889, a group of San Francisco investors decided to develop both the placer fields and newly discovered gold-bearing quartz veins. They bought out most of Ibarra's holdings and began a typical American-type operation, although it was still called the Ibarra Gold Mining Company. Its miners dug wells, found adequate water, built a wagon road to Puerto de Santo Domingo on the Pacific, and brought in steam engines to work ore crushers and other mining machinery. The Ibarra Company built some fine houses for management personnel, some small dwellings for miners, and other necessities such as a general store, workshops, and warehouses.

By 1900 the boom was past and activities gradually slowed. Various individuals and groups have mined there on a diminishing scale ever since. One American, Byron Hall, was mining and in residence to greet Edward Alphonso Goldman's Smithsonian Institution expedition of 1905, and adventurer Alfred Walbridge North in 1906.

At Calmallí, Tacho and Leandro encountered an unexpected opportunity. An American had contracted to run a pipeline to bring water from Calmallí to the new community of El Arco some eight miles to the south over level ground. Leandro Arce soon lost interest in laboring for wages. He tried his hand at being a gambusino and became discouraged, so he went back to the Sierra de San Francisco. But Tacho persevered and spent nearly a year trenching, laying pipe, and handling the American's string of pack animals. When the job was done, Tacho stayed on for some months as a gambusino, using the practices of the 1880s. He dug sandy earth from the edges of a wash, spread it on a slanted table, and separated gold from dross by vibrating the table sharply until the lighter wastes worked their way over the lowest edge, or by blowing across the material with a bellows that tended to carry off sand and earth. In either case, traces of finely divided gold remained on the table and had to be painstakingly swept together.

Fidencio Ibarra, a descendant of the onetime mine owner, kept a little store at Calmallí and bought gold with money or supplies. None of the handful of gambusinos working the digs in 1931 had any exact idea of the value of gold or even the means to weigh it. Ibarra weighed what he bought and paid what he had to. Tacho thought he may have been paid about half price but added with a grin, "Ibarra earned whatever profit he made by having to live at Calmallí and associate with such riffraff as we were." Young Señor Arce soon tired of hard work in such uncongenial surroundings. One day he put all his possessions on a burro and set out for home, four days' hike over desert and into the sierra.

In late 1931, Tacho's older cousin, Loreto Arce, needed help in developing his new ranch at San Gregorio. Tacho passed through San Gregorio on his way from Calmallí. He spent the night talking to Loreto and decided to accept his offer, move in, and go to work. In later years, Loreto and his wife, Josefa—who incidentally was Leandro Arce's sister—reminisced a great deal about Tacho's years with them. Looking at the prodigious work that went into building the huertas, it would be easy to assume that Tacho spent his time moving earth and stones. Surprisingly, he said that was not the case. "I was a collector of mezcales, nothing more." Pressed for details, Tacho added an entirely new aspect to the view of Loreto's accomplishments.

When Loreto first went to San Gregorio, he had no cattle or goats. Even after he had built and planted a few plots of protected soil, he had few crops in prospect for several years. To support his family and finance his construction, Loreto became a *mezcalero*—literally, a maker of the liquor mezcal. This activity was, and is, prohibited in Mexico except as a government-licensed and -inspected enterprise, but it also was an occupation as old as the mountain ranches themselves. In the late eighteenth and early nineteenth centuries, liquor was made as a trade item to supply local demand, since imports were expensive and cash was scarce. Later in Baja California, as in many of the world's remote mountain regions, moonshining flourished. Liquor was heavily taxed. However, in the sierras, it could be hidden from tax collectors and law enforcement officers. Loreto Arce, a cautious man, was prepared to take a gamble on the fact that his location was particularly remote and thus would not be easily discovered. Even so, his *beneficio*, as the entire mezcal work is called, was located in a hidden nook near his spring.

The process that Loreto and Tacho were about to employ had a history four centuries old in Mexico and at least two centuries long in Baja California. Like so many Mexican traditions, it began as a marriage of ancient Indian practices and those of their Spanish conquerors. Aztecs and others in pre-Columbian Mexico had brewed a sort of beer, called *pulque*, by fermenting the hearts of native agaves. The Spaniards simply applied their skill and technology to distill pulque and produce mezcal. Mexico's classic liquor tequila is actually the particular form of mezcal elaborated in the Tequila district of the modern state of Jalisco. Early production of this alcoholic drink on the peninsula is evidenced by Governor Joaquín de Arrillaga's 1794 decree that all goods created in Baja California could be imported freely to Alta California, "except mezcal and other liquors."[8]

At San Gregorio, the moonshiners' first task was harvesting agaves. Tacho was employed to drive a string of burros up onto mesas to the north and west where he could collect a small gray-green agave that grows in clusters of two or three to a dozen heads. Tacho chopped off roots and leaves with his sharp, heavy, ten-inch-long belt knife and loaded each burro with up to five hundred of

---

8. José Joaquín de Arrillaga to the commander of the frontier, September 23, 1794, The Bancroft Library C-A 7, 111–12.

7.12. Loreto Arce, born in 1898, the founder of Rancho San Gregorio, poses with Josefa Arce, his wife and cousin. Both are descended primarily from Hispanic mission servants who settled around San Ignacio nearly two centuries ago.

the mezcal hearts. Back at the beneficio, Loreto would prepare a pit about four feet deep and long enough to hold five or six burro loads of mezcal hearts. The depression was lined with large rocks, and in it a pile of hardwood was laid and ignited. When the blaze was strongly established, the *horno*, or oven, would be partially damped, and the fire would smolder and heat the rocks and surrounding earth to a temperature at which they glowed red.

When the mezcalero knew that the fuel was burned down, he opened the oven, dumped the mezcales in, and covered the hole tightly with a piece of sheet metal and then a heavy layer of thick mud to seal in heat and vapor as much as possible. There the agave hearts roasted for three days before being removed, mashed, put in barrels, and covered with water. Within four or five days, a ferment caused by naturally occurring yeasts ran its course. The mezcalero had only to stir his mash daily. Then entire barrel loads were transferred to a primitive still pot—a fifty-gallon copper vessel that could be tightly sealed—and distilled in more or less the same way most other ferments are converted to strong liquors.

With Tacho's help, Loreto Arce could make about twenty gallons of mezcal per month during the hot season, which he favored for the work. Not only was the horno more efficient and the ferment sweeter and more rapid in that season, but the men could also be employed in light work rather than moving earth and rocks during a time when daytime temperatures ranged from 100 to 120 degrees.

Sales of contraband liquor posed a greater danger than the manufacturing processes, especially to Tacho, who actually delivered it. The final consumers of most mountain mezcal were miners employed by El Boleo Mining Company in relatively nearby Santa Rosalía. But typical of large, isolated industries, El Boleo had a company store that sold legitimately bottled spirits at a very profitable markup and "owned" every government man in the area. Not only were Santa Rosalía officials a danger to visiting mezcaleros, but so too were some of its miners, a notoriously rough crowd that came to know who brought liquor into town and who left

7.13. Narciso Villavicencio was an invaluable guide to his homeland, the Sierra de Guadalupe, an area where his ancestors had been pioneer settlers and, later, moonshiners. Here he points out the remains of an underground oven once used in roasting native agaves as a step in making contraband mezcal, a distilled liquor.

with money. Robberies and violence occasionally took place on the mesas and in the ravines above the mining town. By the time Tacho became a mezcal runner, bootleggers had learned to meet their suppliers in outlying places where transactions and transshipments could take place more secretly.

The product of Loreto's beneficio was usually taken to Cerro Verde, a ranch way station in the canyons northwest of Santa Rosalía. Here an elaborate charade was played out. Tacho would hide his jugs or little barrels of liquor outside the encampment and ride in with one or two burros loaded with cheese, firewood, or whatever sierra commodity was handy. A buyer would come in from Santa Rosalía with a modest load of falluca, perhaps a pile of sombreros, a few shirts, or the like. Each party would check with confidants in order to know that no untrustworthy observers were around, and then both groups would ride out to do business.

Tacho was never actually caught by government or El Boleo men, but he had some anxious times. Once he had to wait two days to finish his task, all the while making a pretense of visiting friends, while his nervous buyers kept their eyes on a company foreman who had no apparent business in camp. On another occasion, Tacho was met on the trail outside Cerro Verde by a cousin who had waited for him for two days because police were watching the camp.

In 1936 the government finally shut down Loreto Arce's production facilities. Gradually, through informers, the locations of active beneficios were being obtained. Eventually soldiers were sent to San Gregorio, and they seized the mezcalero and destroyed his still. He was brought back to Santa Rosalía and jailed for a month before a judge fined him two thousand pesos and made him promise not to break the law again. Loreto agreed and kept his word. Moreover, Tacho remembered that he was philosophical about his loss. The moonshining operation had supported his family for five or six years; it allowed him to build, plant, and bring into production his handsome huerta. "¡Qué será, será!"[9]

---

9. What will be, will be!

7.14. Tacho Arce and Tránsito Quintero taking pack mules up a steep grade.

7.15. A condenser jacket for a mezcal still. Moonshiners once had entire fermentation and distillation rigs handsomely fabricated from heavy sheet copper.

The closing of Loreto's beneficio ended Tacho's employment at San Gregorio. Loreto's sons were able to help more and more as they grew up, and now that his "cash crop" was suppressed, Loreto could not afford paid help. The blow was especially hard on Tacho because he had just married. Now he had to go out and find a new way to support his expected family.

His bride was Ramona Agúndez, only recently acquainted with Tacho but born in San Ignacio to a family long in the area. Ramona's father, Napoleón Agúndez, had worked for years as a foreman on El Boleo ranches. The company had developed about fifty ranches to supply meat, cheese, and vegetables, not only for sale to the miners and their families but also as profitable exports that could be sold to visiting ore ships or coastal traders working the Gulf of California. Agúndez was then foreman at San Carlos,

7.16. Germán Arce makes shoes while recalling with Tacho the days when Germán's father, Loreto, employed Tacho at San Gregorio.

near the gulf coast east of the Sierra de San Francisco. Tacho and Ramona met at the fiesta for San Francisco's patron saint. This local observance probably dates back to the ranch's origin as an outlying chapel of Mission San Ignacio. These mountain gatherings attracted many of the area's inhabitants and, along with wedding celebrations, provided the largest social get-togethers of each year. Visitors would flock into the host ranch bringing food, drink, musical instruments, gifts, and decorations. Dining became

7.17. Even the tiniest and most temporary of ranches has an ample corredor—its shady, open-sided sitting room. Here Tacho Arce and his son Felipe *(left)* visit with Tacho's brother Loreto and his family at Rancho Las Calabazas.

communal, shared by ranchers and guests. The several *corredores*, or covered overhangs of the ranch houses, became dormitories for the several days of the fiesta. Daytime was given over to playing ball or card games and, most of all, to conversation. Nights were spent in singing, dancing, and drinking.

Ramona Agúndez and her family had ridden up from San Carlos to take part. It was their first visit, and it accomplished one of the unspoken but understood purposes of fiesta gatherings by providing a sort of "coming out" for the otherwise rather sequestered ranch maidens. The meeting of Tacho and Ramona resulted in a marriage two months later. It was a civil ceremony at Santa Rosalía because Tacho could not afford to hire a priest or a judge to come to San Francisco. A simple fiesta was held at Rancho San Antonio when the couple and their parents returned.

Tacho's older brother, Ignacio, had married a year or more earlier and had started a tiny goat ranch at Las Calabazas, some four miles west of San Antonio and at the same four-thousand-foot elevation. Tacho and Ramona moved to Calabazas and built a ramada, a house of trunks, branches, and palm thatch that initiates nearly every new settlement. Tacho had little patience with herding and milking goats. He had been grateful to leave these chores at his father's ranch ten years before, but he did relish taking cheese and meat to San Ignacio and returning with *mercancía* (merchandise). Soon he added another source of income. Taking extra burros, he collected firewood on the way to town and found a ready market. Indeed, turning to the trade of a *leñero*, a wood gatherer, served Tacho in some of the worst economic crises of the area and his life. His energy and persistence made him successful at this tiring and unattractive pursuit. His sons learned the lesson and helped themselves in the same way.

Tacho and Ramona began to raise a family, but not without sacrifice and tragedy. After a stillbirth and a miscarriage, their daughter Loreta was born in 1938 and named for her godfather, Loreto Arce of Rancho San Gregorio. In 1940 the couple had a son,

Felipe, then a further series of heartbreaks. Six children were lost before sons Candelario and Ramón were born in 1946 and 1947 and remained healthy. There was no medical service in the sierra, and its people had found it difficult to go into towns and await treatment. Fortunately, problems like those that afflicted Tacho and Ramona were relatively rare. Most sierra couples had eight or ten children and raised all but one or two. Tacho did what he could. He took Ramona and the babies to town and made trips whenever necessary for whatever medicines were prescribed or were believed to be of assistance. He was poor, at best, and became poorer due to medical costs and lost time.

Finally, he turned to the only available source of income that he knew. He took his burros up to the mesas on the south slope of Cerro de La Laguna, the Sierra de San Francisco's highest peak, above six thousand feet. Against that backdrop he and his brothers began to collect mezcales. They built their own beneficio and once again began the risky business of making contraband liquor. They were never apprehended. Tacho was too cautious to go near Santa Rosalía, El Boleo, or the soldiers. He ran his mezcal into San Ignacio or San Lino, the relatively undisciplined suburb across the river. Most of his cargo was purchased by Remigio Camacho, a descendant of an Indian henchman of Tacho's great-great-grandfather, Buenaventura Arce. When the medical crises of Tacho's family were past, the beneficio was abandoned. None of the brothers really had a stomach for danger.

By 1950 Tacho's father was in trouble at San Antonio. The old ranch simply could not support the numbers of goats that the aging Severiano and his brothers, Francisco and Carmen, were trying to run. Much the same problem existed at Rancho Las Calabazas, where Nacho and Tacho had been joined by their younger brother, Loreto. It was decided that Tacho and Ramona would go with his parents and occupy an abandoned El Boleo ranch called El Prospecto in the lowlands, just east of the sierra. The company had run cattle successfully in the area, and Tacho had dreams of building up a herd. A house was built, a few head of cattle were bought, and others were taken in from their owners to be reared for shares. All of the family worked hard at El Prospecto, but the venture soon failed because of drought. In 1953, after three years of effort, Tacho was poorer than ever and had no visible prospects. Casting about for means to feed his family, Tacho, in some desperation, took a job running a ranch at San Carlos Viejo that ironically, had once been a landholding of Buenaventura Arce and was now in possession of another of his descendants, Tacho's distant cousin, Salvador ("Chavalo") Arce, an older brother of Leandro Arce with whom Tacho had partnered in work at Calmallí twenty years earlier.

The four years at San Carlos were the worst, the lowest ebb in Tacho's life. Chavalo Arce was a mean, penurious employer. He paid Tacho and Ramona very low wages and only paid them intermittently. He begrudged them a share of the huerta's crops, and at times the whole family went hungry. At Rancho San Gregorio, Loreto Arce remembered how it was in those days: "We were afraid to send any leather goods out by way of San Carlos. Tacho would eat them!" (this only half-jokingly). Ramona, with a rare flash of anger, called those years "tristes y amargos" (sad and bitter). Tacho toiled away at ranch chores. He cut dates, dried them, and cared for a small herd of cattle, but he came to hate all of it. The only bright spots in his life, besides his family, were friendships with Amado Villavicencio and Manuel Moreno, as well as hunting trips into the nearby ranges of La Reforma and Las Vírgenes, where he was able to bag deer and mountain sheep.

Tacho was not out of Loreto's mold. He did not have a farmer's patience or stay-at-home desires. The meat and skins from his hunting successes helped to support his family, and their pursuit got him away from ranch responsibilities. Before long, he knew the game and the mountains better than anyone. His reputation as a hunter spread over the area, in sierras and towns alike.

When his friend Amado Villavicencio died and Manuel Moreno moved away, Tacho decided to leave Chavalo Arce's employment.

Hunters from the Mexican mainland and the United States were coming into the area and were looking for guides. When Manuel Moreno moved into Rancho Las Vírgenes, on the old wagon road between Santa Rosalía and San Ignacio, he asked Tacho to come and help him. There Tacho worked more as a cowboy than as a farmer. Las Vírgenes's business was selling cheese to manganese miners at the north end of the old El Boleo area. Cattle had to be rounded up constantly and brought to milking pens. Whole herds had to be moved from one grazing area to another. Tacho was happier with the work and the pay, and his friend Manuel Moreno was sympathetic when hunters sought Tacho's services as a guide. By providing a substitute to do his chores, Tacho was free to leave on his own business.

Mule deer are the game for a rancher in and around central Baja California sierras. This animal provides meat and leather in significant quantities. The prospect of encountering deer prompts nearly every man and boy to travel armed with a rifle. But visiting hunters seldom care to stalk deer. The game that attracts them from several continents is *borrego*, the rare bighorn sheep. Heads or horns of this animal are among the most sought-after trophies in the Americas. Bighorn sheep used to range widely over the western United States and northwestern Mexico, but they have been hunted down to a few thousand, most of which live in areas where they are protected by strenuously enforced laws.

Tacho had made himself an authority on borrego haunts and habits all along the eastern sierra slopes from the Sierra de San Juan, near the 28th parallel of latitude, down to the Tres Vírgenes volcanoes. During the 1940s and through the 1960s that area was remote enough that game laws were little enforced. Hunters came without licenses for borrego and got their prizes. They sent other hunters to the area, and Tacho was soon a favored guide. He would arrange for riding and pack animals, get another man to help, and then lead his clients to campsites suitably close to hunting places. Each trip was likely to require a week or ten days' time. Although

A Man of the Mountains

7.18. Every man and boy goes armed for hunting.
The usual game is the common mule deer,
a favorite ranch delicacy and a source of valuable leather.

Tacho charged what now seems to be ridiculously low fees, the guide's pay was high compared to that of a ranch hand.

By 1961, Tacho felt able to strike out on his own again after years of near-servitude. In fact, the move he was to make offered a chance at independence but hardly prosperity. La Esperanza, or "Hope," a ranch abandoned by the El Boleo mining concern, was available for a squatter's claim but required much work in order to be usable. Its only real assets were a reservoir, a corral, and the prize—a well with permanent water.

The location of La Esperanza was especially appealing to Tacho. It lay at the intersection of a complex of roads and trails. The east–west auto road from San Ignacio to Santa Rosalía passed within fifty feet of the corral. Main trails led northwest into the Sierra de San Francisco, and southwest to San Regis and other ranches.

7.19. Tacho Arce visiting a hillside ranch house in the southwest corner of the Sierra de San Juan.

Tacho was a gregarious man, and his life was bound up with travel to and from the sierras. At La Esperanza, most passersby would be his relatives or, at least, his friends, and the commerce of the area would pass his front door.

Rancho La Esperanza was a bargain only in the sense that it was acquired at no initial cost. The area is rocky and sandy. Rains are notoriously intermittent and unreliable. A greater drawback was the prodigious depth of the well, 290 feet and partially caved in at that. Cleaning it out took Tacho and a hired helper nine months of the most exhausting work, but he became philosophical about the effort and expense put into his well. He reasoned that had the well been clear, someone more influential than he would have claimed the ranch before he had the chance.

Although clearing the well required heroic efforts, at least the work had an end. However, because of its depth, the well remained a crushing burden for all the people of La Esperanza. During El Boleo times there had been a windmill, but it had been removed and Tacho could not afford to replace it. Nor could he afford a pump. La Esperanza's residents had to raise water by using a mule or burro to pull a rope attached to a bucket. The bucket, holding seven or eight gallons, was lowered by hand, capsized by an expert jerk of the cord, and then the beast of burden, usually driven by a child, walked along a path until the bucket reached the bar over which the rope was drawn. A man had to wait at the wellhead, lift the bucket to one side, and dump it into a small reservoir that held up to two thousand gallons. All of La Esperanza's water was obtained by this laborious, time-consuming routine. This water had to sustain not only six or eight people, but also whatever livestock was to be reared. Nor did the problem end with labor, since the 300-foot-long well rope wore out in an agonizingly short time and each replacement was expensive.

Fortunately, by the time Tacho took over Rancho La Esperanza, he had help in his immediate family. His eldest son, Felipe, was in his early twenties, and by then he was an experienced hand at most ranch activities. The two younger boys could also help. Ramón became invaluable by the age of sixteen, showing many of his father's talents in handling animals, hunting, and hard work. Their help allowed Tacho to leave for protracted periods during hunting seasons. His guiding fees, paid in cash, were crucially important to family finances. Also, with more hands, wood-gathering became a regular business. Tacho's old friend Frank Fischer, an expatriate German mechanic and fifty-year resident of San Ignacio, had a truck and came regularly to La Esperanza to buy the bundles of wood that the Arce men had collected and tied.

In spite of his long residence, Fischer retained an educated outsider's curiosity about the region. He hunted for the sources of building materials used by Jesuits and Dominicans and collected Indian artifacts. Fischer also became interested in locating rock art and employed Tacho in his searches. The diminutive German was the only qualified auto mechanic in a large area, and he spoke English fluently. In those days before paved roads, it is not surprising that he met nearly every tourist who passed through San Ignacio. Fischer described immense, sharply defined rock paintings to tourists. Before long, he and Tacho Arce were conducting tours of painted sites in the nearby Arroyo del Parral. This was before other local people directed Erle Stanley Gardner to Sierra de San Francisco rock art in 1962. The elderly novelist subsequently brought great publicity to the paintings but was very secretive about their locations. He did not attempt continued explorations, and several years then passed with no significant addition to the knowledge released by Gardner and members of his entourage.

When I first talked to Tacho Arce in 1972, it became apparent that he knew many painted sites that had never been seen by outsiders. For years thereafter, Tacho was instrumental in most of the explorations and information gathering that produced two previous books: my *Cave Paintings of Baja California* (1975), and *La Pintura Rupestre de Baja California*, by my oftentimes sierra companion Enrique Hambleton (1979). Publication of the former

7.20. Tacho Arce leads our cavalcade, crossing a low desert on an eastern approach to the Sierra de San Francisco.

work rearranged Tacho's life. Not long after the book's appearance, the Transpeninsular Highway was completed, and it brought a wave of new tourists, many of whom wished to see the area's great works of ancient art. Tacho soon had opportunities to arrange and guide sightseeing expeditions on an almost continuous basis from midautumn to midspring, the pleasant months in the ancient art-dotted sierras. In this way he found a little prosperity. Finally, in 1980, a used windmill was erected over the well at La Esperanza.

In 1981, an undaunted Eustacio Arce reached the age of seventy. Despite the many hard days of his life and the modest condition of his estate, he was still ebullient and the most resilient and cheerful of men. He rose with a wink and a smile. He never missed an opportunity to exercise a sierra man's penchant for poking fun at everything and everyone, making plays on words and telling stories—*especially* telling stories. His gift for this art, freely shared, has done much to perpetuate old sierra values, to create identity for sierra people, and to make them, however unconsciously, proud of their heritage. Tacho's family and friends have many indelible memories of the man—not grandiose scenes, but human ones, such as an evening at a mountain ranch with Tacho sitting in a candlelit kitchen, surrounded by a family that has not seen him for months, the adults seated in a circle, the youngsters standing behind them, faces shining, rapt, hanging on Tío Tacho's every word.

And fittingly enough, it turned out that many Americans came to know Tacho Arce. Although his means were humbler, this great-great-grandson of Buenaventura Arce outdid his ancestor in the numbers he entertained and sent away in his debt. The mountains and all their contents have created no more vivid memories than the man who opened their doors has.

Much of Tacho's spontaneous wit was so dependent on word-play in Spanish that it cannot be translated. But some stories may give an inkling of his humor—and some insight on sierra culture as well. Tacho often reminisced about the old days before mid-peninsular life was turned topsy-turvy by the paved highway and the influx of new people and ideas. In those slow-moving times, there was a place for everyone in the ancient scheme of things. Old people, or even wanderers or life's worn-out waifs, without families or connections, found a corner to sleep in and a kitchen where they were fed. Tacho recalled a San Ignacio scene in the days of his youth:

> A little old man, tiny and thin, a stranger to all of us, sat every day in the square and smiled at all the people and talked to the regulars who rested in the shade. Mornings and evenings, he walked about with his hat in his hand and was given here a plate of soup and there a place to sleep. He kept all his possessions in a tattered *maleta*, a rolled leather bag, which must have served him for forty years. One day he appeared in a shirt so threadbare and torn that it fluttered on him like ribbons. One of his acquaintances from the square stared so hard at this shirt that the little old man looked down at it himself. "Well, yes," he said, happily enough, "it is all I have—this one and the old one."

7.21. Steep hillside trail crossing the pass between Rancho San Martín and Rancho Pie de la Cuesta in the Sierra de Guadalupe.

There is still a rift between the padres in the towns and the ranchers in the mountains. Priests, during the past century, have usually been Italians and therefore foreign to the area's basic culture as well as its outlying folk. Busy enough with the parishioners under their noses, they had an understandable lack of enthusiasm for the days on steep trails needed to officiate at sierra weddings, fiestas, or imminent deaths. Not surprisingly, Tacho remembered those issues and related events and expressed them with wry

7.22. The kitchen of a sierra ranch is busy all day as a social center and a shop for odd jobs, as well as a place for preparing food and serving meals.

humor rather than bitter rhetoric. Ranch people who had heard Tacho's anecdotes regarding padres prompted him to repeat them, and then waited eagerly for their effects on even a single uninitiated listener. Here is one example.

> Once a priest had to go into the sierra and, at the end of two days, arrived at Rosarito tired of the saddle and out of sorts. When he got to the kitchen, he found only a thin sopa and some beans in preparation, so he suggested stewing one of the chickens he saw pecking about. This was done and he ate with satisfaction and passed the night. As he prepared to leave after breakfast the following morning, the housewife came up to him boldly and asked to be paid for the cock which had gone into the pot. As she was not one of his regular flock, the priest saw no way to refuse. With very little grace, he asked what he should pay. "Thirty pesos," she answered. The priest was taken aback by such a commercial rate. "Are chickens then so rare in these parts?" he asked. "No," she answered, "what is rare in these parts is a priest."

In truth, Tacho's memories seemed boundless and were all recalled in marvelously engaging terms. Many, including the ones that follow, concerned his years as a guide.

One of Tacho's expeditions was ready to take to the trail for the first time when it was discovered that one man had no spurs. Tacho immediately whipped off one of his own as a stopgap measure. The recipient seemed unsure and apologized for inconveniencing the guide. "It is not a problem," said Tacho, "one spur has its usual effect—and the other side of the mule has no choice but to follow."

The same man later had occasion to apologize to Tacho because he could not make his mule go down steep grades at the rate at which others were progressing. "Don't feel bad," advised Tacho, "the poorest riders often go downhill fastest."

On a trip to Santa Teresa, there was little vegetation for the animals to eat for three days and nights. The mules and burros became so sorrowful-looking that someone suggested to Tacho that it was a pity to load them and ride them. "Oh, no," was his response, "they are quite able to carry on. Besides, it is better to count their ribs than our steps."

7.23. Kodalith of a spur. From Maekawa, Sakai, and Hatsutarō, *Kaigai Ibun: A Strange Tale from Overseas*, or, *A New Account of America*, 97. Courtesy Harry Crosby.

Just before a long riding expedition, Tacho's clients were about to make a quick trip by car from Rancho La Esperanza to Santa Rosalía for last-minute odds and ends. Tacho was asked if he needed anything from the city. "Another old wife, nothing more," he called back—within easy earshot of Doña Ramona, naturally!

If Tacho sneezed and no one wished him "¡Salud!," he would wait a couple of beats, then to no one in particular say "¡Gracias!" in a booming, cheerful voice.

On returning from a two-week trip where he served as Tacho's assistant, young Chuy Ojeda had sores on his wrists from rope burns. Someone at La Esperanza remarked about them with a question in his voice. Before Chuy could answer, Tacho cut in, "We had to hobble him to keep him in at night."

Once a trip projected to last a month was stalled at Santa Marta for lack of a couple of burros. An old eccentric named Mata was living there at the time, and he had an ordinary burro. After some hours of other negotiations had failed to produce the needed beasts of burden, Tacho walked over to Mata and asked if he would sell his burro. "Yes, of course," said the jaunty little man. "And how much could it possibly be worth?" Tacho mused aloud. "Three hundred pesos," the man replied. Tacho whistled. "¡*Madre de Dios!* It must have a radio and a spare tire."

7.24. Kodalith of a boy and a mule drawing water from a well.
Courtesy Harry Crosby.

Epilogue

For two centuries after its Hispanic settlement began in 1697, the California peninsula attracted remarkably little attention. In the nineteenth century, when it finally began to enter public awareness, it was the land, not the people, that drew attention. Perhaps it was because these people were not Indians, and early anthropologists showed little interest, since they did not notice any unique or interesting features of their society. Then, before anyone attempted to study this regional subculture, it was diluted or changed in most of its more populated parts. In the north it was overwhelmed by the arrival of many times its number of Mexicans from the interior of the Republic. These people were from very different cultural and ethnic backgrounds. Farther south, in most towns and villages, peninsular ways were pushed aside by foreigners or mainland Mexicans who came to dominate business and social life. In *Californio Portraits: Baja California's Vanishing Culture*, the focus is on the mountain areas where local culture has been least affected, although even there it is in a process of rapid change.

The peninsula's particular Hispanic way of life, like its people, was derived in part from the frontiers of New Spain, where it had already undergone two centuries of adaptation from its original

Spanish model. In Baja California, it was further shaped by isolation, limited raw materials, and restrictions imposed by Church and government. By various quirks of history, these conditions persisted long enough to give Baja California's people a distinctive cultural stamp, but perhaps not distinctive enough to have its imminent demise mourned by anthropologists. This subculture lacked some of the more obvious features that make peoples and regions prime candidates for appreciation and study. For example, the decorative arts do not seem to have developed, except for a few pale imitations of mainland styles. Homes traditionally were without architectural embellishments or painted-on decoration, clothing was simple, and leather items were left plain or tooled perfunctorily in basic patterns. Music and dance were influenced mainly by visiting sailors or immigrants and thus had little regional flavor. Written literature was nonexistent, since literacy itself has always been of the simplest sort. Oral history did not produce stories that were preserved in poetry. Even superstitions were few.

One might conclude from a checklist of standard cultural traits that Baja California culture was drab and that it developed among unimaginative people. But that conclusion would overlook a mass of less tangible, more subjective evidence. Many foreigners who visited the peninsula as early as two centuries ago found much to admire in Baja California people. A recurrent theme in their accounts was flattering comparisons between the people of the peninsula and those of the Mexican mainland. They also noted a certain independence of spirit. The region did not generate dominant leaders. Instead, its people have avoided being led for 150 years. If their society has lacked a power structure, it has also avoided some of the more usual homegrown tragedies. For example, there have been no blood feuds and no lynchings. Neighbor has not turned against neighbor, and strangers are objects of interest, not of fear or suspicion. In the 1890s, Gustav Eisen, of the California Academy of Sciences, made several long trips to remote places on the peninsula. He wrote, "As regards the people, it can be said that they are very friendly and hospitable. . . . There is not the

Epi.1. Created for no weightier purpose than entertaining and housing visitors, the welcoming corredor at Rancho La Soledad shows typically unadorned peninsular folk architecture. However, it also displays the handsome lines and elegant handwork that characterize most products of traditional crafts in the sierras of Baja California.

Epi.2. Kodalith of a horse.
Courtesy Harry Crosby.

least danger to anyone and even the most inexperienced traveler need have no fear."[1]

"Friendly" and "hospitable" are insufficient as descriptive words. The mountain people are good-natured in the best and fullest sense of the term, not merely by nature but as a cultivated trait that one generation encourages in the next. Children learn by example. The generally positive attitude of sierra youth mirrors the quality of their families' influence, but that attitude only begins to demonstrate how deep that influence is. In sierra life, family is the warm, robust, and highly organized heart. Family is the matrix in which everyone matures and continues to have a place. Oral traditions, arising from the home and extending their influence, preserve minute details of people's lives, their triumphs and trials, their joys and mishaps. This Baja California subculture imparts an astonishing amount of personal identity to each of its participants, an identity whose impact is reinforced by the fact that it lasts long after death.

---

1. Eisen, "Explorations in the Central Part of Baja California," 420.

This persistence has a powerful and positive influence on each person's social behavior. There has been little cruelty and less crime in the sierra. The people have a real concern for reputation, and that is based more on a person's character than on material success. These habits of the mind and heart have enabled the mountain people, as money-poor as they were, to take pride in themselves and in those things they had in plenty. Only with the coming of the roads and the beginnings of a desire for manufactured objects has this pride withered somewhat.

The greater modern world suffers from overcrowding, crime, pollution, and overdependence on a myriad of factors beyond everyone's control. In this climate, it would be simple to romanticize Baja California's fast-disappearing regionalism because until recently its people seemed to have escaped most of these difficulties. They lived in such harmony with their land that it might seem that their idyll, if left alone, could go on forever. Realistically, no such projection could have been made. Even if modern life had not found the peninsula and seized it for profit and pleasure, the land of traditional folkways could not have accommodated a much larger population.

However, much about sierra life remains admirable and thought provoking. This small society demonstrates the effectiveness of family life, personal identity, and a tight-knit social structure in preventing crime and the need for assistance from outside agencies. These people's attitudes and accomplishments remind us of the self-reliance popularly associated with our country's own lost frontier and pioneer experiences. But the example set by the mountain people is still present. In the face of so many hardships, they are hardworking people with time for companionship and laughter.

The old California culture is not gone. In the sierras, its influences will be felt for a long time. Some people cling to their traditions and resist changing their rhythms. But clearly an era is ending. The forces that guided the early settlers are losing their strength. Everything has an end.

Among the people of the sierras, there is this saying:

> "Hasta aquí el molino; cada quien por su camino."
> "This is as far as the old mill grinds; every man now his own path finds."

Glossary

Aguaje	Spring or waterhole.
Aguardiente	A distilled liquor made from local alcoholic ferments. In Jesuit California, a grape brandy, a product of several missions.
Alcalde	A local magistrate, usually a member of the municipal council.
Alférez	An ensign; the lowest-ranked military officer, approximately equal to today's rank of second lieutenant.
Alforjas	Pairs of rawhide boxes or hampers slung on either side of a pack animal to contain its load.
Andariego	A rover or wanderer, a restless soul.
Aparejo	A packsaddle made from two thicknesses of leather sewed at their edges. It was draped over the back of pack animals and offered little padding at the spine but, on each side, provided a large pouch, stuffed with straw, to protect the beasts' vulnerable ribs.
Arriero	A muleteer, a driver of pack animals.
Arroyo	A major seasonal watercourse; a creek or stream.
Beneficio	A mezcal works; the place and all equipment used in making distilled liquor from agave hearts.

Boleo	Literally, ball. Word used by the Californios to describe nodules of copper ore.
Borrego	North American mountain sheep (*Ovis canadensis*).
Burro	Small donkey used as a pack animal.
Cal	Lime in powder form, prepared by grinding kiln-fired pieces of limestone. Used for mortar, in leather curing, and as an ingredient in tortilla making.
Californio	Regional name for a non-Indian inhabitant of California. All gente de razón reared or, later, born and reared in California were Californios. The term had been used in Antigua California since 1700 and came into popular use in Alta California by the 1820s, with the growth of the first generation of California-born Mexicans.
Cambiadero	Literally, "one who moves about"; a goat rancher who depends on temporary water supplies and makes planned annual moves as resources are exhausted.
Camino real	A principal road or trail for mounted travelers or pack trains. Originally, a road built or maintained by the Crown.
Cañada	A side canyon; a short, steep watercourse tributary to an arroyo.
Capitán-gobernador	Captain-governor.
Carrizo	A giant grass or false cane (*Phragmites communis*) commonly found growing in permanent springs or streams and used as an indication of immediate subsurface water; the stems were used as a material for thatched roofs, woven infill walls, sleeping mats, coarse baskets, etc.
Chayote	A squashlike member of the cucumber family (*Sechium edule*) of Caribbean origin.
Chubasco	A violent, cyclonic summer storm usually associated with torrential but localized rainfall; common to the Sea of Cortez and surrounding lands.

Colache	A syrupy preserve of any soft fruit, such as peaches, guavas, or papayas.
Color quebrado	Refers to the range of hues apparent in the skin of people with varying amounts of African, Indian, and European blood.
Comal	A flat sheet of earthenware or metal for cooking tortillas.
Compadrazgo	A kinship or relationship between a child's parents and his or her godparents.
Conquistador	Conqueror; term applied to those who led the Spanish conquest of Mexico and Peru in the sixteenth century.
Corredor	A covered, open-sided porch; at a ranch, the corredor serves as the principal meeting and visiting place.
Coyote	Coyote or wolf.
Enjambre	A wild beehive; if accessible, a regular source of honey.
Español	Literally, a Spaniard; on the northwestern frontiers of New Spain in the seventeenth and eighteenth centuries, a person of primarily European blood with the cultural characteristics of a Spaniard; a person considered worthy to be recognized as white, regardless of heritage from other racial stocks.
Falluca	A term that originally was applied to contraband goods. Later it was used for store-bought goods (clothing, utensils, yardage, etc.).
Falluquero	Originally, a term used to describe a smuggler. Later, used to describe one who rides to ranches to sell or trade goods.
Fandango	A Spanish courtship dance in triple time; at the Spanish Colonial frontiers it was a lavish and boisterous social event.
Fiesta	A celebration, festivity.
Gambusino	A hand miner.
Gente de razón	Literally, "people with the capacity to reason"; any non-Indian.

Gracias	Thank you.
Guatamote	An arroyo shrub (*Baccharis glutinosa*) whose straight stems are used to make baskets.
Güéribo	The giant poplar (*Populus brandegeei*) indigenous to the higher sierras of central and southern peninsular California; in Jesuit times its wood was used for shipbuilding.
Hacienda	A rural property typically devoted to raising sheep or cattle. As a unit of measurement, equivalent to five square leagues or 21,690 acres. Also, very large estates were generally called haciendas. Variable factors defining haciendas included capital, labor, land, markets, technology, and social recognition.
Horno	An oven.
Huacal	Homemade crates made from the straight stems of guatamote and bound at the edges and corners with rawhide thongs.
Huerta	A kitchen garden, orchard, or both.
Huitlacoche	A California thrush.
Jarabe	A folk dance for couples, popular in central and southern Mexico, notably in the state of Jalisco. Derived in colonial times from Spanish popular music and dances such as fandangos. The jarabe was also influenced by native Mexican couple dances imitating the courtship of doves.
Jícama	Large, white-fleshed tuber of the species *Pachyrhyzus*, used as a food.
Jota	A Spanish dance in fast triple time, usually to a guitar and voice accompaniment.
Lechuza	An owl.
Leñero	One who gathers firewood.
Madre de Dios	Mother of God.
Maleta	A suitcase.
Mano	A handstone used to grind on a metate, or mortar.
Mantilla	A woman's shawl or scarf.

Masa	Corn treated with limewater, ground to coarse flour, and mixed with water to create the dough from which tortillas are made.
Mayordomo	A foreman or supervisor of a mission under the padre, or of a ranch under the owner.
Mercancía	Merchandise; staple foods, dry goods, etc., purchased at a store.
Mestizo	A person of mixed European and Indian heritage.
Metate	A grindstone or mortar, used with a mano as an all-purpose grinding or mashing tool.
Mezcal	Any of several agave plants; a liquor distilled from fermented agave hearts.
Mezcalero	A person who makes mezcal.
Mezquite	A local hardwood; common name for several species of leguminous plants (*Prosopis palmeri*).
Música norteña	The characteristic country music popular all over northern Mexico.
Muy bronco	When referring to animals, *muy bronco* means wild or not yet broken. When referring to humans, it means coarse or rough around the edges.
Palo blanco	A multitrunked tree with white bark (*Lysiloma candida*); different parts of the plant serve as building material, tanbark, and medicine; chips of its bark, fresh cut, are brewed with water to make the peninsula's basic leather-tanning fluid.
Panocha	Cakes of crude brown sugar made by boiling down cane pressings; the staple sweet of New Spain's frontierspeople and poor.
Pardo	An eighteenth-century term for a person of dark skin color, or a person of mixed race.
Peninsulares	People born and raised on the Baja California peninsula.
Pila	A small reservoir used to accumulate water during the night so that the volume needed for irrigating a planted area was available as needed; a tank made of masonry to hold water.

Pitahaya dulce	*Lemaireocereus thurheri*, the tallest and most common organ-pipe cactus, whose summer and early fall maturing fruit formed the major part of the Indian diet; an important food crop for native peoples and Hispanic pioneers alike.
Polainas	Leather leggings worn as protection against spines, snakes, etc.; universal garb for men in Baja California's central mountains.
Pulque	An alcoholic drink made by fermenting a watery slurry of roasted mezcal hearts.
Ramada	Literally, a house of branches; a simple structure made by setting forked posts in the ground as corners, laying other posts across them as superstructure, and roofing the whole with thatch.
Ranchería	An organized, autonomous band of hunting and gathering Indians occupying a well-defined territory; after mission contact, such a band was named for the principal geographical site in its territory.
Represa	An artificial pool formed by damming a section of a watercourse that has a solid rock bed.
Salud	Literally, health; an interjection after a person has sneezed ("Bless you") or as a toast ("Cheers").
Sombrero	A hat.
Sopa	Soup.
Subdelegado	A government representative.
Sur, El	Literally, the south. Refers to the cape region of Baja California.
Templo	Church or temple.
Tequila	A form of mezcal made from the blue agave plant.
Tina	A tub or vat.
Tinaja	A water catchment in the bedrock of a watercourse; a cask of about eleven-gallon capacity.
Tinta	Ink.
Tromba	Localized cloudbursts.

Vaquero	A cowherd; on the peninsula, primarily one who rounds up cattle that have spread out untended.
Vecino	A neighbor; a resident of a town.
Venado	A deer.
Zaya	A parsniplike plant (*Amoreuxia* species) found on mesas and used as food.

Bibliography

This bibliography has been compiled by the series editors. We took Harry Crosby's original bibliography for the first edition of Last of the Californios and supplemented it with the work he used to revise that edition. In addition, we have included relevant books and articles from the bibliography we prepared for the Guía de manuscritos cited below. We hope in this way to assist scholars and others interested in the history of Baja California during its colonial and early national periods.

Aguilar Marco, José Luis, et al. *Misiones en la península de Baja California*. Mexico City: Instituto Nacional de Antropología e Historia, 1991.

Aguirre, Amado. *Contribución para la historia de la Baja California: Compilación de datos y documentos ordenada por el gobernador del territorio sur de la Baja California*. La Paz: 1928.

———. *Documentos para la historia de Baja California*. Introductory study by Miguel León-Portilla. Mexico City: Universidad Nacional Autónoma de México, Instituto de Investigaciones Históricas; Tijuana: Universidad Autónoma de Baja California, Centro de Investigaciones Históricas, 1977.

Aguirre Bernal, Celso. *Breve historia del estado de Baja California*. Mexico City: Ediciones Quinto Sol, 1987.

———. *Geografía básica del estado de Baja California*. Mexicali: Celso Aguirre Bernal, 1990.

Alric, Henry J. A. *Sketches of a Journey on the Two Oceans and to the Interior of America and of a Civil War in Northern Lower California*. Translation from the French by Norah E. Jones; edited and with introduction and notes by Doyce B. Nunis, Jr. Baja California Travels Series, 24. Los Angeles: Dawson's Book Shop, 1971.

Altman, Ida, and James Lockhart. *Provinces of Early Mexico: Variants of Spanish American Regional Evolution*. Los Angeles: UCLA Latin American Center Publications, University of California, 1976.

Álvarez, José Rogelio. *Diccionario enciclopédico de Baja California*. Mexico City: Compañía Editora de Enciclopedias de México; Instituto de Cultura de Baja California, 1989.

Álvarez, Robert R. *Familia: Migration and Adaptation in Baja and Alta California, 1800–1975*. Berkeley: University of California Press, 1987.

Álvarez de Williams, Anita. *Primeros pobladores de la Baja California: Introducción a la antropología de la península*. Mexicali: Talleres Gráficos del Gobierno del Estado de Baja California, 1975.

———, comp. *Travelers among the Cucupá*. Baja California Travels Series, 35. Los Angeles: Dawson's Book Shop, 1975.

Amao Manríquez, Jorge Luis. *Mineros, misioneros y rancheros de la Antigua California*. Mexico City: Instituto Nacional de Antropología e Historia; Editorial Plaza y Valdés, 1997.

Andrews, Thomas, ed. *English Privateers at Cabo San Lucas: The Descriptive Accounts of Puerto Seguro by Edward Cooke and Woodes Rogers*. Comments by George Shelvocke and William Betagh. Baja California Travels Series, 41. Los Angeles: Dawson's Book Shop, 1979.

Archer, Christon I. *The Army in Bourbon Mexico, 1760–1810*. Albuquerque: University of New Mexico Press, 1977.

Arrillaga, José Joaquín de. *José Joaquín de Arrillaga: Diary of His Surveys of the Frontier, 1796*. Translated by Froylan Tiscareño; edited by John W. Robinson. Baja California Travels Series, 17. Los Angeles: Dawson's Book Shop, 1969.

Aschmann, Homer. *The Central Desert of Baja California, Demography and Ecology*. Berkeley and Los Angeles: University of California Press, 1959.

———. *The Natural and Human History of Baja California*. Baja California Travels Series, 7. Los Angeles: Dawson's Book Shop, 1966.

Atondo y Antillón, Isidro. *First from the Gulf to the Pacific: The Diary of the Kino-Atondo Peninsular Expedition, December 14, 1684–January 13, 1685*. Transcribed, translated, and edited by W. Michael Mathes. Baja California Travels Series, 16. Los Angeles: Dawson's Book Shop, 1969.

Auger, Edouard. *Voyage en Californie (1852–1853)*. Paris: L. Hachette et Cie., 1854.

Bibliography

Baegert, Johann Jakob. *The Letters of Jacob Baegert, 1749–1761.* Edited and with an introduction by Doyce B. Nunis, Jr.; translated by Elsbeth Schulz-Bischof. Baja California Travels Series, 45. Los Angeles: Dawson's Book Shop, 1982.

———. *Noticias de la península americana de California.* Introductory notes by W. Michael Mathes and Raul Antonio Cota; translated from the German by Pedro R. Hendrichs. 2nd ed. La Paz: Gobierno del Estado de Baja California Sur, 1989.

———. *Observations in Lower California.* Translation, introduction, and notes by M. M. Brandenburg and Carl L. Baumann. Berkeley and Los Angeles: University of California Press, 1952.

Bancroft, Hubert Howe. *The History of California.* 7 vols. San Francisco: The History Company, 1884–90.

———. *The History of the Northern Mexican States and Texas.* 2 vols. San Francisco: The History Company, 1884.

Barbosa E., Lupita. *From Velicatá to San Diego—De Velicatá a San Diego.* Mexico City: Editorial Luz y Arte, 1984.

Barco, Miguel del. *Ethnology and Linguistics of Baja California.* Translated by Froylan Tiscareño; introduction and notes by Miguel León-Portilla. Baja California Travels Series, 44. Los Angeles: Dawson's Book Shop, 1981.

———. *Historia natural y crónica de la Antigua California.* Edited and with introduction, notes, and appendixes by Miguel León-Portilla, with additional writings by Barco. Mexico City: Universidad Nacional Autónoma de México, Instituto de Investigaciones Históricas, 1988.

———. *The Natural History of Baja California.* Translated by Froylan Tiscareño; introduction by Miguel León-Portilla. Baja California Travels Series, 43. Los Angeles: Dawson's Book Shop, 1980.

Bartlett, John Russell. *Personal Narrative of Explorations and Incidents in Texas, New Mexico, California, Sonora and Chihuahua connected with the United States and Mexican Boundary Commission during the years 1850, '51, '52, and '53.* 2 vols. New York: Appleton and Company, 1854.

Bayle, Constantino. *Misión de la Baja California.* Madrid: Editorial Católica, 1946.

Beebe, Rose Marie, and Robert M. Senkewicz, eds. *Guía de manuscritos concernientes a Baja California en las colecciones de la biblioteca Bancroft.* Guadalajara: Published for The Bancroft Library, University of California, Berkeley, by Ediciones de la Noche, 2002.

Bendímez, Mary Julieta. "Wenceslaus Linck y la última frontera jesuita en Baja California." *Meyibó* 2, no. 6 (December 1985): 73–85.

Bendímez-Patterson, Julia. "Antecedentes históricos de los indígenas de Baja California." *Estudios fronterizos* 5, no. 14 (September–December 1987): 11–45.

Bennett, Frederick Debell. *Narrative of a Whaling Voyage Round the Globe from the Year 1833 to 1836.* 2 vols. Amsterdam: N. Israel; New York: Da Capo Press, 1970.

Bernabéu Albert, Salvador. "La religión ofendida: Resistencia y rebeliones indígenas en la Baja California colonial." *Revista complutense de historia de América* 20 (1994): 169–80.

Bolton, Herbert Eugene, ed. "The Iturbide Revolution in the Californias." *Hispanic American Historical Review* 2, no. 2 (May 1919): 188–242.

———. *Rim of Christendom: A Biography of Eusebio Francisco Kino, Pacific Coast Pioneer.* Foreword by John L. Kessell. Tucson: University of Arizona Press, 1984.

Boneu Companys, Fernando. *De Catalunya a California: Gaspar de Portolá.* Lérida, Spain: Diputación de Lérida, 1986.

———. *Documentos secretos de la expedición de Portolá a California: Juntas de Guerra.* Lérida, Spain: Instituto de Estudios Ilerdenses, 1973.

———. *Don Gaspar de Portolá: Conquistador y primer gobernador de California.* Lérida, Spain: Instituto de Estudios Ilerdenses, 1970.

———. *Don Gaspar de Portolá: El noble militar leridano, descubridor y primer gobernador de California.* Madrid: Publicaciones Españolas, 1970.

———. *Gaspar de Portolá: Explorer and Founder of California.* Translated and revised by Alan K. Brown. Lérida, Spain: Instituto de Estudios Ilerdenses, 1983.

Bowman, J. N. "History of the Provincial Archives of California." *Southern California Quarterly* 64, no. 1 (1982): 1–97.

Browne, John Ross. "Explorations in Lower California." *Harper's Magazine* 37 (October 1868): 577–91; 38 (November 1868): 9–23.

———. *Explorations in Lower California.* Tucson: Arizona Silhouettes, 1952.

———. *Resources of the Pacific Slope: A Statistical and Descriptive Summary of the Mines and Minerals, Climate, Topography, Agriculture, Commerce, Manufactures, and Miscellaneous Productions of the States and Territories West of the Rocky Mountains. With a Sketch of the Settlement and Exploration of Lower California.* New York: Appleton and Company, 1869.

Buffum, Edward Gould. *Six Months in the Gold Mines: From a Journal of Three Years Residence in Upper and Lower California, 1847–49.* Philadelphia: Lea and Blanchard, 1850.

Bull, James Hunter. *Journey of James H. Bull, Baja California, October 1843 to January 1844.* Edited by Doyce B. Nunis, Jr. Baja California Travels Series, 1. Los Angeles: Dawson's Book Shop, 1965.

Burrus, Ernest J., ed. *Jesuit Relations, Baja California, 1716–1762.* Baja California Travels Series, 47. Los Angeles: Dawson's Book Shop, 1984.

———. *Kino and Manje, Explorers of Sonora and Arizona: A Study of Their Expeditions and Plans.* Rome: Jesuit Historical Institute, 1971.

———. *Kino and the Cartography of Northwestern New Spain.* Tucson: Arizona Pioneers' Historical Society, 1965.

———, ed. *Kino's Plan for the Development of Pimería Alta, Arizona, and Upper California: A Report to the Mexican Viceroy.* Tucson: Arizona Pioneers' Historical Society, 1962.

———. *La obra cartográfica de la Provincia Mexicana de la Compañía de Jesús, 1567–1967.* Madrid: Ediciones José Porrúa Turanzas, 1967.

———. *Misiones norteñas mexicanas de la Compañía de Jesús, 1751–1757.* Mexico City: Antigua Librería Robredo de José Porrúa e Hijos, Sucs., 1963.

Burrus, Ernest J., and Félix Zubillaga, eds. *Misiones mexicanas de la Compañía de Jesús, 1618–1745: Cartas e informes conservadas en la "Colección Mateu."* Madrid: Ediciones José Porrúa Turanzas, 1982.

———, eds. *El noroeste de México: Documentos sobre las misiones jesuíticas, 1600–1769.* Mexico City: Universidad Autónoma Nacional de México, 1986.

Caballero Carranco, Juan. *The Pearl Hunters in the Gulf of California, 1668: Summary Report of the Voyage Made to the Californias by Captain Francisco de Lucenilla.* Translated and edited and with an introduction by W. Michael Mathes. Baja California Travels Series, 4. Los Angeles: Dawson's Book Shop, 1966.

California. Junta de Fomento. *Plan para el arreglo de las misiones de los territorios de la Alta y de la Baja California propuesto por la Junta de Fomento de aquella península.* Mexico City: Imprenta de Galván a cargo de Mariano Arévalo, 1827.

Cariño Olvera, Martha Micheline. *Historia de las relaciones hombre-naturaleza en Baja California Sur (1500–1940).* La Paz: Universidad Autónoma de Baja California Sur; Promarco, 1996.

Carron de Fleury, S. E. L. "Notas geológicas y estadísticas sobre Sonora y la Baja California. Situación geográfica. Descripción Física. Origen de la población actual." *Boletín de la sociedad mexicana de geografía y estadística* 2, no. 1 (1869): 44–52.

Castañares, Manuel. *Colección de documentos relativos al departamento de Californias*. Mexico City: Imprenta de la Voz del Pueblo, 1845.

Castillo Negrete, Francisco. "Geografía y estadística de la Baja California, 1853." *Boletín de la Sociedad Mexicana de Geografía y Estadística* 1, no. 7 (1859): 338–59.

Castro Agúndez, Jesús. *Patria chica*. La Paz, Mexico: n.p., 1958.

———. *Resumen histórico de Baja California Sur*. Mexico City: YOLVA, 1986.

Chapman, Charles E. *A History of California: The Spanish Period*. New York: Macmillan, 1921.

Chaput, Donald, William M. Mason, and David Zárate Loperena. *Modest Fortunes: Mining in Northern Baja California*. Baja California Travels Series, 51. Los Angeles: Natural History Museum of Los Angeles County, 1992.

Cheape, G. C. *Letter from Captain G. C. Cheape: Descriptive of a Trip Made by Him on a Portion of the Territory of the International Company of Mexico, Dated 27th June, 1886*. London: Henmen and Sons, 1886.

Clavigero, Francisco Xavier. *Historia de la Antigua o Baja California*. Edición de Miguel León-Portilla. Mexico City: Editorial Porrúa, SA, 1990.

———. *The History of [Lower] California*. Translated from the Italian and edited by Sara E. Lake and A. A. Gray. Palo Alto, Calif.: Stanford University Press, 1937.

Cleland, Robert Glass. *A History of California: The American Period*. New York: Macmillan, 1922.

Clyde, Norman. *El Picacho del Diablo: The Conquest of Lower California's Highest Peak, 1932 and 1937*. Introduction and bibliography by John W. Robinson. Photographs by Nathan Clark. Baja California Travels Series, 36. Los Angeles: Dawson's Book Shop, 1975.

Combier, Cyprien. *Voyage au Golfe de Californie*. Paris: A. Bertrand, 1864.

Contribución para la historia de la Baja California. Compilación de datos ordenada por el Sr. Gral. Amado Aguirre, Gobernador del Distrito Sur de la Baja California. Cuaderno número 1. La Paz: Talleres Tipográficos del Gobierno del Distrito, 1928.

Cook, Sherburne F. *The Extent and Significance of Disease among the Indians of Baja California, 1697–1773*. Ibero-Americana 12. Berkeley: University of California Press, 1937.

Coronado, Eligio Moisés. *Los apuntes históricos de Manuel Clemente Rojo sobre Baja California*. La Paz: Gobierno del Estado de Baja California Sur, 1996.

———. *Baja California Sur*. La Paz: Imprenta Israel, 1986.

———. *Descripción e inventarios de las misiones de Baja California, 1773*. Presentation by B. Font Obrador; prologue by W. Michael Mathes. Palma de Mallorca: Institut d'Estudis Balearics, 1987.

———. *La diputación territorial de Baja California en 1835*. La Paz: H. Congreso del Estado de Baja California Sur, 1978.

———. "Dos de octubre de 1847, Mulegé: Baluarte de México en sudcalifornia." *Panorama* 11 (January–February 1979): 16–19.

———. "Franciscanos en Baja California." *Some Reminiscences about Fray Junípero Serra*. Edited by Francis J. Weber. Glendale: Published for the California Catholic Conference by the Knights of Columbus, 1985.

———. *Heróico Mulegé*. La Paz: Archivo Histórico "Pablo L. Martínez" de Baja California Sur, 1980.

Costansó, Miguel. *Diario histórico*. Facsimile of the 1771 original reproduced in *The Costansó Narrative of the Portolá Expedition: First Chronicle of the Spanish Conquest of Alta California*. Translated and edited by Ray Brandes. Newhall, Calif.: Hogarth Press, 1970.

Cota Sandoval, José Andrés. *Archivo Histórico de Baja California Sur "Pablo L. Martínez," Catálogo, Ramo I, La Colonia 1744–1821*. Cuaderno de Divulgación, 40. La Paz: Gobierno del Territorio de Baja California Sur, Dirección General de Acción Social y Cultural, 1974.

———. *De la rebelión indígena a la independencia: Dos ensayos sudcalifornianos*. Loreto: Colegio de Bachilleres del Estado de Baja California Sur, 1997.

Cota Sandoval, José Andrés, Antonio Padilla Corona, and Jorge Martínez Zepeda. *Santa Rosalía, Baja California Sur: Tres enfoques históricos*. Santa Rosalía, Baja California Sur: VII Ayuntamiento de Mulegé. Tijuana: Universidad Autónoma de Baja California, Instituto de Investigaciones Históricas, 1992.

Coyle, Jeanette, and Norman C. Roberts. *A Field Guide to the Common and Interesting Plants of Baja California*. La Jolla, Calif.: Natural History Publishing Co., 1975.

Crosby, Harry W. *Antigua California: Mission and Colony on the Peninsular Frontier, 1697–1768*. Albuquerque: University of New Mexico Press, 1994.

———. *The Cave Paintings of Baja California*. San Diego: Sunbelt Publications, 1997.

———. *Doomed to Fail: Gaspar de Portolá's First California Appointees*. Border Series Studies, 2. San Diego: Institute for Regional Studies of the Californias, 1989.

———. *Gateway to Alta California: The Expedition to San Diego, 1769*. San Diego: Sunbelt Publications, 2003.

———. *The King's Highway in Baja California*. San Diego: Copley Books, 1974.

———. *Last of the Californios*. San Diego: Copley Books, 1981.

———. *Los últimos californios*. Translated and with an introduction by Enrique Hambleton. La Paz: Gobierno del Estado de Baja California Sur, 1992.

———, ed. "The 1849 Journal of W. C. S. Smith: From San José del Cabo to San Diego." In *Gold Rush Desert Trails to San Diego and Los Angeles in 1849, Brand Book Number Nine*, edited by George M. Ellis, 126–50. San Diego: San Diego Corral of Westerners, 1995.

Cruz, Francisco Santiago. *Baja California, biografía de una península*. México Heróico, 99. Mexico City: Editorial Jus, 1969.

Cunningham, William H. *Log of the "Courier," 1826–28*. Early California Travels Series, 44. Los Angeles: Glen Dawson, 1958.

Decorme, Gerard. *La obra de los jesuitas mexicanos durante la época colonial, 1572–1767*. Mexico City: Antigua Librería Robredo de J. Porrúa e Hijos, 1941.

De Kay, Drake. *In Relation to Occurrences at Magdalena Bay, Lower California, Mexico, 1871*. San Francisco: E. Bosqui and Company, 1871.

De la Torre Villalpando, Guadalupe, Juan Antonio Siller Camacho, and Nora Gabriela Álvarez Pliego. *Catálogo nacional, monumentos históricos inmuebles*. Mexico City: Secretaría de Educación Pública; Instituto Nacional de Antropología e Historia; Programa Cultural de las Fronteras, 1986.

Díaz, Marco. *Arquitectura en el desierto: Misiones jesuitas en Baja California*. Mexico City: Universidad Nacional Autónoma de México, 1986.

Díaz Mercado, Joaquín. *Bibliografía sumaria de la Baja California*. Bibliografías Mexicanas, 2. Mexico City: DAPP, 1937.

Diguet, León. *Territorio de la Baja California, reseña geográfica y estadística*. Mexico City and Paris: Librería de la Viuda de Ch. Bouret, 1912.

Dimayuga, Rosalba Encarnación. *Medicina tradicional y popular de Baja California Sur*. La Paz: Secretaría de Educación Pública; Universidad Autónoma de Baja California Sur, 1996.

Dobyns, Henry F. *Spanish Colonial Tucson: A Demographic History*. Tucson: University of Arizona Press, 1976.

Ducrue, Benno. *Ducrue's Account of the Expulsion of the Jesuits from Lower California*. In Latin and English. Translated and edited by Ernest J. Burrus. Rome: Jesuit Historical Institute, 1967.

Dunne, Peter Masten. *Black Robes in Lower California*. Berkeley and Los Angeles: University of California Press, 1952.

———. "The Record Book of a Lower California Mission." *Mid-America* 29, no. 3 (1947): 185–200.

Du Pont, Samuel Francis. *Extracts from Private Journal Letters of Captain S. F. Du Pont while in command of the "Cyane," during the War with Mexico, 1846–1848*. Printed for the family. Wilmington, Del.: 1885.

———. *Official Dispatches and Letters of Rear Admiral Du Pont, U.S.N., 1846–1848, 1861–1863*. Wilmington, Del.: Press of Ferris Brothers, 1883.

Du Shane, Helen. *The Baja California Travels of Charles Russell Orcutt*. Baja California Travels Series, 23. Los Angeles: Dawson's Book Shop, 1971.

Echenque March, Felipe I. "Sociedades prehistóricas o históricas en las Californias. Ensayo de un momento de su historicidad." *Estudios fronterizos* 24–25: 161–215.

Eisen, Gustav. "Explorations in the Central Part of Baja California." *Journal of the American Geographical Society of New York* 32, no. 5 (1900): 397–429.

Engelhardt, Zephyrin, Fr. *The Missions and Missionaries of California*. 2nd ed. 4 vols. Santa Barbara: Mission Santa Barbara, 1929.

Engstrand, Iris Wilson. *Royal Officer in Baja California, 1768–1770: Joaquín Velázquez de León*. Drawings by Alexander-Jean Noël. Baja California Travels Series, 37. Los Angeles: Dawson's Book Shop, 1976.

Equihua, Serafín, and Miguel Sánchez. *El puerto de San Felipe, breve relato histórico*. Historia Para Todos, 8. Tijuana: Universidad Autónoma de Baja California, 1983.

Espinoza Arroyo, Alejandro. *Los rosareños: Memorias del nacimiento y vida de un pueblo Baja Californiano, 1774–1992*. El Rosario: Sector Pesquero de El Rosario; Ensenada: Museo de Historia de Ensenada, 1992.

Faulk, Odie B. *The Leather Jacket Soldier; Spanish Military Equipment and Institutions of the Late 18th Century*. Pasadena, Calif.: Socio-Technical Publications, 1971.

Fernández Galiano, María José. *El régimen misional de la Orden de Santo Domingo en las misiones californianas*. Seville: Studium Generale, 1989.

Flores Damasceno, Jorge. *Documentos para la historia de la Baja California*. 2 vols. Papeles Históricos Mexicanos, 2–3. Mexico City: Talleres Gráficos de la Nación, 1940–1946.

Forbes, Alexander. *California: A History of Upper and Lower California from their First Discovery to the Present Time*. London: Smith, Elder and Company, 1839.

Gastélum Arce, Roberto. *Centenario de Santa Rosalía, 1885–1985*. La Paz: Edición del Gobierno del Estado de Baja California Sur, 1985.

Geiger, Maynard. *Franciscan Missionaries in Hispanic California, 1769–1848: A Biographical Dictionary*. San Marino, Calif.: Huntington Library, 1969.

———. *Palóu's Life of Fray Junípero Serra*. Washington, D.C.: Academy of American Franciscan History, 1955.

Gerhard, Peter. "Gabriel González: Last Dominican in Baja California." *Pacific Historical Review* 21 (1953): 123–27.

———. *A Guide to the Historical Geography of New Spain*. Rev. ed. Norman: University of Oklahoma Press, 1993.

———. "Misiones de Baja California." *Historia Mexicana* 3, no. 4 (1954): 600–605.

———. *The North Frontier of New Spain*. Princeton, N.J.: Princeton University Press, 1982.

———. "Pearl Diving in Lower California, 1533–1830." *Pacific Historical Review* 25 (1956): 239–49.

———. *Pirates in Baja California*. Tlapalán, Mexico: Editorial Tlilán, 1963.

Gerhard, Peter, and Howard E. Gulick. *Lower California Guidebook: A Descriptive Traveler's Guide*. 4th ed. with revision notes. Glendale, Calif.: Arthur H. Clark Company, 1967.

Gerhard, Peter, and W. Michael Mathes. "Peregrinaciones de los registros de misiones de Baja California." *Calafia* 8, no. 4 (1996): 7–11.

———. "Peregrinations of the Baja California Mission Registers." *The Americas* 52, no. 1 (July 1995): 71–80.

Gibson, Charles. *Spain in America*. New York: Harper & Row, 1966.

Gómez Canedo, Lino. *De México a la Alta California: Una gran epopeya misional*. Mexico City: Editorial Jus, 1969.

———. *Un lustro de administración franciscana en Baja California*. La Paz: Gobierno del Estado de Baja California Sur, Dirección de Cultura, 1983.

Grant, Campbell. *Rock Art of Baja California*. With notes on the pictographs of Baja California by León Diguet (1895). Translated by Roxanne Lapidus. Baja California Travels Series, 33. Los Angeles: Dawson's Book Shop, 1974.

Guillén, Clemente. *Explorer of the South: Diaries of the Overland Expeditions to Bahía Magdalena and La Paz, 1719, 1720–1721*. Translated and edited by W. Michael Mathes. Baja California Travels Series, 42. Los Angeles: Dawson's Book Shop, 1979.

Gutiérrez, Alfonso René. *Edición crítica de la vida del V.P. Juan María de Salvatierra escrita por el V.P. César Felipe Doria*. Mexico City: Consejo Nacional para la Cultura y las Artes; Fondo Regional para la Cultura y las Artes del Noroeste, 1997.

Gutiérrez Martínez, María de la Luz. *Arte rupestre, Baja California Sur*. Mexico City: Instituto Nacional de Antropología e Historia; Salvat, 1994.

Halleck, Henry W. *The Mexican War in Baja California: The Memorandum of Captain Henry W. Halleck Concerning His Expeditions in Lower California, 1846–1848.* Introduction by Doyce B. Nunis, Jr. Baja California Travels Series, 39. Los Angeles: Dawson's Book Shop, 1977.

Hambleton, Enrique. *La pintura rupestre de Baja California.* Mexico City: Fomento Cultural Banamex, 1979.

Hansen, Woodrow James. *The Search for Authority in California.* Oakland, Calif.: Biobooks, 1960.

Hardy, Robert William Hale. *Travels in the Interior of Mexico in 1825, 1826, 1827, 1828.* Edited by David J. Weber. Glorieta, N.Mex.: Río Grande Press, 1977.

Henderson, David A. *Men and Whales at Scammon's Lagoon.* Baja California Travels Series, 29. Los Angeles: Dawson's Book Shop, 1972.

Herrera Carrillo, Pablo. "Proclamación de la independencia en Baja California." *Calafia* 1, no. 2 (April–June 1970): 36–45.

Hilton, John W. *Hardly Any Fences: Baja California in 1933–1959.* Baja California Travels Series, 38. Los Angeles: Dawson's Book Shop, 1977.

Hinojosa, Salvador. *Arquitectura misional de Baja California Sur.* La Paz: Gobierno del Estado de Baja California Sur, 1988.

———. *Cuaderno histórico del templo misional de San Francisco Javier Viggé Biaundó.* Ruta de las misiones. Cuaderno 1. La Paz: Ayuntamiento de Loreto; Gobierno del Estado de Baja California Sur; Instituto Nacional de Antropología e Historia; Fondo Nacional de Fomento al Turismo; Revista Compas, 1999.

Hutchinson, C. Alan. *Frontier Settlement in Mexican California: The Híjar-Padrés Colony and Its Origins, 1769–1835.* New Haven, Conn.: Yale University Press, 1969.

Hyland, Justin. "Debunking the Myth: Jesuit Texts and History and Archeology in Baja California." *Kroeber Society Anthropology Papers* 79 (1995).

Iselin, Isaac. *Journal of a Trading Voyage around the World, 1805–1808.* Fairfield, Wash.: Ye Galleon Press, 1999.

Ives, Ronald, L. *José Velásquez: Saga of a Borderland Soldier (Northwestern New Spain in the 18th Century).* Tucson: Southwestern Mission Research Center, 1984.

Jackson, Robert H. "Congregation and Population Change in the Mission Communities of Northern New Spain." *New Mexico Historical Review* 69, no. 2 (1994): 163–83.

———. "Demographic Patterns in the Missions of Central Baja California." *Journal of California and Great Basin Anthropology* 6, no. 1 (1984): 91–112.

———. "Grain Supply, Congregation, and Demographic Patterns in the Missions of Northwestern New Spain: Case Studies from Baja and Alta California." *Journal of the West* 36, no. 1 (January 1997): 19–25.

———. *Indian Population Decline: The Missions of Northwestern New Spain, 1687–1840.* Albuquerque: University of New Mexico Press, 1994.

———, ed. *The Spanish Missions of Baja California.* New York: Garland Publishing, 1991.

Janes, John F. *The Adventures of Stickeen in Lower California, 1874.* Edited by Anna Marie Hager. Baja California Travels Series, 28. Los Angeles: Dawson's Book Shop, 1972.

Jones, Oakah L. *Los Paisanos: Spanish Settlers on the Northern Frontier of New Spain.* Norman: University of Oklahoma Press, 1996.

Jordán, Fernando. *Mar Roxo de Cortés: Biografía de un golfo.* Prologue and notes by Felipe Gálvez. Colección Baja California: Nuestra Historia, 10. Mexicali: Secretaría de Educación Pública; Universidad Autónoma de Baja California, 1995.

———. *El otro México: Biografía de Baja California.* Prologue, research, and bibliography by Felipe Gálvez; notes by Aidé Grijalva. Colección Baja California: Nuestra Historia, 3. Mexicali: Secretaría de Educación Pública; Universidad Autónoma de Baja California, 1993.

Junta de Fomento de Californias. *Colección de los principales trabajos que se ha ocupado la Junta nombrada para meditar y proponer al supremo gobierno, los medios más necesarios para promover el progreso de la cultura y civilización de los territorios de la Alta y de la Baja California. Año de 1827.* Mexico City: Imprenta de Galván a cargo de Mariano Arévalo, 1827.

Kino, Eusebio Francisco. *Crónica de la Pimería Alta: Favores celestiales.* 3rd ed. Hermosillo, Mexico: Gobierno del Estado de Sonora, 1985.

———. *First from the Gulf to the Pacific: The Diary of the Kino-Atondo Peninsular Expedition, December 14, 1684–January 13, 1685.* Transcribed, translated, and edited by W. Michael Mathes. Baja California Travels Series, 16. Los Angeles: Dawson's Book Shop, 1969.

———. *Kino Reports to Headquarters: Correspondence of Eusebio F. Kino from New Spain with Rome.* Translation and notes by Ernest J. Burrus. Rome: Jesuit Historical Institute, 1954.

———. *Kino Writes to the Duchess: Letters of Eusebio Francisco Kino to the Duchess of Aveiro.* Translated and edited by Ernest J. Burrus. Rome: Jesuit Historical Institute, 1965.

———. *Kino's Historical Memoir of the Pimería Alta: A Contemporary Account of the Beginnings of California, Sonora, and Arizona.* Translated and edited by Herbert E. Bolton. 2 vols. Berkeley and Los Angeles: University of California Press, 1948.

———. *Las misiones de Sonora y Arizona*. Mexico City: Editorial Porrúa, SA, 1989.

Konsag, Ferdinand. *Descripción compendiosa de lo descubierto y conocido de la California*. Introduction and notes by Catalina Velázquez Morales. Mexicali: Universidad Autónoma de Baja California, Centro de Investigaciones Históricas UNAM-UABC, 1985.

Krmpotic, M. D. *Life and Works of the Reverend Ferdinand Konscak, S.J., 1703–1759: An Early Missionary in California*. Boston: The Stratford Company, 1923.

Lassépas, Ulises Urbano. *De la colonización de la Baja California y decreto de 10 de marzo de 1857*. Mexico City: Imprenta de Vicente García Torres, 1859.

———. *Historia de la colonización de la Baja California y decreto del 10 de marzo de 1857*. Prologue by David Piñera Ramírez. Colección Baja California: Nuestra Historia, 8. Mexicali: Secretaría de Educación Pública; Universidad Autónoma de Baja California, 1995.

Lemoine Villicaña, Ernesto. "Evolución demográfica de la Baja California." *Historia mexicana* 9, no. 2 (October–December 1959): 249–68.

León-Portilla, Miguel. *Baja California: Algunas perspectivas en términos de historia universal*. La Paz: Universidad Autónoma de Baja California Sur, 1983.

———. *La California mexicana: Ensayos acerca de su historia*. Serie Historia Novohispana, 58. Mexico City: Universidad Nacional Autónoma de México, Instituto de Investigaciones Históricas; Mexicali: Universidad Autónoma de Baja California, 1995.

———. *Cartografía y crónicas de la Antigua California*. Mexico City: Universidad Nacional Autónoma de México, Instituto de Investigaciones Históricas y Fundación de Investigaciones Sociales, 1989.

———, ed. *Loreto, capital de las Californias: Las cartas fundacionales de Juan María de Salvatierra*. Mexico City: Universidad Autónoma de Baja California; Fondo Nacional de Fomento al Turismo; Consejo Nacional para la Cultura y las Artes; Centro Cultural Tijuana, 1997.

———. *Loreto's Key Role in the Early History of the Californias*. Santa Clara: California Mission Studies Association, 1997.

———. *Testimonios sudcalifornianos: Nueva entrada y establecimiento en el puerto de La Paz, 1720, por Jayme Bravo, Juan de Ugarte y Clemente Guillén*. Mexico City: Universidad Nacional Autónoma de México, 1970.

———. *Voyages of Francisco de Ortega: California, 1632–1636*. Baja California Travels Series, 30. Los Angeles: Dawson's Book Shop, 1973.

León-Portilla, Miguel, and José María Muriá. *Documentos para el estudio de Baja California en el siglo XIX*. 3 vols. Mexico City: Futura, 1992.

León Velazco, Lucila. "Conflictos de poder en la California misional (1768–1775)." In *Memoria 2001: Undécimo ciclo de conferencias, seminario de historia de Baja California*, 149–60. Mexicali: Instituto de Cultura de Baja California, n.d.

———. "Indígenas y misioneros en Baja California." In *Memorias de balances y perspectivas de la antropología e historia de Baja California 2002–2004*, 247–52. Mexicali: Instituto Nacional de Antropología e Historia, 2005.

Linck, Wenceslaus. *Wenceslaus Linck's Diary of His 1766 Expedition to Northern Baja California*. Edited by Ernest J. Burrus. Baja California Travels Series, 5. Los Angeles: Dawson's Book Shop, 1966.

———. *Wenceslaus Linck's Reports and Letters, 1762–1778*. Translated and edited by Ernest J. Burrus. Baja California Travels Series, 9. Los Angeles: Dawson's Book Shop, 1967.

Lingenfelter, Richard E. *The Rush of '89, the Baja California Gold Fever and Captain James Edward Friend's Letters from the Santa Clara Mines*. Baja California Travels Series, 8. Los Angeles: Dawson's Book Shop, 1967.

Lo Buglio, Rudecinda, Bartolomé T. Sepúlveda, and Nadine Marcía Vásquez. "Lista de los Individuos que Sirvieron en los Nuevos Establecimentos." In *Antepasados*. Janesville, Calif.: Los Californianos, 1977.

Longinos Martínez, José. *Diario de las expediciones a las Californias de José Longinos*. Edited by Salvador Bernabéu. Theatrum naturae. Serie Textos Clásicos. Aranjuez: Doce Calles, 1994.

———. *Journal of José Longinos Martínez: Notes and Observations of the Naturalist of the Botanical Expedition in Old and New California and the South Coast, 1791–1792*. Translated and edited by Lesley Byrd Simpson. [San Francisco]: J. Howell-Books, 1961.

Lucero Antuna, Héctor. *Evolución político-constitucional de Baja California Sur*. Mexico City: Universidad Nacional Autónoma de México, Instituto de Investigaciones Jurídicas, 1979.

Maekawa, Bunzō, Junzō Sakai, and Hatsutarō. *Kaigai Ibun: A Strange Tale from Overseas, or, A New Account of America*. Baja California Travels Series, 20. Los Angeles: Dawson's Book Shop, 1970.

Magaña, Mario Alberto. *Población y misiones de Baja California: Estudio histórico demográfico de la Misión de Santo Domingo de la Frontera, 1775–1850*. Tijuana: El Colegio de la Frontera Norte, 1998.

Márquez de Romero Aceves, María del Carmen, and Ricardo Romero Aceves. *Geografía e historia de Baja California*. Mexico City: Costa-Amic, 1987.

Martínez, Alejandro D. *Resumen histórico-gráfico de un pueblo singular: De las cuevas pintadas a la era misional.* Biblioteca de Historia Regional de "Las Californias." La Paz: Gobierno de Baja California Sur; Secretaría de Bienestar Social; Dirección de Cultura, 1989.

Martínez, Pablo L. *Las cinco fundaciones de La Paz, Baja California Sur.* La Paz: Archivo Histórico "Pablo L. Martínez," 1984.

———. *Efemérides californias: Trescientas fechas históricas.* Mexico City: Tipografía Pardo, 1950.

———. *Guía familiar de Baja California, 1700–1900.* Mexico City: Editorial Baja California, 1965.

———. *Historia de Baja California.* Mexico City: Libros Mexicanos, 1956.

———. *A History of Lower California.* Translated by Ethel Duffy Turner. Mexico City: Editorial Baja California, 1960.

Martínez Zepeda, Jorge, comp. *Testimonios sobre la invasión norteamericana a Baja California, 1846–1848.* Mexicali: Universidad Autónoma de Baja California, 1984.

Mathes, W. Michael, coord. *Baja California cartografía: Catálogo de mapas, planos y diseños del siglo XIX que se encuentran en el Archivo Histórico de Baja California Sur "Pablo L. Martínez."* La Paz: Gobierno de Baja California Sur, Archivo Histórico del Estado, 1979.

———. *Baja California: Textos de su historia.* 2 vols. Mexico City: Instituto de Investigaciones "Dr. José María Mora," Secretaría de Educación Pública; Programa Cultural de las Fronteras; Gobierno del Estado de Baja California, 1988.

———. "Baja California Indians in the Spanish Maritime Service, 1720–1821." *Southern California Quarterly* 62, no. 2 (Summer 1980): 113–26.

———, ed. *Californiana I: Documentos para la historia de demarcación comercial de California 1583–1632.* 2 vols. Colección Chimalistac, 22. Madrid: Ediciones José Porrúa Turanzas, 1965.

———, ed. *Californiana II: Documentos para la historia de la explotación comercial de California, 1611–1679.* 2 vols. Colección Chimalistac, 23. Madrid: Ediciones José Porrúa Turanzas, 1970.

———, ed. *Californiana III: Documentos para la historia de la transformación colonizadora de California, 1679–1686.* 3 vols. Colección Chimalistac, 29. Madrid: Ediciones José Porrúa Turanzas, 1974.

———, ed. *Californiana IV: Aportación a la historiografía de California en el siglo XVIII.* Colección Chimalistac, 45–46. Madrid: José Porrúa Turanzas, 1987.

———. *The Capture of the Santa Ana, Cabo San Lucas, November, 1587: The Accounts of Francis Pretty, Antonio de Sierra, and Tomás de Alzola*. Transcribed, translated, and annotated by W. Michael Mathes. Baja California Travels Series, 18. Los Angeles: Dawson's Book Shop, 1969.

———. *Cattle Brands of Baja California Sur, 1809–1885: Los registros de marcas de Baja California Sur*. Published for the Archivo Histórico de Baja California Sur "Pablo L. Martínez," La Paz. Baja California Travels Series, 40. Los Angeles: Dawson's Book Shop, 1978.

———. *The Conquistador in California: 1535. The Voyage of Fernando Cortés to Baja California in Chronicles and Documents*. Translated and edited by W. Michael Mathes. Baja California Travels Series, 31. Los Angeles: Dawson's Book Shop, 1973.

———. *Cronistas y crónicas jesuitas del noroeste de Nueva España*. Serie Cuadernos, 44. Culiacán, Mexico: El Colegio de Sinaloa, 1998.

———. "El establecimiento de la ruta transpeninsular." *Calafia* 4 (June 1983): 35–46.

———. "Estadísticas de Baja California: Extractos de libros de registro de misiones." *Calafia* 7, no. 6 (1994): 3–117.

———, ed. *Ethnology of the Baja California Indians*. New York: Garland Publishing, 1992.

———. *The Father President of the Missions Recalls the First Centenary of the Founding of Nuestra Señora de Loreto*. Santa Clara: California Mission Studies Association, 1997.

———, ed. *Jesuítica californiana, 1681–1764*. Colección Chimalistac, 49. Madrid: Ediciones José Porrúa Turanzas, SA, 1998.

———. *Las misiones de Baja California 1683–1849*. La Paz: Gobierno del Estado de Baja California Sur; Editorial Aristos, SA, 1977.

Meade, Adalberto Walther. *Baja California: Tierra extremosa y riqueza en los mares*. Mexico City: Secretaría de Educación Pública, 1982.

———. *El distrito norte de Baja California*. Mexicali: Universidad Autónoma de Baja California, 1986.

Meadows, Donald Charles. *The American Occupation of La Paz*. Early California Travels Series, 31. Los Angeles: Glen Dawson, 1955.

———. *Baja California, 1533–1950. A Biblio-history*. Los Angeles: Glen Dawson, 1951.

Meighan, Clement Woodward. *The Testimony of Prehispanic Rock Paintings in Baja California*. Baja California Travels Series, 13. Los Angeles: Dawson's Book Shop, 1969.

Meigs, Peveril. *The Dominican Mission Frontier of Lower California*. Berkeley and Los Angeles: University of California Press, 1935.

———. *La frontera misional dominica en Baja California*. Translation by Tomás Segovia; prologue by Miguel León-Portilla; notes by Carlos Lazcano Sahagún. Colección Baja California: Nuestra Historia, 7. Mexicali: Secretaría de Educación Pública; Universidad Autónoma de Baja California, 1994.

Memoria I: Semana de información histórica de Baja California Sur. La Paz: Gobierno de Baja California Sur, Fonapas, 1982.

Memoria II: Semana de información histórica de Baja California Sur. La Paz: Gobierno de Baja California Sur, Fonapas, 1982.

Memoria III: Semana de información histórica de Baja California Sur. La Paz: Gobierno de Baja California Sur, Dirección de Cultura, 1983.

Memoria IV: Semana de información histórica de Baja California Sur. La Paz: Gobierno de Baja California Sur, Dirección de Cultura, 1984.

Memoria V: Semana de información histórica de Baja California Sur. La Paz: Gobierno de Baja California Sur, Dirección de Cultura, 1984.

Memoria VI, VII y VIII: Semanas de información histórica de Baja California Sur. La Paz: Gobierno de Baja California Sur, Dirección de Cultura, 1985.

Memoria del primer congreso de historia regional, celebrado en Mexicali, Baja California, 1956. Mexicali: Dirección General de Acción Cívica y Cultural, 1958.

Messmacher, Miguel. *La búsqueda del signo de Dios: Ocupación jesuita de la Baja California*. Mexico City: Fondo de Cultura Económica, 1997.

Meza León, Carlos. *Baja California (la península del noroeste), reseña histórica geográfica*. Mexico City: DAPP, 1937.

Moorhead, Max L. *The Presidio: Bastion of the Spanish Borderlands*. Norman: University of Oklahoma Press, 1991.

Mora, Vicente de. *Edificar en desiertos: Los informes de fray Vicente de Mora sobre Baja California en 1777*. Edited and with an introduction by Salvador Bernabéu Albert. Mexico City: Embajada de España, 1992.

Morgan, Dale P., and George P. Hammond, eds. *A Guide to the Manuscript Collections of the Bancroft Library*, vol. 2: *Manuscripts Chiefly Relating to Mexico and Central America*. Edited by George P. Hammond. Berkeley: Friends of The Bancroft Library, University of California Press, 1972.

Mörner, Magnus. *Race Mixture in the History of Latin America*. Boston: Little, Brown, 1967.

Moyano Pahissa, Ángela. *California y sus relaciones con Baja California, síntesis del desarrollo histórico de Baja California y sus repercusiones sobre Baja California*. SEP/80 48. Mexico City: Fondo de Cultura Económica, 1983.

———. *La resistencia de las Californias a la invasión norteamericana, 1846–1848*. Mexico City: Consejo Nacional para la Cultura y las Artes, 1992.

———, comp. *Testimonios sobre la invasión norteamericana a Baja California, 1846–1848*. Tijuana: Universidad Autónoma de Baja California, Centro de Investigaciones Históricas UNAM-UABC, 1984.

Nápoli, Ignacio María. *The Cora Indians of Baja California: The Relación of Ignacio María Napoli, September 20, 1721*. Translated and edited by James Robert Moriarty III and Benjamin F. Smith. Baja California Travels Series, 19. Los Angeles: Dawson's Book Shop, 1970.

———. *Relación del Padre Ignacio María Nápoli acerca de la California, hecha el año de 1721*. Edited by Roberto Ramos. Mexico City: Editorial Jus, 1958.

Navarro García, Luis. *Don José de Gálvez y la comandancia general de las provincias internas del norte de Nueva España*. Seville: Escuela de Estudios Hispano-americanos, 1966.

Nieser, Albert Bertrand. "The Dominican Mission Foundations in Baja California, 1769–1822." PhD diss., Loyola University, 1960.

———. *Las fundaciones misionales dominicas en Baja California, 1769–1822*. Translated by Esteban Arroyo G. and Carlos Amado L.; prologue by Salvador Bernabéu Albert. Colección Baja California: Nuestra Historia, 14. Mexicali: Secretaría de Educación Pública; Universidad Autónoma de Baja California, 1998.

North, Arthur Walbridge. *Camp and Camino in Lower California*. Edited by W. Michael Mathes. Glorieta, N.Mex.: Río Grande Press, 1977.

———. *The Mother of California*. San Francisco and New York: P. Elder, 1908.

Northrop, Marie E. *Spanish-Mexican Families of Early California: 1769–1850*. Vol. 1. Burbank: Southern California Genealogical Society, 1987.

———. *Spanish-Mexican Families of Early California, 1769–1850*. Vol. 2. Burbank: Southern California Genealogical Society, 1984.

———. *Spanish-Mexican Families of Early California*. Vol. 3. Burbank: Southern California Genealogical Society, 2004.

Noticias y documentos acerca de las Californias, 1764–1795. Madrid: J. Porrúa Turanzas, 1959.

Nunis, Doyce B., ed. *The 1769 Transit of Venus: The Baja California Observations of Jean-Baptiste Chappe d'Auteroche, Vicente de Doz, and Joaquín Velázquez Cárdenas de León*. Translations by James Donahue, Maynard J. Geiger, and Iris Wilson Engstrand. Baja California Travels Series, 46. Los Angeles: Natural History Museum of Los Angeles County, 1982.

Palóu, Francisco. *Cartas desde la península de California, 1768–1773*. Edited by José Luis Soto Pérez. Mexico City: Editorial Porrúa, 1994.

———. *Historical Memoirs of New California*. 4 vols. Edited by Herbert E. Bolton. Berkeley: University of California Press, 1926.

———. *Noticias de la Antigua y Nueva California*. Documentos Para la Historia de México, 4 vols. Mexico City: Imprenta Vicente García Torres, 1857.

———. *Recopilación de noticias de la Antigua y de la Nueva California (1767–1783)*. New edition with notes by José Luis Soto Pérez; introductory study by Lino Gómez Canedo. 2 vols. Mexico City: Editorial Porrúa, SA, 1998.

———. *Vida de Fray Junípero Serra y misiones de la California septentrional*. Edited by Miguel León-Portilla. Mexico City: Editorial Porrúa, SA, 1990.

Piccolo, Francisco María. *Informe del estado de la nueva cristiandad de California, 1702, y otros documentos*. Edited by Ernest J. Burrus. Colección Chimalistac, 14. Madrid: Ediciones José Porrúa Turanzas, 1962.

———. *Informe on the New Province of California, 1702*. Translated and edited by George P. Hammond. Baja California Travels Series, 10. Los Angeles: Dawson's Book Shop, 1967.

Pineda Gómez, Fernando. "Desarrollo de la península de Baja California." *Calafia* 2, no. 6 (April 11, 1975): 41–44.

Piñera Ramírez, David. *Ocupación y uso del suelo en Baja California: De los grupos aborígenes a la urbanización dependiente*. Mexico City: Instituto de Investigaciones Históricas, Universidad Nacional Autónoma de México; Tijuana: Centro de Investigaciones Históricas, Universidad Autónoma de Baja California, 1991.

———. *Panorama histórico de Baja California*. Tijuana: Centro de Investigaciones Históricas Universidad Nacional Autónoma de México–Universidad Autónoma de Baja California, 1983.

———, coord. *Relación de materiales del Archivo de Microfilm*. Mexico City: Universidad Nacional Autónoma de México, Centro de Investigaciones Históricas; Tijuana: Universidad Autónoma de Baja California, Centro de Investigaciones Históricas, 1979.

———. "La tenencia de la tierra en Baja California de la época prehispánica a 1888." MA thesis. Mexico City: Universidad Nacional Autónoma de México, 1975.

Pitt, Leonard. *The Decline of the Californios: A Social History of the Spanish-Speaking Californians, 1846–1890*. Berkeley: University of California Press, 1966.

Pleasants, Joseph Edward. *The Cattle Drives of Joseph E. Pleasants from Baja California in 1867 and 1868*. Edited by Donald Meadows. Baja California Travels Series, 3. Los Angeles: Dawson's Book Shop, 1965.

Polzer, Charles W. *Rules and Precepts of the Jesuit Missions of Northwestern New Spain*. Tucson: University of Arizona Press, 1976.

Polzer, Charles W., and Thomas E. Sheridan, eds. *The Presidio and Militia on the Northern Frontier of New Spain: A Documentary History*. Vol. 2, part 1: *The Californias and Sinaloa-Sonora, 1700–1765*. Tucson: University of Arizona Press, 1997.

Preciado Llamas, Juan, and María Eugenia Altable Fernández, eds. *Sociedad y gobierno en el sur de la Baja California: Cinco aproximaciones históricas*. La Paz: Universidad Autónoma de Baja California Sur, 1991.

Priestley, Herbert Ingram. *José de Gálvez, Visitor-General of New Spain (1765–1771)*. Berkeley: University of California Press, 1916.

Ramos, Roberto, ed. *Tres documentos sobre el descubrimiento y exploración de Baja California por Francisco María Piccolo, Juan de Ugarte y Guillermo Stratford*. Mexico City: Editorial Jus, 1958.

Revere, Joseph Warren. *A Tour of Duty in California with Notices of Lower California, the Gulf and Pacific Coasts, and the Principal Events Attending the Conquest of the Californias*. New York: C. S. Francis and Company, 1849.

Reyes Silva, Leonardo. *La vida y la obra de Manuel Márquez de León: Estudio monográfico*. La Paz: Edición del Gobierno de Baja California Sur, 1985.

Río, Ignacio del. *Breve historia de Baja California Sur*. Mexico City: El Colegio de México; Fideicomiso Historia de las Américas; Fondo de Cultura Económica, 2000.

———. *Conquista y aculturación en la California jesuítica, 1697–1768*. Serie Historia Novohispana, 32. Mexico City: Instituto de Investigaciones Históricas, Universidad Nacional Autónoma de México, 1984.

———, ed. *Crónicas jesuíticas de la antigua California*. Mexico City: Universidad Nacional Autónoma de México, 2000.

———. *A la diestra mano de las Indias: Descubrimiento y ocupación colonial de la Baja California*. La Paz: Gobierno del Estado de Baja California Sur; Dirección de Cultura, 1985.

———. *La época colonial en Baja California: Tareas, temas y problemas de investigación*. La Paz: Universidad Autónoma de Baja California Sur, 1983.

———. *Guía del Archivo Franciscano de la Biblioteca Nacional de México*. Preliminary study by Lino Gómez Canedo; index by Ramiro Lafuente López. Mexico City: Instituto de Investigaciones Bibliográficas, Universidad Nacional Autónoma de México, 1975.

———. *El noroeste del México colonial: Estudios históricos sobre Sonora, Sinaloa y Baja California*. Mexico City: Universidad Nacional Autónoma de México, 2007.

———. "Población y misiones de Baja California en 1772: Un informe de Fray Juan Ramos de Lora." *Estudios de Historia Novohispana* 5 (1974): 241–71.

———. *El régimen jesuítico de la Antigua California*. Mexico City: Universidad Nacional Autónoma de México, 2003.

———. *Todos Santos: Una misión californiana*. La Paz: Archivo Histórico "Pablo L. Martínez," 1983.

———. "Utopia in Baja California: The Dreams of José de Gálvez." Translated by Arturo Jiménez-Vera. *Journal of San Diego History* 18, no. 4 (Fall 1972): 1–13.

Rivera Cambas, Manuel. *México pintoresco, artístico y monumental*. Mexico City: Imprenta de la Reforma, 1880–1883.

Rivera Granados, Ángel. "Antecedentes históricos-políticos en la conformación de los ayuntamientos del estado de Baja California." *Calafia* 4, no. 5 (1981): 19–30.

Rivera y Moncada, Fernando de. *Diario de Fernando de Rivera y Moncada*. Edited and with a prologue and notes by Ernest J. Burrus. Madrid: Ediciones José Porrúa Turanzas, 1967.

Robinson, W. W. *Land in California: The Story of Mission Lands, Ranchos, Squatters, Mining Claims, Railroad Grants, Land Scrip, Homesteads*. Berkeley: University of California Press, 1948.

Rojo, Manuel C. *Historical Notes on Lower California with Some Relative to Upper California Furnished to The Bancroft Library*. Edited by Philip O. Gericke. Baja California Travels Series, 26. Los Angeles: Dawson's Book Shop, 1972.

Rubio y Mora, Alberto. *Los jesuitas en Baja California*. Madrid: Ediciones Cultura Hispánica, 1991.

Rudkin, Charles, trans. "Conditions in Baja California, 1824–25: Two Unpublished Reports to the Central Government of Mexico." In *Los Angeles Corral of Westerners Brand Book No. 6*, 107–17. Los Angeles: Los Angeles Corral of Westerners, 1956.

Ryan, William Redmond. *Personal Adventures in Upper and Lower California in 1848–49, with the Author's Experiences at the Mines*. London: William Shoberl, 1950.

Salazar Rovirosa, Alfonso. *Cronología de Baja California del territorio y del estado de 1500 a 1956*. Mexico City: Litografía Artística, 1957.

———. *Geografía del estado de Baja California: Una lección visual de geografía*. Mexico City: n.p., 1962.

———. *Historia del estado de Baja California: Una lección visual de historia*. Mexico City: Ediciones Económicas, 1962.

Sales, Luis de. *Noticias de la Provincia de California, 1794*. 2 vols. Colección Chimalistac, 6. Madrid: Ediciones José Porrúa Turanzas, 1960.

———. *Observations on California, 1772–1790.* Translated and edited by Charles N. Rudkin. Los Angeles: Dawson's Book Shop, 1956.

Salgado Salgado, José Eusebio. *La bahía histórica de California.* Mexico City: Editorial Diana, 1976.

Salvatierra, Juan María de. *La fundación de la California jesuítica: Siete cartas de Juan María de Salvatierra, S.J. (1697–1699).* Edited and with an introduction and notes by Ignacio del Río; biographical study of Juan María de Salvatierra by Luis González Rodríguez. Mexico City: Universidad Autónoma de Baja California Sur; Fondo Nacional de Fomento al Turismo, 1997.

———. *Juan María de Salvatierra: Selected Letters about Lower California.* Translated and edited by Ernest J. Burrus. Baja California Travels Series, 25. Los Angeles: Dawson's Book Shop, 1971.

———. *Misión de la Baja California.* Compiled and with an introduction and notes by Constantino Bayle. Madrid: Editorial Católica, 1946.

Sánchez Vásquez, Luis. *Salvatierra, 300 Años.* Mexicali: Instituto de Servicios Educativos y Pedagógicos de Baja California; Instituto Salvatierra, 1997.

Santos, Robert LeRoy. *A Bibliography of Early California and Neighboring Territory through 1846: An Era of Exploration, Missions, Presidios, Ranchos and Indians.* Turlock, Calif.: Privately printed, 1992.

Scammon, Charles Melville. *Journal Aboard the Bark "Ocean Bird" on a Whaling Voyage to Scammon's Lagoon, Winter of 1858–1859.* Edited by David A. Henderson. Baja California Travels Series, 21. Los Angeles: Dawson's Book Shop, 1970.

Schurz, William Lytle. *The Manila Galleon.* New York: E. P. Dutton, 1939.

Shipek, Florence C., comp. *Lower California Frontier: Articles from the San Diego Union, 1870.* Baja California Travels Series, 2. Los Angeles: Dawson's Book Shop, 1965.

Southworth, John R. *El territorio de la Baja California, México, su agricultura, comercio, minería e industrias.* San Francisco: Press of the Hicks-Judd Company, 1899.

Stein, Stanley J., and Barbara H. Stein. *The Colonial Heritage of Latin America; Essays on Economic Dependence in Perspective.* New York: Oxford University Press, 1970.

Stern, Norton B. *Baja California, Jewish Refuge and Homeland.* Baja California Travels Series, 32. Los Angeles: Dawson's Book Shop, 1973.

Tamayo Sánchez, Jesús. *La ocupación española de las Californias: Una interpretación del primer impulso urbanizador del noroeste mexicano a partir de algunas fuentes históricas.* Mexico City: Plaza y Valdés, 1992.

Taraval, Sigismundo. *The Indian Uprising in Lower California, 1734–1737, as described by Father Sigismundo Taraval*. Translation, introduction, and notes by Marguerite Eyer Wilbur. Los Angeles: The Quivira Society, 1931.

———. *La rebelión de los californios*. Edited by Eligio Moisés Coronado. Aranjuez and Madrid: Doce Calles, 1996.

Taylor, Alexander S. *A Historical Summary of Baja California from Its Discovery in 1532–1867*. Edited by Walt Wheelock. Pasadena, Calif.: Socio-Technical Books, 1971.

Terrazas Basante, Marcela. *En busca de una nueva frontera: Baja California en los proyectos expansionistas norteamericanos, 1846–1853*. Mexico City: Universidad Nacional Autónoma de México, 1995.

Tibesar, Antonine, ed. *Writings of Junípero Serra*. 4 vols. Washington, D.C.: Academy of American Franciscan History, 1956–65.

Tirsch, Ignacio. *The Drawings of Ignacio Tirsch, a Jesuit Missionary in Baja California*. Edited and with an introduction by Doyce B. Nunis, Jr.; translated by Elsbeth Schulz-Bischof. Baja California Travels Series, 27. Los Angeles: Dawson's Book Shop, 1972.

Torre Iglesias, Manuel. *Geografía del territorio sur de la Baja California*. Mexico City: N.p., 1957.

———. *Historia del territorio sur de la Baja California, 1535–1951*. Mexico City: Ediciones El Nacional, 1956.

Trasviña Taylor, Armando. *Estado de Baja California Sur*. 3rd ed. La Paz: N.p., 1977.

———. *Loreto: Madre y cuna de las Californias/Loreto: Mother and Cradle of the Californias*. 2nd ed. La Paz: Patronato del Estudiante Sudcaliforniano, 1977.

———. *Territorio de Baja California*. Cuadernos de Lectura Popular, 178. Serie Monografías de México. Mexico City: Subsecretaría de Asuntos Culturales, 1969.

Trejo Barajas, Dení. "Propiedades y propietarios en la Baja California a mediados del XIX." *Siglo XIX: Cuaderno de Historia* 12, no. 4 (1995): 29–45.

Trejo Barajas, Dení, and Marco Antonio Landavazo Árias. *Población y grupos de poder en la península de Baja California: Dos estudios históricos del siglo XIX*. La Paz: Seminario de Investigación en Historia Regional, Universidad Autónoma de Baja California Sur, 1994.

Trujillo, G. P. *Bibliografía de Baja California*. Tijuana: Editorial Californidad, 1967.

Valadés, Adrián. *Historia de la Baja California, 1850–1880*. Prologue by Miguel León-Portilla. Mexico City: Universidad Nacional Autónoma de México, 1974.

———. *Temas históricos de la Baja California*. Mexico City: Editorial Jus, 1963.

Valadez, José C. *Apuntes sobre la expedición de Baja California*. Mexico City: Imprenta Ymmex, 1956.

Velázquez, María del Carmen. *Notas sobre sirvientes de las Californias y proyecto de obraje en Nuevo México*. Mexico City: Centro de Estudios Históricos, Colegio de México, 1985.

Velázquez de León, Joaquín. *Descripción de la Antigua California: 1768*. Transcription, presentation, and notes by Ignacio del Río. Colección Cabildo, 2. La Paz: Edición del H. Ayuntamiento de La Paz, 1975.

Venegas, Miguel. *Juan María de Salvatierra*. Translated, edited, and with notes by Marguerite Eyer Wilbur. Cleveland: Arthur H. Clark Company, 1929.

———. *Obras californianas del Padre Miguel Venegas, S.J.* Edited by Michael W. Mathes. 5 vols. La Paz: Universidad Autónoma de Baja California Sur, 1979.

Weber, Francis J. *The Missions and Missionaries of Baja California*. Baja California Travels Series, 11. Los Angeles: Dawson's Book Shop, 1968.

———. *The Peninsular California Missions, 1808–1880*. Los Angeles: Dawson's Book Shop, 1979.

Wheelock, Walt, and Howard E. Gulick. *Baja California Guidebook: A Descriptive Traveler's Guide*. 5th ed. Clark Guidebooks, 1. Glendale, Calif.: Arthur H. Clark Company, 1975.

Xántus, János. *Travels in Southern California*. Detroit: Wayne State University Press, 1976.

———. *Xántus: The Letters of John Xántus to Spencer Fullerton Basird from San Francisco and Cabo San Lucas, 1859–1861*. Introduction, notes, and illustrations by Ann H. Zwinger. Baja California Travels Series, 48. Los Angeles: Dawson's Book Shop, 1986.

Zambrano, Francisco. *Diccionario bio-bibliográfico de la Compañía de Jesús en México*. Mexico City: Editorial Jus, 1961.

Zevallos, Francisco. *The Apostolic Life of Fernando Consag, Explorer of Lower California*. Translation, annotations, and introduction by Manuel P. Servín. Baja California Travels Series, 15. Los Angeles: Dawson's Book Shop, 1968.

Zugliani, Domingo. *Noticias histórico-religiosas de Baja California*. La Paz: Ciudad de los Niños, 1976.

Index

Photographs and maps are indicated by page numbers in italics.

Acapulco, 53
African descent peoples, 47
agaves, 145, 147
agriculture: creating cultivable earth, 17; intensive, 7. *See also* cattle; goat ranching
aguardiente (distilled liquor), 104
Aguilar, Buenaventura, 132
Aguilar, Casimiro, 133
Aguilar, Fernando, xiv, xv
Aguilar, Javier, Smith's baptismal name, 4
Aguilar, José María, 136
Aguilar, Juana, 176
Aguilar, Juan Antonio, 139
Aguilar, Luis, 138–39, 149, 191–92; cattle brands, 135
Aguilar, Luis Ignacio, 131–32, 133–34, 133

Aguilar, María Mónica, 183
Aguilar, Pedro, 132
Aguilar, Xavier, 4
Agúndez, Napoleón, 212–13
Agúndez, Ramona, 212, 213, 215–16
Ahome, 135
alcohol, 173; moonshining, 205–206, 208, 210, 212, 216
alforjas (rawhide boxes or hampers), 17
Alta California: after gold rush, 6; cattle industry, 131, 139; economic development compared, 6; foreign colony, 149; foreign influx, 92–93; geography compared, 140; grazing lands, 75; great ranches, 92, 131, 149; Jesuit impact, 66; leather tanning, 32–33; *mayordomo* descendants, 139;

Alta California *(continued)*
  Mexican independence era, 84–85; modern inhabitants compared, 9–10; natural disasters compared, 143–45; pioneer family names, 66; pioneer settlers, 66; post-independence era, 139–40; presidios, 75; pueblos, 75; ranches compared, 77–78, 140; ranching legacy compared, 147; road access, 71; ships visiting, 85; Sinaloa origins of pioneers, 52; social development, 75; trade, 81; typical landholdings, 92
Amador, Francisco, *138*
Amador, Inocencio, *138*
Amador, Porfirio, *138*
andariegos (rovers), 181
Antigua California, 66
aparejo (packsaddle for burros), 31–32, *33*
Arce, Agustín, 33–34, 36, 39
Arce, (Ignacio) Buenaventura, 183–86; affluence, 191, 193, 197; character in book, 192; children, 197; death, 197; descendants, 149, 197–98; influence, 186, 189; patriarchal style, 193; Rancho San Francisco, 198–99; sharp dealings, 190, 191
Arce, Candelario, 216
Arce, Carmen, 216
Arce, Eustacio ("Tacho"), *15*, *23*, *180*, *213*, *214*; as cowboy, 218; childhood home, 199, *199*, *201*; early life, 199–200; family line, 197; goat ranching, *163*, 199–200; gold mining, 202–205; hunting trips, 217–19, *219*, 222; marriage, 212, 213, 215–16; moonshining, 205–206, 208, 210, 212, 216; with pack mules, *211*; on padres in towns, 225, 227; Rancho La Esperanza, 219, 221–22; rock art tours, 222–23; special gift, 200; storytelling, 181–83, *185*, 223–27
Arce, Felipe, 214, 216, 221–22
Arce, Francisco, 26–27, *28*, *30*, 31–32, *33*, 36–37, 39, 216
Arce, Gabriel, 139
Arce, Germán, 39, 213
Arce, Ignacio María, 183
Arce, Josefa, *25*, 26, 205, 207; shrines, *38*, 39
Arce, Josefa (daughter of José Gabriel Arce), 136
Arce, José Gabriel, 135, 136
Arce, José Gabriel de, 183
Arce, Juan ("Rango"), 34, *35*, 36, 39
Arce, Juan Bautista Ignacio, 136
Arce, Juan de, 183
Arce, Leandro, 202, 204, 217
Arce, Loreta, 215
Arce, Loreto, *15*, *207*; as godfather, 215; background, 17; help from Tacho, 205–206, *207*; jailed for moonshining, 210; moonshining, 205–206, 208, 210, 212; work routine, 14–16, 21, 22, 33, 36, 37
Arce, Lucas, 197
Arce, Manuel, 136
Arce, Ramón, 216, 222
Arce, Ramona (née Agúndez), 212, 213, 215–16, 217, 228
Arce, Salvador ("Chavalo"), 217
Arce, Sebastián, 135–36, 139
Arce, Sebastián Constantino de, 183
Arce, Severiano, 200, 216

Argüello, José Darío, 134
Argüello, Luis Antonio, 85
Arizona, 44
arrieros (muleteers), 70, 71–73
Arrillaga, José Joaquín de, 68, 206
arroyo (watercourse), 22, *187*; Sierra de Guadalupe, 128
Arroyo Comondú, *123*
Arroyo del Parral, *222*
Arroyo de Rosarito, *141*
Arroyo Guajademí, 128
Arroyo Rondín, 135
Arroyo San Pablo, *79*
Arviña, Rafael, 102
Ávila, Ramón, 181–82
Avilés, Simón, 73–75

Baegert, Jacobo, 49–50, 95
Bahía de la Concepción, 7
Bahía de Los Ángeles, 7
Bahía Magdalena, 54
Baja California: after gold rush, 6; as Antigua California, 66; border cities, 6; Crosby's research on, xix–xx; early settlements, 55, 56; early ships visiting, 3–4; early U.S. contacts, 3–4, 5; economic development compared, 6; El Sur (cape region), 57; foreigners, 149; geography, 13; geography compared, 140; Gold Rush, 120–22; governors, 77–78; growth in 1970s, 6–7; immigration, 6, 8, 122–24, 231; impact of independence, 84; inhabitants described, 98; lack of change, 6; loss of mules and *arrieros*, 70, 71–73; loss of resources to Monterey expedition, 69; Mexican War era, 93; missionary efforts in north, 70; modern inhabitants compared, 9–10; natural disasters compared, 143–45; policies in independence era, 96–97; post-independence era, 139–40; post-independence leadership, 87–88, 91–92; ranches compared, 77–78, 140; ranching legacy compared, 147; regional character, 96; regional subculture, 231; roads lacking, 71; secular economy, 122; sierras described, 13; Spanish exploration of, 42; U.S. annexation, 113–14; U.S. invasion, 112–15

baptismal names, 160–62
Barco, Miguel del, 32
Bastida, Teódolo, 173
bathing, 108
Bay of La Paz, 57
beef jerky, 103, 117, 119
Bennett, Frederick Debell, 103, 105
Beron, 109–10, 112
bighorn sheep, 218
blind mountain residents, 33–34
Boleo Mining Company, 193–97; contraband trade, 208, 210; ranches to supply, 212–14, 216
borrego (bighorn sheep), 218
Bourbon Reforms, 62–63
Bravo, Jaime, 59
Buffum, Edward Gould, 115
buildings: architecture, 233; *corredor*, 24, 25, *214, 215, 233*; materials, 175; *ramadas*, 215. *See also* housing; kitchens
Bull, James Hunter, 99–102, 192

Burton, Henry S., 114–15

Caballero, Félix, 186
Cabo San Lucas: Gálvez on, 68; Japanese castaways, 105–107; ship supplies, 81, 102; tourism, 7
Cabrillo. *See* Rodríguez Cabrillo, Juan
cacti, 147
California: as island, 42; early exploration, 42–43; early settlements, 55, 56; Manila trade, 43
California Academy of Sciences, 232
California Review, xi
Californios: control after Mexican War, 93; family names, 138; *gente de razón* as, 95–96; kodalith, 10–11; origin of term, 54; use of term, 4; in U.S. era, 93
The Call to California (Crosby), xix
Calmallí, 123, 202–205
Camacho, Remigio, 216
cambiaderos (those who move about), 150, 151, 152
Camino Real, 8, 22; as mule trail, 71, 73; forty-niners, 120; traveler Bull on, 99–100
cañada watercourse, 15, 144
Cape Sierra, 125
Carlos III (King), 63, 65
Carrillo, Isabel, 87
carrizo, for thatch, 106n
Castro, Don Santa María de, 171
cattle: Arroyo San Pablo, 79; boys' labor, 155; brands, 135; Cabo San Lucas, 102, 107; dependence on, 98; El Sur region, 79, 81; hides, 27, 119; Jesuit restrictions on, 52; Ocio, 61; Rancho San Gregorio, 27; Santa Ana, 67; seasonal movement, 141–43; Sierra de Guadalupe, 130–31; significance, 131; trade in hides, 97–98; wild herds, 73, 98. *See also* leather curing; leather work
cattle barons, 85
Cerro Verde, 210
children: family attention to, 165, 171; learning skills, 158; work, 154–55
Choza, Miguel, 108–12, 112–13, 114
chubascos (cyclonic summer storms), 16, 143, 144–45
Ciudad Constitución, 7
climate, 143–45
clothing, 232; fiestas, 173; Japanese traveler, 109; men, 104, 108, 110, 111; ranch inhabitants, 98; San José, 108; soldiers, 74–75; *vaqueros*, 71; women, 99, 104, 108, 110, 111
Cochimí people, 54; conversion, 54; descendant, 82; Sierra de Guadalupe, 127; tensions with Guaycura, 58
colache (fruit preserves), 182
Colorado River expedition, 63
Combier, Cyprien, 97–99
Comondú: Californio occupation of, 121–22, 123; cattle brands, 135; Dominicans at, 81; festivals, 170; guide at, xiii; music, 173; return to, xiv; Smith-Aguilar at, 4
Compagnie Du Boleo, 194–97
conquests: common elements, 43; descendants of conquerors, 46; military, 42, 44; New Spain, 42; religious, 43–44

contraband trade, 81; El Boleo
   Mining Company, 208, 210;
   employees of El Boleo, 196;
   fallqueros and, 200; smuggling
   priest, 186. *See also* moonshining
cook stoves, 25, 27
Copley, James, xii
Copley Press, xii
copper mining, 194–97
Coronado, Eligio Moisés, xx
corredor, 214, 215; architecture, 233;
   dining area, 24, 25
Cortés, Hernán, 42
cowboys, 218

dancing, 100–102, 173, 232
date palms, 80
death, 166
dental hygiene, 117
dipugo trees, 146
Doak, Thomas, 3
Dominican missionaries, 70,
   73–74, 81, 85, 90, 134
drainage basins, 142–43
dried fruit industry, 79, 80
drought, 145, 149, 217; mission era,
   69

economic growth, 6–7, 9
education: lacking, 88–89, 153;
   literacy, 232; ranch folk, 95, 153;
   reading habits, 33
egalitarianism, 84
Eisen, Gustav, 232, 234
El Álamo mining, 124
elderly people, 166, 172, 224
El Patrocinio, 136; cattle brands, 135
El Rosario, 150
El Sur region, 57, 60; cattle raising,
   79, 81; in transition, 60–62

El Triunfo, mining, 123
enajambres (bee nests), 35
English incursions, 65
Ensenada, 6, 150
extended families, 160, 162; as
   social pattern, 165–66; attention
   to children, 165, *171*

fallqueros, 200, 202
families: death of members, 166;
   elderly members, 166, 172;
   extended, 160, 162, 165–66;
   illegitimacy, 177, 179; influence
   on identity, 174; Jesuit problems
   with problem generation, 52–53;
   Jesuit requirements for, 45;
   origins of pioneer families, 52;
   portraits, *154, 170*; work, 153–54
family groups, 165, *169*
family life: communal interest
   in children, 165, *171*; domestic
   chores, 163; effectiveness of, 235;
   travel accounts, 98–99; warmth
   of, 234
family names: Alta California
   pioneers, 66; baptismal names,
   160–62; first names, 160–62;
   later immigrants, 124; old
   Californio, 138
family size, 99
fandango at San Ignacio, 100–102,
   101
farm collectives, 9
Felipe V (King), 62
fiestas and celebrations, 169–70,
   173; Alta California, 75–76;
   clothing, 173; fandango at San
   Ignacio, 75–76, *101*; mission era,
   74; San Francisco fiesta, 213, 215;
   women, 169, 173

Finch, Robert H. ("Bob"), xi–xii
firewood, 75
Fischer, Frank, 222
food, 26, 27; for animals, *146*; beef jerky, 103, 117, 119; cooking utensils, 118–19; forty-niners on, 121; goat cheese, 156; La Paz, 115; *panocha*, 115, *116*, 117; reliance on beef, 131; tortillas, 26, 118–19; travel accounts on, 104, 108; wild food, 145, 147; wild honey, 34–35, *36*
forty-niners, 120–22, 189–92; behavior, 192
foster parents, 165
Franciscan missionaries, 59, 65, 68, 69–70; Alta California, 85; finances, 85
Franciscan Order, 43
French incursions, 65
Frenchmen marrying local women, 196–97
Fronteras region, 78
fruit, 121–22, *123*, 169–70, 192, 193; dried fruit industry, 79, *80*
furnishings, 103, 106, 175

Gabb, William, 192
Gálvez, José de, 64, 65–68; economic development plans, 67–68; greatest responsibility, 66; report on civilian life, 68
gambusinos (hand miners), 203–205
Ganster, Paul, xii, xiv–xv
Gardner, Erle Stanley, 222
generations: after 1920, 150, 152; child rearing practices, 165, *171*; housing, 162; Jesuit problems with, 52–53; mayordomos, 140–41; mobility of some men, 182

gente de razón: Baegert's description, 95; Cabo San Lucas, 102–103; disappearance of term, 124; Gálvez impact on, 65; late mission era, 73; Loreto personnel, 49–50; marriage patterns, 47, 124; post-mission era, 61; private property, 50; reliance on beef, 131; San Ignacio post-independence, 197; secular leadership, 68; slow growth of colony, 52; social status, 47–48, 50; unused mission lands, 133; use of term, 46, 47. *See also* Hispanic population
goat cheese, 156; grinding salt for, 164; salt added, *167*
goat ranching, 150; cheese making, 156, *159*, *160*, *164*, *167*; children, 155; drying goat meat, *163*; jerky, *163*, *168*; Las Calabazas, 215; milking, 156, *161*; practices, 155–56; products, 159; shift from cattle, 155; slaughtering, *168*; Tacho Arce, 199–200
gold finds (placer gold), 185, 202–205
Gold Rush of 1849, 6, 120, 122; forty-niners, 120–22, 189–92
gossip, 34, 168–69, 173
governors, 77–78
Green, John, 3
guatamote (bush), 159
Guaycura people, 54; conversion, 57; conversion challenges, 57–58; tensions with other peoples, 57
Guaymas, 194
güéribo, giant poplar tree, 128; chairs, 175
Guerrero Negro Lagoon, 6

guides to Baja California, xiii–xv

Hall, Byron, 204
Hambleton, Enrique, xx, 222
Hatsutarō, 104–12
Hawks, J. D., 189, 190–92
hide-and-tallow trade, 85
Hispanic population: aftermath of rebellion, 61; geography of settlement, 125; origins of, 45. *See also gente de razón*
honey, 34–35, 36
horses, 234; Cabo San Lucas, 107; forty-niners, 121; Mexican War era, 117; mules compared to, 70–71
hospitality, 115, 121, 232, 234
housing, 110, 111, 232; flood paths and, 144; Luis Aguilar, 191–92; Mexican War era, 117, 118; San José, 108; Sierra de San Juan, 220; thatch, 106, 111; travel accounts on, 106–108
huacales (homemade crates), 32, 37
Huasinapí, 127
huertas (orchard gardens), 122, 123, 192; droughts, 145; mission era, 18; Rancho San Gregorio, 18, 21
huitlacoche (bird), 39
hunting, 217–19, 219, 222, 227

Ibarra, Emiliano, 204
Ibarra, Fidencio, 205
Ibarra Gold Mining Company, 204
identity, 173–74, 234–35
illegitimacy, 177, 179
immigration, 122–24, 231; and marriage patterns, 124
independence era, 78, 83, 84; challenges to military, 87; Church lands, 89–90; Mission Guadalupe area, 133–39; social classes, 96; trade, 85, 97
"Indies," 42
indigenous peoples: decline and labor force, 133; decline and land use, 81; decline in independence era, 90; decline through disease, 73, 128; disease, 45; displacement over time, 83; early numbers, 45, 54; fears about misemployment, 52; influence on dance, 101; insurrection, 59–60; Jesuit protection of, 52; major groups, 54; mission lands for, 90; mission ranches, 76–77; occupations, 48. *See also individual indigenous peoples*
intermarriage. *See* marriage patterns
irrigation system, Rancho San Gregorio, 14–18, 20, 37

Japanese travel account, 104–12
Jesuit expulsion, 63, 65, 69
Jesuits: authority declining, 61; broad powers of, 44, 62–63; control over military, 50; criticisms of, 62–63; dates introduced, 80; financial management by, 85; Hispanic people as servants, 96; impact on Alta California, 66; impact on baptismal names, 162; license to land, 90; missions established, 43–44; need for military escorts and skilled labor, 45; protection of Indians, 52; recruiting soldiers for occupation, 48–50; settlers versus, 44; Sierra de Guadalupe, 127, 128–30

jícama, 147
Juárez, Benito, 149

Kino, Eusebio Francisco, 44, 54
kitchen chores, 26
kitchens, 22, 25, 27, 226; *cambiadero* goat ranches, 151; in caves, 151

land concessions, 123
land grants, 50, 68, 75, 85; Guadalupe Mission area, 132
landholding patterns, 48; inheritance of land, 140; Sierra de Guadalupe, 149
landownership: Alta California, 92, 149; Church lands after independence, 89–90; ex-mayordomos, 81–83; Mexican independence era, 78
land reform, 186, 189
La Paz: cattle, 79; food, 115; founding, 42; Gálvez on, 68; history published in, xx; mission founded, 57; oyster shells, 97; revolt, 59–60; tourism, 7; Uchití people near, 58; U.S. occupation, 5, 113, 114–15
La Purísima (village), 139, 170
Las Flores mining boom, 123
The Last of the Californios (Crosby), xx
leather curing, 26–27, 28, 29, 30, 31
leather tanning, mission era, 32–33
leather working, 26, 30, 31–33, 232; mission era, 32–33
lechuza pouches, 173
leñero (wood gatherer), 215, 222
Liberal Party, 91
liming treatment for hides, 29
livestock, 83, 107; droughts and, 145; *represas*, 150; switch to goats, 155
locusts, 69
Longinos Martínez, José, 90
López, Domingo, 135, 136
López, Juan Miguel, 135, 139, 149
Loreto (presidio), 45, 49–50; galleon port issue, 54, 57; Nueva California service, 66; Ruíz as captain, 87–88; ship's carpenter, 4; soldier at, 139; uprising, 59–60
Loreto (town): author following Portolá Trail, xiii; Arce's arrival in, 183; as Buenaventura Arce's hometown, 184; dancing women, 173; founding, 44; late mission era, 73; sailing launches based at, 185; tourism, 7; town council, 86; travel accounts, 97–99
Los Ángeles (town), 75
Lydia (ship), 3

Magdalena Plain, 7
Manila trade: galleon ports, 54, 57; missions nearby, 57; need for coastal base, 43, 53, 54; port established, 58–59; reports on Indians, 54
marriage ceremonies, 215
marriage opportunity, 177, 179
marriage patterns, 137; cousin marriage, 160; immigration and, 124
Maryland (ship), 3–4
Mason, Richard B., 114
Mayoral, Pedro, 134
Mayoral, Raymundo, 134
Mayoral, Salvador, 134
mayordomos, 76–83, 76; bonds among, 137–38; Buenaventura

Arce as, 185; catching bull, 76; duties, 131; land claims, 82; Mission Guadalupe, 131–32, 133–34, 133; Sierra de Guadalupe, 139; status of, 137; successive generations, 140–41

Mazatlán, 109–12

mealtimes, 24, 25–26; sitting order for meals, 24, 25, 103–104

Mejía, Cayetano, 202

merchants, mounted, 200, 202

mesquite, 29, 146

mestizos, 47

Mexican War of 1846–48: collaboration of Californios, 5, 114–15; foreigners in Alta California, 149; forty-niner behavior after, 192; impact on Alta California, 93; impact on Baja California, 93; invasion of Baja California, 112–15; occupation, 5

Meza, María, 4

mezcalero (maker of mezcal), 205–206, 208, 210, 216; condenser jacket for still, 212; underground oven, 208, 209

migration, isolation of men, 179

military in Baja California, 44; clothing, 49, 74–75; duties, 49–50; independence era, 87–88; Jesuit control, 52; Jesuit control renounced, 63; marriage patterns, 46–47; as mayordomos, 77; missionaries handling finances, 85; recruiting, 48–50; spartan living conditions, 74; squatters' claims, 81–82; working with missionaries, 48–50

miners, influence feared, 52

mining: booms, 123–24; copper, 194–97, 195; Osio, 61

Mission Comondú, *huertas* (orchard gardens), 18

mission era: cash wages, 74; changing employees, 50–52; conversion of El Sur, 57; creating cultivable earth, 18–19; dispersion from mission centers, 75; drought, 69; frontier culture, 45–48; growth of outside influences, 53–58; historical sources on, 95; *huertas* (orchard gardens), 18; impact on Guadalupe range, 127; independence era, 84, 85; leather working, 32–33; maps, 55, 56; marriage patterns, 46–47; missions, ranches and chapels (map), 56; mules, 70, 71–73; number of Indians, 45; outside influences, 53–58; popular image of mission frontier, 45; recruiting, 48–50; regimentation described, 73–74; San Gregorio water sources, 17; skilled labor needs, 49; solidarity among pioneer families, 74; stagnation, 73; urban preferences, 45–46

Mission La Purísima, xiv, 130, 136

Mission Los Dolores, 57

Mission Nuestra Señora de Guadalupe, 127, 128, 130; cattle brands, 135; independence era, 133–39; mayordomos, 131–32, 133–34, 133

mission ranches, 56, 76–77, 129; independence era, 85; Mission Guadalupe, 128–30

Mission Rosario, 78
missions: duty to assist military, 78; independence era, 90; mission lands issue, 89–92; neophytes on ranches, 76–77; phantom missions post-independence, 88, 90; resources depleted, 70; support of converts, 76
Mission San Borja, 63, 82
Mission San Diego, 78
Mission San Fernando de Velicatá, 135
Mission San Ignacio, 82, 129, 130, 188; Arce at, 135; Buenaventura Arce at, 185; church buildings, 191, 192–93; described, 189–91; fandango at, 100, *101*; Ignacio María Arce's baptism, 183; mayordomo, 136; post-independence, 186; Rancho San Francisco, 199, 213
Mission San Javier, 121
Mission San José del Cabo, 57, 59
Mission Santa Clara, 32
Mission Santa Gertrudis, 63, 82, 129
Mission Santa Rosa (later Todos los Santos), 57
Mission Santa Rosalía de Mulegé, 128, 130, 132; Arce as godparent to Indian child, 184–85; dependencies, 136; Dominicans at, 81; mayordomo, 135
Mission Santiago, 57; insurrection, 59
Mission Santo Domingo, 183
Mission Santo Tomás, 191
Mission Todos Santos, insurrection, 59–60

Montaño, Juan Miguel, 139
Montaño, María Dolores, 139
Monterey: as capital, 75; Californios transferred to, 5; strategic importance, 70
Monterey expedition, 66, 69
moonshining, 205–206, 208, 210
Moreno, Manuel, 217, 218
mountain people: admirable qualities, 235; after gold rush, 6; archaic ways, 10–11; as good-natured, 234; clothing, 99; education, 95, 153; family portrait, *154*; forty-niners on, 121; geography of settlement, 125; isolation of, 41, 83, 162, 165, 169–70, 176, 179, 224, 232; lack of change, 9, 179; mayordomo origins, 82–83; Mexican War era, 93; migration, 179; mining boom, 124; mules' importance, 72; occupations and skills, 153; origins of culture, 231–32; post-independence secularization disputes, 92; sources for studying, 41, 95; traditional character, *118*; travel accounts, 41, 73–75, 97–99; typical settlements, 2
mule deer, 218
Mulegé (village): arroyo at, 128; Bull at, 99; fiestas, 170; mayordomo descendants, 139; tourism, 7
mules: and *arrieros*, 70, 71–73; as transportation, 157; breaking, 177; breeding, 71; horses compared, 70–71; importance in Baja California, 70–73, *72*; Mexican War era, 117; mission

era, 70, 71–73; with packsaddles, 37, *211*; pack trip in Sierra de San Francisco, *12*; roping, *229*; on steep grades, *211*; Tacho's stories, 227, 228; trade, *148, 203*; travelers' woes, 190
Murillo, Antonio, 202
Murillo, Jaime, 184–85
Murillo, José Julián, 132
Murillo, José María, 134
Murillo, Romaulda, 184, 197
music, 22, 39, 232; fandango, 100, *101*; violin, 173

natural disasters, 143–45
New Spain, 42; contraband trade, 81; Jesuits reacting to criticism, 63
North, Alfred Walbridge, 204
Nuestra Señora de Loreto, 162
Nueva California, 66

Ojeda, Chuy, 228
oral history, 232, 234
Osio, Antonio María, xix
Osio, Manuel de, 61; cattle herds, 130; compared to other Hispanic families, 74; Crosby research on, xix; fortunes diminished, 70
oyster shells, 97

pack train, 22, 203
palo blanco trees, 16, 21; tanning fluid, 28
panocha, 115, *116*, 117, 193
pardos, 47
Paso Hondo (village), xiv
pearl fishing, 43, 52, 61
peer groups, 165
Pérez, Diego, 185

Pérez, Petra, 185
Pericú people, 54; cape region, 102; conversion challenges, 58; location, 57; missions and, 57; tensions with Guaycura, 58
Péripuli, Heriberto, xiii–xiv
personal identity, 173, 174, 234–35
Peru, 139
photographer, author's living as, xi
pila (reservoir), 21
pioneer families: mission ranches, 77; origins of, 52
pitahaya dulce, 147
Pitic Presidio, 4
polainas (leather leggings), 31
Polynesian islanders, 103, 104
population growth, 149, 150, 152
Portolá Expedition: *panocha*, *116*; Rafael Villavicencio, 139; research on, xii–xiii
Portolá Trail, xii–xv
Pourade, Richard, xii
poverty, independence era, 86, 88, 137
presidios, 44; Alta California, 75; El Sur region, 60; social life, 75
pride and independence, 98, 99, 115, 117, 232, 235
private property, 60, 78, 130; former mission ranches, 81–82
pueblos: Alta California, 75; Gálvez report on, 68; use of term, 68
Puerto de Santo Domingo, 204
pulque (agave beer), 206

Quintero, Tránsito, 211

ranch, use of term, 77
rancherías, 57

ranches: Arroyo San Pablo, 79;
    dependence on cattle, 104;
    independent nature and, 98;
    life seen in travel accounts, 103;
    Mexican War era, 93; mission era
    and post-mission, 56, 81; Mission
    Guadalupe, 128, 130; mules and
    horses, 117; oasis character of,
    121–22, 123; padres in towns and,
    225, 227; pre-independence, 96
Rancho El Patrocinio, 132, 140
Rancho El Prospecto, 216–17
Rancho El Valle, 140
Rancho El Zorrillo, 151
Rancho La Esperanza, 219, 221–22,
    223
Rancho Las Calabazas, 214, 215,
    216
Rancho Las Jícamas, 2, 148
Rancho La Soledad, 233
Rancho Las Vírgenes, 218
Rancho Pie de la Cuesta, hillside
    trail, 225
Rancho Rosarito, 169, 176, 227
Rancho San Antonio, 199, 199, 201
Rancho San Carlos, 186; El Boleo
    supplies, 212–13
Rancho San Carlos Viejo, 217
Rancho San Francisco, 186, 198–99
Rancho San Gregorio: buildings,
    22, 25, 27, 38, 39; irrigation
    system, 14–18, 20, 21; leather
    curing, 26–27, 28, 29, 30,
    31; location, 22, 127; mezcal
    operation shut down, 210;
    moonshining, 206, 208, 210;
    roads to, 22; water flume, 19, 21
Rancho San José de Gracia, 132, 140
Rancho San José de Magdalena,
    136, 140
Rancho San Marcos, 181
Rancho San Martín, xv, 137;
    hillside trail, 225
Rancho San Miguel, 140
Rancho San Nicolás, 185
Rancho San Pedro, 181
Rancho Santa Marta, 22, 186, 228
Rancho Vivelejos, 132
reading habits, 33, 232
Real del Castillo mining, 124
rebellion, 59–61
rennet, 156, 159
represa (artificial catchment traps),
    150
Republic of Mexico era, 85–89;
    federal policies, 96–97
reputation, importance of, 235
reservoir, stone, 191
Resources of the Pacific Slope, 192
Ritchie, Thomas, 107, 107n
Rivera y Moncada, Fernando de,
    68, 69
rock art, xv, 16–17, *16*, 128;
    publications, 222; Tacho Arce
    and, 222–23
Rodríguez, Bernardo, 53
Rodríguez Cabrillo, Juan, 42–43
Rodríguez de Montalvo, Garcí, 42
Rodríguez, Captain Esteban, 54, 63
Rojo, Manuel Clemente, 73–75
Romero, María de Jesús, 184
Rosas Villavicencio, José, 134
Rothschild group, 194
Roy, Louis le, 4
Ruíz, Francisco María, 87
Ruíz, José Manuel, 85–88, 115, 134,
    137
Ruíz, Juan María, 8
Ruíz, María Amparo, 115
Russian explorations, 65

Ryan, William Redmond, 115–19, 118

salt-harvesting complex, 6
Salvatierra, Juan María de, 44, 53–54
San Antonio (mining center), 4
San Bernabé, 58–59
San Diego, forty-niner trip to, 121
San Diego County, honey industry, 35
San Diego Old Town, 87
San Fernado, 182
San Ignacio (village): Arce as *alcalde*, 186; described, 192; Dominicans at, 81; Francisco's leather work, 26; mayordomo descendants, 139; mezcal sales, 216; natural conditions, 198; smuggler priest at, 186; trade with, 22, 36–37; viewed later, 14
San Ignacio de Loyola, 162
San Javier (village), xiii, 170, 173
San José (Alta California town), 75
San José (Baja California town), 109
San José (de los Arces), 136
San José del Cabo, 4; forty-niners, 121; housing, 103; insurrection, 59; mission, 57; U.S. occupation, 5, 113
San Lino, 216
Santa Águeda, 136, 137, 182, 193–94
Santa Ana, 62; ranches, 67, 68
Santa Bárbara Presidio, 32–33
Santa Rosalía, 14, 123, 129; contraband mezcal, 208; mining town, 194, 195, 196; music, 173
schools, 89
secularization of mission lands,

86, 88; decrees, 91–92; Sierra de Guadalupe, 132
self-reliance, 235
Las sergas de Esplandián (Rodríguez de Montalvo), 42
sexual adventurism, 102
shrines, 38, 39
Shubrick, Commodore, 114
Sierra de Guadalupe: backgrounds of people, 139–40; cattle, 130–31; compared to other ranges, 127; daily routines, 153; geology, 127–28; height of population, 150; hillside trail, 225; landholding, 149; land rentals, 134; mayordomo influence, 139; mission origins, 127, 128–30, 129; proliferation of ranches, 149; ranch society, 125; secularization of mission lands, 132; typical settlements, 2; uplands, 126
Sierra de la Giganta, 7; compared to other ranges, 127; forty-niners at, 121
Sierra de San Borja, 202
Sierra de San Francisco: Arce family, 197–99; Arroyo San Pablo, 79; compared to other ranges, 127; described, 13–14; eastern approach, 223; pack trip, 12; Rancho San Nicolás, 185; Rancho San Pedro, 181; roads nearby, 22. *See also* Rancho San Gregorio
Sierra de San Juan, 218, 220
sierras described, 13
Sinaloa: El Fuerte, 87; insurrection response, 60; Jesuit missions, 44; population centers, 55; recruiting for missions, 49, 50, 51

Smithsonian Institution expedition (1905), 204
Smith, Thomas ("Javier Aguilar"), 4–5
Smith, W. C. S., 120–22, 189–90
smuggling, 186
social mobility, 48
social status, 47–48
social stratification, 47–48, 96, 232; mayordomo status, 137
Sonora: Jesuit explorations, 63; Jesuit missions, 44; Yaqui mercenaries, 113; Yuma region war, 99
sopa (of varied contents), 26
Spain: support of missions and presidios, 78; threats in Western North America, 65–66
spurs, 227, 228
storytelling, 173–74, *178*, 181–83
sugarcane presses, 115, *116*, *117*
supernatural, views of, 166
superstitions, lack of, 166, 232
switchback trails, *148*

Tamaral, Padre, 59
tanbark, 29
tanning solution, 31
Texas independence, 93
timber trees, 128
tinajas (catchment pools), 141, *142*, 145, 149–50
tinas (tanning vats), 29, 31
tinta (tanning solution), 31
Toba, Fernando de la, 134
Todos Santos (village): Dominicans at, 81; ship supplies, 81
Tokugawa Shogunate, 105
tortillas, 26; corn, 118–19

tourism, 7, 223; rock art, 222–23
trade, 22; Alta California, 81; contraband, 81; goat cheese, 156; hides, 97–98; independence era, 85, 97; late mission era, 71, 73; mining boom, 124; ship supplies, 79, 81; transport, *148*
Transpeninsular Highway, 7, *8*, 223
travel accounts, 41, 73–75, 97–99, 104–12, 115, 120–22
Treaty of Guadalupe Hidalgo, 114
Las Tres Vírgenes, 186
trombas (cloudbursts), 143–44

Uchití people, 58
Ugarte, Juan de, 54, 57, 59
United States, invasion of Baja California, 112–15

vaqueros, 70; clothing, 71; wild cattle, 98
vecinos (neighbors, residents), 82
Velasco, Ana Gertrudis, 183
verbal exchange, 168
Verduzco, Anastasio, 137
Viétez, José, 134
Villa de Sinaloa, 50, *51*, 55, 183
Villavicencio, Amado, 217
Villavicencio, Anastasio, 182
Villavicencio, Dolores, 136
Villavicencio, Domitilia, 197, *198*
Villavicencio, Elías, 169–70, 173, 176
Villavicencio, José Rosas, 136, 137, 193–94
Villavicencio, José Urbano, 136, 149
Villavicencio, Narciso, *209*
Villavicencio, Rafael, 139
violin music, 173
Vizarrón y Eguiarreta, Juan Antonio de, 59

Vizcaíno expedition, 54
Vizcaíno Plain, 6

water flume, 19, 21
water sources: *arroyo* (watercourse), 22, 187; gold mining, 203, 204; missionary systems, 17; mission era, 17; pipeline, 204; Rancho San Gregorio, 14–17; San Ignacio, 191, 193; stone reservoir, 191; wells, 221
water systems: Mexican War era, 118; mission era, 18; Rancho San Gregorio, 19
whaling, 103
wild cattle, 98
wild food, 145, 147
wild honey, 34–35, 36
women: clothing, 99, 104; described, 103–104; domestic chores, 163; fiestas, 169, 173; isolation of, 176; marriage opportunity, 177, 179; sitting order for meals, 24, 25, 103–104; skills and occupations, 153–54
work, 153–55; children, 154–55; elderly, 172

Yaqui Indians, 194

zayas (roots), 145
Zensuke, 109, 110–12

www.ingramcontent.com/pod-product-compliance
Lightning Source LLC
Chambersburg PA
CBHW020745160426
43192CB00006B/252